CARRIED TO THE WALL

CARRIED TO THE WALL

AMERICAN MEMORY AND THE
VIETNAM VETERANS MEMORIAL

KRISTIN ANN HASS

UNIVERSITY OF CALIFORNIA PRESS
BERKELEY   LOS ANGELES   LONDON

University of California Press
Berkeley and Los Angeles, California

University of California Press, Ltd.
London, England

© 1998 by
The Regents of the University of California

Library of Congress Cataloging-in-Publication Data

Hass, Kristin Ann, 1965-
    Carried to the wall : American memory and the Vietnam
Veterans Memorial / Kristin Ann Hass.
        p.   cm.
    Includes bibliographical references and index.
    ISBN 0–520-20413-1 (cloth : alk. paper).—ISBN 0–520-
21317-3 (pbk. : alk. paper)
    1. Vietnam Veterans Memorial (Washington, D.C.)
2. Funeral rites and ceremonies—United States.
3. Patriotism—United States.   4. War memorials—United
States.   5. Vietnamese Conflict, 1961–1975—Public
opinion.   6. Public opinion—United States.   I. Title.
DS559.83.W18H33   1998
959.704'36—dc21   97-46807
                                                              CIP

Printed in the United States of America
9 8 7 6 5 4 3 2 1

The paper used in this publication meets the minimum
requirements of American National Standard for Information
Sciences—Permanence of Paper for Printed Library Materials,
ANSI Z39.48-1984.

For Cameron and Finn

CONTENTS

ACKNOWLEDGMENTS

I want to thank David Scobey for his tremendous help at every stage of this project; his keen, close readings, his expansive comments, his dedication as a teacher, and his true friendship have been invaluable to me. I am also indebted to the rest of my dissertation committee at the University of Michigan: Robin Kelley and Diane Kirkpatrick were generous with their time, their thoughtful responses, and their encouragement; Pete Daniel, at the National Museum of American History, was incredibly kind to read and respond to my dissertation—his comments were with me as I worked through my revisions; and June Howard, as the director of the Program in American Culture at the University of Michigan, as a teacher, and as a friend, inspired and instructed me from the very first stages of this project. The faculty—past and present—of the Program in American Culture, in particular David Hollinger, Robert Berkhofer, Joanne Leonard, and George Sanchez, taught me a great deal about the value of American studies scholarship. George Sanchez, as the director of the program, provided me with crucial support so that I could work on this manuscript. The program staff, especially Linda Eggert and Heather Dornoff, helped me at every turn.

I am also deeply grateful to David Guynes and Duery Felton for letting me into MARS (Maryland Area Regional Storage) to review the Vietnam Veterans Memorial Collection log books and for sharing their insights with me. Tony Porco, at MARS, was also very kind and helpful.

Frank "everyday we wrote the books" Mitchell, Diane Sampson, Martha Umphrey, Joe Won, Michelle Risdon, Austin Booth, Eric Porter, Jean Henry, Marsha Ackermann, and my friends in the Program in American Culture provided me with a rich intellectual community in which to work. (Frank, Diane, and Michelle also made sure that I actually did work.) My friends at the National Museum of American History, especially Marvette Perez and Charlie McGovern and Dierdre Cross, encouraged and inspired me throughout. My students at the University of Michigan, in particular Jodi Smith, Pilar LaValley, Estella Chung, Robert Kamins, Marifrances Conrad, Brian Murray, and Nicole Bates, kept me on my toes and pushed me to think about monuments and memorialization in new ways.

There are also many scholars whose work has shaped this project— Laura Palmer, Edward Linenthal, Thomas Laqueur, James Mayo, John Michael Vlach, Terry Jordan, Blanche Linden-Ward, Karen Krepps, Lynn Gosnell, Susan Gott, and H. Bruce Franklin are just a few of those to whom I am indebted.

This project has been generously supported by the Program in American Culture, the Rackham School of Graduate Studies, the Henry Ford Museum, the Smithsonian Institution, Eileen Colon, who took such good care of me whenever I was in Washington, and Ann Stevenson, who took such good care of Finn while I finished up.

Thanks also to Hank Savage for the fine photographs.

William Murphy at the University of California Press was blessedly patient, encouraging, and insightful. Sue Heinemann, Naomi Schneider, and Carlotta Shearson have all been tremendously helpful. I am grateful to each of them.

I also want to thank my fabulous parents, Earlene Hass and Robert Hass, and my brothers—Leif, Luke, and Tommy. The rest of my dear and extended family, including Marilyn and Duncan Magoon, Brenda Hillman, Tom McCoy, Margaret Handley, Jean Mandel, Sioban Scanlon, and Dahlia Petrus, know how helpful they have been. Finally, of course, I want to thank my beloved Cameron and Finn Magoon—it's not that I couldn't have done it without them, it's just that I wouldn't have.

A RESTLESS MEMORY OF WAR

teddy bear
birthday card
Christmas tree

A mother travels to the Vietnam Veterans Memorial a couple of times a year, usually once around Christmastime and then close to her son's birthday. She comes with her pride, we might guess, and her grief, for sure—but she also brings a gift. A birthday card, a loved childhood toy, or a small Christmas tree decorated with strands of silver tinsel and bright red globes. This book is about the ways in which her gifts, and the many thousands like them, are not only poignant individual memories but also part of a noisy, unsolicited conversation at the Wall about post-Vietnam America. All of the still vital questions that surround the Vietnam War—all of the ways in which this war challenged so many citizens' ideas about what it means to be American—are asked and answered and asked and answered and asked again by the leaving of these gifts. Together, these gifts let us listen in on this unexpected outpouring about the war, its lost bodies, and its indelible mark on American patriotism. These things also demonstrate a new impulse in the making of American public memory—the abiding desire on the part of so very many visitors to the Wall to speak, publicly and privately, to the problematic memory of this war. Why?

Things appear at the Wall because the Vietnam War has a restless memory. More than twenty years after its official end, it continues to haunt the American imagination. On April 22, 1994, a few hours after

1

the death of Richard Nixon, Henry Kissinger was interviewed about the former president on national television. He spoke proudly of opening China and of treaties with the Soviet Union; he celebrated a record of softening relations with the very communists Nixon had built his career warning against. When asked if Nixon had been concerned that his long political career would be misconstrued, Kissinger did not talk about Watergate but instead asked Americans to come to peace with the memory of Vietnam. He did not ask that Nixon's waging of the war be reinterpreted; he simply expressed the hope that with the former president's death the memory of the Vietnam War could rest in peace.

A few days later in Yorba Linda, California, after the elaborate and much documented westward journey of the former president's body, his flag-draped coffin was presented to the public for viewing in the Richard Nixon Library. Forty-two thousand mourners came, and many of them left personal offerings at a makeshift shrine near the library's entrance. Thousands of wreaths and flags were joined by handwritten notes, a Chinese scroll, a pink toy raccoon, and other personal mementos. This swelling collection of gifts in memory of Richard Nixon is a part of his political legacy. The war in which Nixon asked so many Americans to fight had a deeply unsettling effect on the nation. It changed the ways in which Americans imagined and understood their community, and in doing so it changed American memorial practices.

The things carried to the funeral for Nixon represent an attempt by his mourners to articulate what his life and death mean for them. This need to articulate meaning is also what drives people to leave things at the Vietnam Veterans Memorial. The restive memory of the war changed American public commemoration because the memory could not be expressed by or contained in Maya Lin's powerful and suggestive design alone. The deep need to remember the war and the challenges that it presented to the idea of the nation, the soldier, and the citizen met in Lin's design and inspired hundreds of thousands of Americans to bring their own memorials to the Wall. These intensely individuated public memorials forge a richly textured memory of the war and its legacies.

This book is about war and memory and bodies and things and the connections between them; it is an exploration of the thousands of offerings carried by ordinary Americans to the Vietnam Veterans Memorial. I believe that the liminal, contested place of the Vietnam War in

American culture has disrupted the expectation that dead soldiers can be retired to a stoic, martyred memory of heroism and sacrifice and, in so doing, has disrupted American memorial practices. I see the gifts Americans bring to the Wall as part of a continuing public negotiation about patriotism and nationalism. These gifts forge a new mode of public commemoration that suggests ordinary Americans deeply crave a memory, or a thousand memories together, that speaks to ways in which this war disrupted their sense of American culture and their place in it.

The impulse to make personal memories of difficult public grief emerged at the Vietnam Veterans Memorial, but it has been expressed throughout the culture and has opened up an amazing dialogue about the shape of the nation and the place of its citizens. It has changed memorial practices for Americans struggling to make sense of other painful aspects of their culture. For Americans struggling to face the enormous grief and the outcast social position of those suffering and dying from AIDS, the AIDS quilt is, in part, a response to the kind of memory made at the Wall. In the wake of the public rage at the Rodney King verdict in Los Angeles, a wall was constructed and inscribed with the names of all those killed in the violence, and people carried all kinds of personal gifts to this wall. In Crown Heights and Bedford-Stuyvesant, Brooklyn, walls have been painted with the names of those killed in urban violence. In Detroit a portrait of Malice Green was painted on a wall near where he was beaten to death, and for weeks people brought offerings to this spontaneous memorial. And, most dramatically, in Oklahoma City more than a million gifts have been carried to the fences that surround the remains of the bombed-out Federal Building. Such memorial impulses reflect both a need to negotiate the public meanings of these deaths and a determination on the part of ordinary citizens to do this work themselves.

This book is about death, but it is also about the failure of death. It is about the life sustained in the work of making American public memory. In order to reveal the problems of representation to which the things are a response, the first chapter sketches the fight to build the Vietnam Veterans Memorial. The story of the Vietnam Veterans Memorial is one of struggle over the representation of contested terrain. It is an allegory for the Vietnam War itself and the ways in which the war has stayed alive in American culture since the fall of Saigon.

The second chapter is an exploration of the history of memorializing. It argues that the Vietnam Veterans Memorial and the things that people leave there are part of a continuing conversation about the relationship of individuals and bodies to nations and to patriotism and nationalism. The memorial also marks, I will argue, a shift in the way that the relationship between the individual and the nation is imagined and articulated. This is, I know, a lot of work for one memorial, but a close look at the history of memorializing war, and at the shifting ideas about nationalism and individualism that this history reflects, places this memorial in a developing conversation about individual sacrifice and national ideals. Paying particular attention to the memory of the American Civil War, French memorials to World War I, and the bridges and auditoriums that constitute American memorials to World War II, chapter 2 argues that the shifting shapes of these monuments reflect shifting ideas about bodies and nations that are implicitly expressed in and at the Wall.

The third chapter explores American funerary traditions. It argues that rich traditions of grave decoration, which mirror much of what happens at the Wall, have shaped the ways in which people participate at the memorial. It argues that the working-class African Americans, Mexican Americans, and white ethnic Americans who fought this war have been bringing their complicated traditions of grave decoration to the Wall in order to negotiate the liminal position of the dead, and the veterans, in relationship to the nation. The history of these funerary traditions creates a dense context in which to try to understand a fishing lure or a Bible or the thousands of other things left at the Wall. The history makes the intensity of the response to the Wall and some of the things—crosses and photographs and holiday cards and even tea cups—more comprehensible. The people who come to speak at the Wall are not only claiming the national monument as their own, but they are also taking responsibility for making a memory of the war themselves. At the Wall, they are forging a memory of the war and its legacy that is far more complicated, more richly textured than any national memorial has ever been. The things are a loud—if not finely tuned—interjection into the memorial conversations with which we have defined the nation.

The fourth chapter focuses on the particular symbolic work of the things within the collection. Most of the offerings left at the Wall seem to make a memory of a name on the Wall or the experience of a specific veteran, and yet taken together the objects, which I see as a response to a crisis of public memory, articulate a struggle on the part of ordinary Americans to be part of a conversation about how the war should be remembered and, therefore, part of a conversation about the shape of the nation. Using a handful of rough categories of objects to draw out the terms of this conversation, I argue that the objects, while not a coordinated effort of people with a clearly articulated vision of how to remember or reimagine the nation, are nevertheless the work of people who feel compelled to respond to the problem of remembering the war and the nation.

The final chapter closely examines one category of artifacts left at the Wall: the POW/MIA artifacts. I argue that these articulate a wide range of anxieties not necessarily directly related to the war, that they are not only a means of forging a bridge across the ever widening gulf between patriotic nationalism and the rage inspired in veterans and their communities by the disregard with which the federal government had treated them but also a response to the changing social and economic structures of the late twentieth century that are displacing working-class men and women. Through missives left at the wall, these communities struggle to protest the inaction of the United States government without aligning themselves with antiwar, antigovernment, or, perhaps most important, antipatriotic positions. This chapter explores the mourning of unnamed losses—the loss of masculinity, patriotism, working-class idealism and pride—manifest in the tremendous outpouring for POWs at the Wall. It argues that the work of imagining the nation and of constructing public memory at the Wall has given Americans a powerful grassroots vernacular for negotiating the grief and the trials of this imagined community.

Together these arguments are intended to help us hear the cacophony of voices speaking at the Wall. I want these arguments to help us listen in on this tremendous, unmediated community of citizens. I want to map out the terrain from which the making of memorials at the Wall has emerged. I want to tune our ears to the places where these things, alive with desire, strike common cords. I also, however, want this book to explore the lives of these things without pretending to contain them—both because they are produced by so many individual acts and because these acts seem to be very much a process—one of intervention or communication—rather than distinct pieces of a finished memory, or a new vision of America constructed at the Wall. All of my thinking about the things and the stories around them has convinced me that the best gift that I can offer in response to these gifts is a guide for carefully, and respectfully, witnessing what is alive at the Wall—the work of ordinary citizens getting their hands dirty in the forging of public memory. I hope that is what I have given here.

MAKING A MEMORY OF WAR

BUILDING THE VIETNAM VETERANS MEMORIAL

American materialism is . . .
the materialism of action and abstraction.

—Gertrude Stein, in *Gertrude Stein's America*

In 1971 angry Vietnam veterans gathered outside the White House gates and on the steps of Capitol Hill. Chanting and jeering, they hurled their Purple Hearts, their Bronze Stars, their awards of valor and bravery, over the White House fence and against the limestone Capitol.[1] In a radical breach of military and social decorum, these highly decorated military men spit back their honors. They had been betrayed, lied to, and abandoned. They had had no chance to be Hollywood heroes; instead they had fought an ugly war, survived, and lost.

In 1982, in the calm of the Constitution Gardens, these medals started to appear at the base of the Vietnam Veterans Memorial.[2] They were set carefully under a name (or a group of names of soldiers who lost their lives together) by the owners of the medals and the fathers of the dead. Chances are good that there was no chanting or jeering as the medals were laid down; the Wall is a startlingly quiet place. And although the medals and ribbons were sometimes accompanied by a photograph or a note hastily written on stationery from a local hotel, the awards were left at the Wall one at a time. At first, they were set down without publicity or organized purpose. Thousands of Americans had the same unanticipated response to the memorial. They came and left their precious things. Why?

Hurling your Purple Heart at the powers that be and setting it at the foot of a memorial to your dead friends are very different acts. The veterans' throwing of their medals is not difficult to interpret as the rejection of an honor, a disdainful public protest against betrayal. However defiant, these veterans were still acting within commonly understood social codes. The things they threw had clearly defined social meanings.

The things offered at the memorial were given new meaning in a much less clear social context. Mainstream funerary and memorial traditions in American culture do not involve the offering of things. Flowers and flags are for memorials. Medals of valor and old cowboy boots are for mantels and attics. This new response to a veterans memorial, then, raises some fascinating questions. Why did so many people have the same unconventional, unanticipated response to the memorial? Where did it come from? What meaning do these things have? Are these offerings left for the dead or the living? Is the medal left as a show of respect? Or of anger?

More than 20 million visitors, about one in ten Americans, have visited the Wall,[3] and every day for fifteen years some of these visitors have left offerings. The flowers and flags have been accompanied by long letters to the dead, poems, teddy bears, wedding rings, human remains, photographs, ravaged military uniforms, high school yearbooks, fishing lures, cans of beer, collections of stones, Bibles, and bullets. In November of 1990, eight years after the dedication of the monument, nearly six hundred objects were left, including seventy military medals, one urn containing human ashes, and a large sliding glass door.[4] Why?

THE MEMORIAL

Dear Smitty,

Perhaps, now I can bury you; at least in my soul. Perhaps, now I won't again see you night after night when the war reappears and we are once more amidst the myriad hells that Vietnam engulfed us in. . . . I never cried. My chest becomes unbearably painful and my throat tightens so I can't even croak, but I haven't cried. I wanted to, just couldn't. I think I can today. Damn, I'm crying now. Bye Smitty. Get some rest.

—Anonymous note left at the Wall[5]

The average age of the soldiers killed in Vietnam was nineteen; most of those who died had been drafted. The Vietnam Veterans Memorial was born out of a clear vision of what was to be represented: the dead, the veterans, and the sense of community that had made the war palatable to some Americans between 1957 and 1975. The problem, however, of what the death, the veterans, and the lost community suggested together and how they might be represented was the subject of many public and private battles. The work of any memorial is to construct the meaning of an event from fragments of experience and memory. A memorial gives shape to and consolidates public memory: it makes history. As historian James Mayo argues, "how the past is commemorated through a country's war memorials mirrors what people want to remember, and lack of attention reflects what they wish to forget."[6] The veterans fighting to shape the meaning of the Vietnam War found that their efforts to commemorate this country's longest war were met with all of the conflicting emotions and ideologies expressed about the war itself. There was no consensus about what the names represented, about what to remember or what to forget.

The deeply controversial nature of the war, its unpopularity, and the reality that it was lost created an enormous void of meaning that compounded the difficult work of memorializing. What it meant to die in this war was as unclear as what it meant to fight in it. Moreover, the duration of the war, the military's system of rotation, and the defeat precluded the ticker-tape parades young boys going to war might have anticipated.[7] Veterans came home to changing ideas about patriotism and heroism; they returned to a society riven by the civil rights movement, Watergate, and the assassinations of the men who had inspired many of them to fight. There was no clear ideology around which a community of grief could have formed. It was a muddled, lost war waiting to be forgotten even before it was over. People who lost their children, husbands, fathers, sisters, and their own hearts were without a public community for the expression of grief or rage or pride. This lack of community not only made them deeply crave a remembrance of the experience of Americans in Vietnam but also made the work of remembering especially difficult. Commemorating the war and the deaths required giving new shape to the broken meanings of the war. It required a reimagination of the nation.

In March of 1979 Jan Scruggs, a vet and the son of a rural milkman, went to see *The Deer Hunter*. He came home terrified and inspired. This Hollywood movie, about the horrors of the war, the impossibility of coming home, and the struggles of a small, working-class Pennsylvania community to come to terms with its losses, convinced Scruggs that it was time for the nation to publicly remember the war. In the movie a community shattered by the war regains its bearings in a tentative return to the patriotic ideals that had inspired its boys to fight. It is a troubling response, but it offered Scruggs some hope; the possibility of a community healing itself inspired in him the idea of building a memorial. So with a few of his veteran friends, Scruggs formed the Vietnam Veterans Memorial Fund (VVMF) in April of 1979.

The fund's first attempts to gain public support were not entirely successful. No more than a dozen reporters showed up for the first press conference, on May 28, 1979. Scruggs and his friends tried to launch a national fundraising campaign, but they received a handful of heart-wrenching letters and worn dollar bills instead of the generous checks for which they had hoped.[8] The veterans fighting for a memorial were angry and determined, but they were not socially or politically powerful; and their cause was not easily or quickly embraced. They did, however, attract the attention of a few influential Vietnam veterans. Jack Wheeler, a Harvard- and Yale-educated West Pointer, joined the VVMF and began to draw in Vietnam veterans from high places throughout Washington. And although the founders of the VVMF had wanted to oppose the power structures whose work they were trying to memorialize, they learned that they could not raise public interest— let alone funds—without the aid of a few Washington power brokers. The fund's first major contributions came after a brunch for defense contractors organized by Senator John Warner.[9]

The men and women who came to form the core of the VVMF were by no means politically or socially unified. Some had protested after serving in the war, and others continued to believe in the ideals of the conflict; nearly all, however, were white veterans who were keenly aware of their outcast social position as survivors of a deeply unpopular war. They wanted a national monument to help them reclaim a modicum of recognition and social standing.

As the money began to trickle in, the VVMF made several key decisions that determined a great deal about the character of the memorial and the kind of community that it rebuilt. The fund wanted a monument that listed all the names of those killed, missing in action, or still held as prisoners of war in Vietnam. Although the dead became the heart of the project because they were, in an important sense, all these veterans could agree upon, there was no easy agreement about how the memorial should remember the dead. The fund imagined a *veterans* memorial not a *war* memorial; the former would ensure a memory that emphasized the contributions of the soldiers rather than the federal government. The members of the fund did not ask for federal money because they did not want to be perceived as more Vietnam vets looking for a handout and because after Ronald Reagan cut $12 million from the Veterans Administrations budget in 1980, the vets did not trust his administration to give them the kind of memorial they hoped for.[10] Building it with private contributions would also prove that a larger American public wanted to remember,[11] and they wanted the memorial built on the Mall in Washington, D.C., to assure the memory of the veterans a place of national prominence.

The VVMF found itself in a complicated political position. The fund expected strong opposition from the antiwar movement and from the Washington bureaucracy; so it had to negotiate a public memory without either celebrating or explicitly renouncing the war, which would have been politically disastrous for any administration.[12] As a result, strange alliances were formed at every step of the memorializing process. In 1980 the VVMF raised money through letters from Bob Hope calling for a reward for sacrifices made. Gerald Ford, Rosalynn Carter, Nancy Reagan, James Webb, Admiral James Stockdale, General William Westmoreland, and George McGovern made unlikely companions on the fund's letterhead.[13] Few of the alliances were easily made, and not all of them held.

Early on the average donation to the $10 million project was $17.93,[14] and envelopes were sent in with $2 in change. Eventually, however, the campaign worked, and the success clearly demonstrated to the VVMF organizers that there was a population that wanted to publicly remember this war. Building this community of supporters and contributors, tenuous though it may have been, was an essential first step in the work of making a public meaning of the war. To memorialize the war, to solidify its shape and meaning, the fund had to bring together diverse experiences and ideologies. The seeming impossibility of the project was not only in facing the "myriad hells that Vietnam engulfed" the country in but also in repairing the social and political understandings that the war had fractured. In the end, the design of the memorial was a response to the problem of making memory in the wake of the Vietnam War; this is the history they made.

THE DESIGN

I came down today to pay respects to two good friends of mine. Go down to visit them sometime. They are on panel 42E, lines 22 and 26. I think that you will like them.

—Anonymous note left at the Wall

Most war memorials in America—statues, schools, stadiums, bridges, parks—proudly salute American triumph. How do you memorialize a painfully mired, drawn-out defeat that called into question the most fundamental tenets of American patriotism?[15]

The design of the Vietnam Veterans Memorial was bound to be controversial. Its promoters understood that it would be impossible to find a representation of the war that could satisfy a deeply polarized society. The leaders of the VVMF decided to hold an open, juried contest because they wanted to cast a wide net and because they knew that without the participation of some recognized bearers of cultural capital they would never get a design through Washington's notoriously difficult architectural gatekeepers—the National Planning Commission, the Department of the Interior, and the Fine Arts Commission.[16] Choosing the jury was difficult, though. Who should decide how the war would be represented? There was some noise made about including a Vietnam veteran, an African American, and a woman; but it was feared that jurors might defer too much to the opinions of a vet, and, oddly, they were unable to locate a qualified woman or a qualified African American.[17] So the decision was turned over to the most traditional bearers of culture: early in 1981 a panel of distinguished architects, landscape architects, sculptors, and critics was organized by Washington architect Paul Spreiregen.[18] The unpaid veterans who had worked long hours to bring the memorial to this point were impressed by the prestige of the jury but nervous about turning their project over to men "the same age as the people who sent [them] to 'Nam."[19]

The jury and the contestants were given only a few simple, if wildly

ambitious, instructions: the design should "(1) be reflective and con-
templative in character; (2) harmonize with its surroundings; (3) contain the names of those who had died in the conflict or who were still
missing; and (4) make no political statement about the war."[20] The most
important task of the design, however, was the creation of a memorial
that would, as Scruggs wrote, "begin a healing process, a reconcilia-
tion of the grievous divisions wrought by the war."[21] One of the great
ironies of these guidelines is that Vietnam's death toll of fifty-eight thousand is, compared with that of most other American wars, so low that
all of the names could actually be reproduced on one memorial. (The
effect is overwhelming, of course, but possible only because so relatively few Americans died.)

By April 26, 1981, more than fourteen hundred designs had been entered. On May 1, 1981, the jurors, after remarkably little deliberation, unanimously selected a simple black granite V, set into a small hill in the Constitution Gardens, carved with the name of every man and woman who never came back from Vietnam. They were impressed with the eloquence and the simplicity of the design. The jurors, one of whom noted of the designer, "he knows what he's doing, all right,"[22] were no doubt startled to discover that their winner was a remarkable impossibility: a twenty-one-year-old art student at Yale University—young, intellectual, female, and Chinese American.

In imagining her design, Maya Ying Lin made a clear decision not to study the history of the war, or to enmesh herself in the controversies surrounding it. Her design lists the names of the men and women killed in Vietnam in the order in which they were killed. The names are carved into black granite panels that form a large V at a 125-degree angle and suggest the pages of an open book. The first panel cuts only a few inches into the gently sloping hillside, but each panel is longer than the last and cuts more deeply into the ground, so that you walk downhill toward the apex, at which point the black panels tower three or four feet above your head. At the center you are half buried in a mass of names; pulled toward the black granite, you see yourself and the open lawns of the mall behind you reflected in the memorial. The center of the monument is a strangely private, buffered public space. Literally six feet into the hillside you are confronted simultaneously with the names and with yourself. The black granite is so highly reflective that even at night visitors see their own faces as they look at the Wall. The Wall manages to capture the unlikely simultaneous experiences of reflection and burial. This brilliant element of the design asks for a personal, thoughtful response.[23] As you exit, the panels diminish in size, releasing you back into the daylight. Lin's design did not initially include the word "Vietnam"; she gave form not to the event that caused the deaths but to the names of the dead, to the fact of the deaths.[24]

The names are carved out of polished granite from Bangalore, India.[25] The carving invites tangible interaction. Each name has a physical presence. It asks to be touched. Lin wanted visitors to be able to feel the names in many different ways, and she wanted people to be able to take something of the Wall away with them—a rubbing of a name.

The Wall tries to make a somehow individuated memory of a war. The events in Vietnam are remembered through the names of the dead; these men and women—many of whom, even those drafted against their will, might have imagined, at least in part, that their experience would be like that portrayed in the movie *How I Won the War with John Wayne*—are each remembered as tragically fallen individuals.[26] The power of the design lies in the overwhelming presence of individual names, which represent complicated human lives cut short. This attention to individual lives lost would not, however, be as potent if it were separated from the black expanse of all of the names together, the effect of which is so overwhelming that it both foregrounds the individual names and hides them.[27] Lin's organization of the names also contributes to this tension between particular names and the whole formed by the names together. The dead appear on the Wall not alphabetically but rather in the order in which they died in Vietnam. Soldiers who died together are listed together on the Wall, so that on every line on every panel stories of particular times and places are inscribed with the names. This placement of the names, however, makes finding an individual name in the list impossible without the aid of the phone book–like alphabetical indexes at the entrances to the memorial.[28] Although the index provides information about every name—including hometown, birth date, and death date—it requires a certain amount of participation on the part of any visitor interested in a particular name.[29]

Maya Lin's design earned her a B in her funerary architecture class at Yale, but that was the least of her troubles. She was thrown into a noisy "firestorm of the national heart." Her design was dubbed the "black gash of shame."[30] Its shape was considered an affront to veteran and conservative manhood especially when compared to the shape of the neighboring Washington Monument: the V shape hinted at the peace sign, or a reference to the Vietcong; the black stone was more mournful than heroic.[31] It seemed to many too clear an admission of defeat. The public outcry reflected outrage with Lin's design and with the principles that the VVMF required of all designs: the Wall was too abstract, too intellectual, too reflective. It was, in the minds of many, high art, the art of the class that lost the least in the war. It was not celebratory, heroic, or manly. James Webb, a member of the VVMF's National Sponsoring Committee, called it a "wailing Wall for future antidraft and anti-nuclear demonstrators."[32] Tom Carhart, a veteran who had been awarded a Purple Heart and had submitted a design of his own, coined a key phrase for those who hated the design when he wrote in a *New York Times* op-ed piece that it was "pointedly insulting to the sacrifices made for their country by all Vietnam veterans . . . by this we will be remembered: a black gash of shame and sorrow, hacked into the national visage that is the mall."[33]

The popular press offered some support for the design, but the conservative press was enraged by it. In the *Moral Majority Weekly* Phyllis Schlafly called it a "tribute to Jane Fonda."[34] *National Review* described it as an "Orwellian glob." In an open letter to President Reagan, Republican Representative Henry Hyde complained that it was "a political statement of shame and dishonor." And in September of 1981 an editorial in *National Review* demanded that Reagan intervene, arguing: "Okay, we lost the Vietnam war, okay the thing was mismanaged from start to finish. But American soldiers who died in Vietnam fought for their country and for the freedom of others, and they deserve better than the outrage that has been approved as their memorial . . . the Reagan administration should throw the switch on the project."[35]

Its implicit admission that the war was disastrous, of course, is precisely what others loved about the design. A great many Vietnam veterans reacted with cautious approval. The VVMF and all leading veterans organizations, including the Veterans of Foreign Wars and the American Legion, officially approved of the design. The best evidence of the reaction of the larger community of veterans was their continued effort to support the monument despite the barrage of bitter publicity about the design. Veterans held garage sales, bingo games, and "pass the helmet" campaigns to raise funds for construction. At one of these events in Matoon, Illinois, a vet remarked to Scruggs that "everything Vietnam touches seems to go sour. . . . I may never have the money to get to D.C., but it would make me feel good to know that my buddies' names are up there."[36]

Of course, since the official dedication of the Wall in 1982 volumes of praise have been written for the design and the reflection that it has inspired.[37] The Wall's emphasis on the tragedy of each death has appealed to critics and supporters alike. Strong hopes that this monument will guard against future wars have been expressed; James Kilpatrick, a nationally syndicated columnist, wrote, "this will be the most moving

memorial ever erected . . . each of us may remember what he wishes to remember—the cause, the heroism, the blunders, or the waste."[38] One vet carried a sign at the memorial's opening that expressed a commonly held sentiment: "I am a Vietnam Veteran / I like the memorial / And if it makes it difficult to send people to battle again / I like it even more."[39] A *New York Times* editorial reprinted in the Gold Star Mothers Association newsletter argued, "Nowadays, patriotism is a complicated matter. Ideas about heroism, or art, for that matter, are no longer what they were before Vietnam. . . . But perhaps the V-shaped, black granite lines merging gently with the sloping earth make the winning design seem a lasting and appropriate image of dignity and sadness."[40]

Understanding the design as an attempt to represent a new, complicated patriotism may have appealed to many veterans and Gold Star Mothers, but to the newly elected leaders of the "Reagan revolution" it was an abomination. The design flew in the face of the recently revived strain of relentlessly nostalgic patriotism that had sent them to the capital. It is not surprising that in this political climate the czars of

American conservatism resented the abstraction and the ambiguity of the proposed war memorial, or that opposition to the design came from high places in Washington. James Watt, then secretary of the interior, was a key figure in the design controversy.[41] It was Watt—with the support of irate VVMF contributor H. Ross Perot—who demanded that Lin's design be supplemented, if not supplanted, by a more heroic, representational, figural memorial. Watt would not let the Wall be *the* Vietnam War memorial. Sculptor Frederick Hart made himself and his concrete bronze design, *The Three Fightingmen*, readily available to Watt, Perot, and the press. His intense lobbying efforts were well rewarded.[42] Watt took to Hart's figures and threatened to hold up construction indefinitely unless the VVMF agreed to use the sculpture. With their backs against the wall, the VVMF decided that the memorial was worth the compromise.[43]

Ultimately, this compromise reflects the impossibility of finding a single design that could represent the Vietnam War for all Americans. Hart's figural sculpture satisfied powerful voices that required concrete representation, but it did not solve the problem of representation presented by the war. His figures, a white man flanked by an African American man and a third man whose race is unclear,[44] stand a hundred feet away facing the Wall, apparently transfixed by its power. They are strong, highly masculinized, and heroic. The white man holds his hands out slightly to his side as if to warn his companions, in a patrician gesture that mimics the imperial nature of the war, of some impending danger. Although frozen, they, like the human figures who walk the memorial's path, are drawn to the black granite that recedes into the earth and then delivers into the light. Hart had intended the figures to look warily into the distance for the ubiquitous, hidden Vietnamese enemy, but the negotiations involved in the addition of the sculpture turned their gaze on the Wall and opened up a broad range of interpretive possibilities. This ironic fate for Hart's symbolically stable, heroic figures is indicative of the difficulty he faced in trying to divert attention from Lin's design. The sculpture in the end dramatizes the difficulties of representation and the power of the names; the main attraction of the memorial continues to be the Wall.

Even after the addition of the figures in 1984, the official commemoration of the war was not yet finished. In 1993, nearly ten years later, another battle over the memory of the war took shape on the Mall.

After years of struggling to raise money and interest, Vietnam veteran Diane Carlson Evans presided over the dedication of the Vietnam Women's Memorial. This memorial is the first national memorial to female veterans.[45] Its four figures—a prone, blindfolded, injured male soldier, a white nurse who holds him in her arms, an African American woman comforting the nurse and looking to the sky, and a third woman kneeling over medical equipment—stand about three hundred feet from the Wall, sheltered in a grove of tall trees. It is a very straightforward figural memorial. And while the sculptor, Glenna Goodacre, was swiftly written off by art critics for whom her pietà is uninspiring,[46] the principal argument against a memorial to the women who served in Vietnam was that it would set a precedent for a whole slew of other "special interest memorials."[47] This complaint, as hollow as it might seem in light of the utter lack of memorials to the sacrifices made by American women at war, held considerable sway with the Park Service and the Fine Arts Commission; it is a reminder of the strength of the ideal that one symbolic gesture should be able to make a memory of this twenty-year war.

Evans wanted a women's memorial because the Wall did not heal the particular, complicated alienation of women veterans she had experienced, and it did not make women visible at the memorial. But her efforts to make the work of women in this war an obvious part of its official memory became a struggle against the firmly held ideal of a singular public memory. This struggle was particularly frustrating because the monument already included two sculptures and because women's war work in the United States has been invisible for so long despite the central role of women in the forging of public memory. The Mount Vernon Ladies' Association of the Union, the Daughters of the Confederacy, the Gold Star Mothers Association, and other women's volunteer associations have been essential to the history of memorializing in America.[48] They have worked to ensure that national memories have been preserved and respected, but their contributions to the history of commemoration have not been recorded. Their roles in the work of making memory have been carefully prescribed—they have nurtured the memories of war as mothers, daughters, wives, and sisters but have not been seen as participants worth remembering. Women were undoubtedly a part of the life of the Vietnam Veterans Memorial in its first ten years, but they were principally visible as grievers, not as veterans. Diane Evans wanted to rewrite this history with the figure of a nurse.

Maya Lin sagely observed about the first statue, "In a funny sense the compromise brings the memorial closer to the truth. What is also memorialized is that people still cannot resolve the war, nor can they separate the issues, the politics from it."[49] This is true about both of the added statues. Hart's sculpture memorializes a need to remember these veterans as manly and heroic; Goodacre's sculpture, eight years later, memorializes a victory for women veterans over the perceived threat to patriotism posed by the idea of making any memory of war that is not singular and masculine. Hart's and Goodacre's additions to the Wall commemorate the difficulty of making memory in the midst of shifting cultural values. It is, in part, this sense of the impossibility of representation that pulls personal, individual memorials from visitors to the Wall; with their things people are bringing the monument "closer to the truth."

In the statement she submitted with her design proposal, Maya Lin wrote, "it is up to each individual to resolve or to come to terms with this loss. For death is in the end a personal and private matter and the area containing this within the memorial is a quiet place, meant for personal reflection and private reckoning."[50] Lin was entirely right. She probably could not have anticipated the extent to which visitors to this memorial would take on the responsibility for the memory of the war, but she did appreciate the constantly unfinished, contested nature of the memory of this war. She understood that memorializing the war necessarily meant undoing the traditional idea of patriotic nationalism in the shape of a singular, heroic memorial. The multiplication of memorials, names, and objects at the Wall has, indeed, replaced the possibility of a singular memory of the war; the single figure of the male citizen embodying the nation has been supplanted by three official memorials and a steady stream of combat boots, bicycle parts, and St. Christophers. People come to this memorial and they make their own memorials.

THE GIVING

I have seen the names of those I know, and, yes, I have cried.
My problem is I don't know the names of those I tried to help
only to have them die in my arms. In my sleep I hear their

cries and see their faces. . . . Attached to this letter are my
service medals. These belong to you and your family and your
friends. I don't need them to show I was there. I have your
faces in my sleep.

'Tell me your names'

Love your brother,

Glen 68–69

—Letter left at the Wall[51]

On November 12, 1982, when the memorial was officially dedicated, Park Service volunteers were faced with an unanticipated problem. People visiting the memorial left behind more than the flowers, flags, and hot dog wrappers the Park Service had expected. From the first day, the volunteers were faced with a growing collection of photographs, medals, letters, clothing, and teddy bears. They had anticipated that people would take rubbings of names important to them. They did not expect people to leave things.

The Wall elicits a physical response. It has inspired visitors to represent their own grief, loss, rage, and despair. Contributing their private representations to public space, they cross a boundary between the private and the public, the nation and the citizen, powerfully claiming the memorial as their own. People affected by the war have the sense that staking a personal claim is an appropriate response to a public space. What inspires this response? Why do people leave more than their tears? The source of the impulse to contribute a personal representation is difficult to pin down. It comes out of the reflective, abstract nature of the design, the impossibility of representing the war, the heartbreak of years of repression of the war and its costs, the social position of veterans, and the traditions of the population that fought in this war. All of these possible explanations will be explored in greater detail in the arguments that follow.

Glen gave his medals for the nameless men who died in his arms—as a bridge between him and them. He left the medals to connect himself to the men whose names he could not find on the Wall, to his experience, which was not represented in the monument. He felt compelled to remake what was in his dreams and not on the Wall.[52] His was an act of self-expression and self-extension. For Glen leaving his things at the memorial was an effort to more completely represent his experience. This, the impossibility of creating a singular monument that could forge a whole account of the Vietnam war, and what seems to be a heightened expectation that this national memorial should somehow name (and in so doing remember) the riot of experiences, ideas, and bodies that such an account would include, leave room for and demonstrate the desire for more representation.

THE COLLECTION

My Dearest Ben,

I miss you and think of you so much. Every day in my prayers, I thank God and Jesus for caring for you and pray that will continue. I'm bringing "Teddy Bear" and a picture of your loved race car. I realize they can't stay there long, but they are yours and I want them to be with you. In time, I hope we can all be together.

Love to you my dear, dear Ben,

Mama

Much love, Dad

—Note left at the Wall[53]

From the beginning, the Park Service staff watched with amazement as the objects piled up at the foot of the monument. Sensing that these things had a certain sanctity, they collected everything set down and stored it all in a nearby toolshed. They saved everything—bubble gum wrappers and wedding rings—with the same respect and attention. Eventually, the Vietnam Veterans Memorial Collection (VVMC) was founded to house and protect the artifacts.

This collection is compelling because it collects itself. No curator rummages the attics of the war dead looking for essential objects to represent them to future generations of Americans. No museum committee establishes parameters for collecting or lays down an epistemological framework defining what has meaning for post-Vietnam-era America and what does not. In a period when virtually all museums are crying out for history from the "bottom up," when research dollars are being spent to disassemble and collect abandoned sharecroppers' homes, the Vietnam Veterans Memorial is inspiring a collection that literally makes itself.

The collection was officially organized in 1984.[54] The objects are sent to an enormous warehouse in suburban Maryland to sit in acid-free

containers and airtight storage cabinets for perpetuity. The Park Service hoped eventually to open the collection to the public as a Vietnam-era museum, but the first task before them was to somehow organize the artifacts and to document them as fully as possible. This was no small task. Objects began to arrive before the Wall was completed, and by 1993 the collection included well over 250,000 objects of every shape, size, and description. The flow of objects continues unabated; things are left every day, all year round; Veterans Day and Memorial Day usually inspire a sharp rise in the number of offerings.[55] Simply managing a collection of this kind is an enormous undertaking.

The scope of the collection is breathtaking. Some types of objects appear repeatedly at the foot of the monument: medals, bottles of booze, military uniforms, photographs of the dead, dog tags, letters, yearbooks, POW/MIA placards, C rations, baseball gloves, Agent Orange cards, Bibles, cigarettes. Other kinds of objects—a brown paper turkey or a Chambers Brothers album, for example—appear only once. It is nearly impossible to know anything about the donors except that they felt strongly enough to leave their things. It is most often impossible to know even for whom an object was left. Some fathers, mothers, wives, siblings, children, grandchildren, and friends identify themselves on the artifacts, but even so not every object is left for a specific individual. The memorial acts in part as a clearinghouse for political protests and celebrations in Washington. Signs and artifacts from these events are brought to the Wall. The five yellow ribbons, for instance, left at the Wall in November of 1990 are likely to be a reference to the American soldiers already gathering in Saudi Arabia for Operation

Desert Storm. Other objects are absolute mysteries. Why would someone leave a full-size sliding glass door at the memorial? There is the same sort of anarchy at the heart of this collection of things that there is in experience and sensation. The range of the objects in the collection is a testament not only to how intensely the war is still felt but also to the continuing need to negotiate its memory.

These things come to the Wall one at a time. They all make their own particular memorials. Yet together they are a noisy, insistent response to the problem of the memory of all Vietnam veterans. Not only does the presence of one object likely inspire the leaving of another, but collectively, as a response to this crisis of public memory, they transform the memory of the soldier. A generic, uniformed soldier remembered by a name in stone was sufficient to shape the nation during the Civil War, but the people bringing their own memorials to the Wall are insisting that the belated naming at the Vietnam Veterans Memorial is only a start in the work of remembering this war and its dead.

The things left at the Wall are collected by the trained Park Service volunteers who staff the Wall twenty-four hours a day, 365 days a year. These volunteers help visitors to locate names on the Wall, help them to take rubbings of names on the Wall, and pick up the things a couple of times daily. (Only a very few things—for example, a signed Presidential proclamation or a print of the film *In Country*—are picked up immediately after they are set down.) The volunteers collect the items and record the panels at which they were left, a very brief description of the objects, and the date and time they were picked up.

Since 1985 David Guynes and Duery Felton, the collection's passionately committed curators, have made weekly trips to pick up the black trash bags full of amazing treasures.[56] Guynes and Felton are responsible for cataloging and preserving these things, but beyond the physical control of the unwieldy, unpredictable collection, they have a responsibility to protect the integrity of the Wall and the experience of visitors leaving things. This responsibility is terribly important to Guynes and Felton and to everything that happens at the Wall. They believe that in order to protect the integrity of the memorial, they must avoid mediating the leaving of things at the Wall. This task has been difficult, impossible really, because from the beginning the press has been keenly interested in the collection. Journalists want to write articles, publish photographs, and tell personal stories.[57] Guynes and Felton provide information about the things, but they do not want to publicize or in any way solicit the offering of more things. They worry that if people read that it is acceptable to leave offerings and read that all the offerings will be saved forever, people will be more likely to bring things for the collection rather than for the dead or themselves. They were particularly concerned that their 1992 exhibit of things in the collection at the National Museum of American History would inspire the leaving of things at the Wall for exhibit in the museum. These concerns were well founded: not long after the tremendously popular exhibit opened, people began to leave things with attached notes granting the Park Service permission to display the artifacts at the Smithsonian.

Since 1982 hundreds of stories have been written about the collection. Virtually every major American magazine has done at least one feature story on the collection, and hundreds of local newspapers have written about people bringing their precious things to the Wall.[58] Most of the stories are relatively straightforward reports about the phenomenon and the collection. Nearly all the reports of these visits to the collection have included lists of the kind of things that people leave. A 1986 story in the *Asbury Park Press* under the headline "America's Wailing Wall" quotes David Guynes describing the things as "icons of a sacred site" and lists "a pair of boots, a champagne glass, a hat, a glove, a jacket, a poem, a cheerleader's pompom." A 1987 story in *GQ* lists "beat-up combat boots, dog tags, Zippo lighters, medals, boonie hats, diaries." A 1989 article in the *San Diego Union* describes the leaving of twelve Marine Corps ribbons at the Wall as "an act of gratitude" and lists other things in the collection, "a high school year book, a chicken stew ration package, a car stereo speaker."[59] The handful of books that have been published contribute to this process. Thomas Allen's 1995 collection of photographs of objects left at the memorial—*Offerings at the Wall*—is a stunning series of images. Laura Palmer's wonderful *Shrapnel in the Heart* is a collection of letters left at the Wall. These reports have, no doubt, influenced visitors to the memorial. People who might never have thought to carry a football jersey or a photograph from San Diego or Baton Rouge or Chicago to Washington have probably been inspired by these stories.

All of the information available about the leaving of things surely must influence visitors to the memorial. Indeed Guynes argues that there are unquestionably two collections: the collection of spontaneous, unmediated offerings and the collection of offerings left to be saved in the warehouse, exhibited at the Smithsonian, or written about in the press.[60] He and his colleagues at the VVMC understand the offerings that mark a direct connection to the war, the dog tags and p-38 can openers, to be part of the spontaneous and authentic collection. They think of the toys and the posters and the framed plaques as part of the collection that is consciously constructed for posterity. They see the impulse to leave things at the Wall as contaminated by the efforts of those who explicitly articulate their desire to be a part, or make their son a part, of the history that is being made. The impulses of the first bearers of Purple Hearts and torn uniforms have, in fact, likely been co-opted by Americans whose sense of loss has a less specific focus. Saving the things creates this problem,[61] but hiding the things for the sake of maintaining the integrity of the first collection would be im- possible and would disrupt the making of this history from the bottom up. The collection is as much a part of the history of this moment as the things themselves are. The building of this collection is part of the process of renegotiating the memory of the war.

Felton's and Guynes's concern about the corruption of the collec- tion by "inauthentic" things is, in part, a concern about whose crisis of memory is being negotiated at the Wall. It implies that the crisis is more real for those with a direct connection to the war. It implies that if you have dog tags or an old Zippo lighter to bring, your stake in the mak- ing of this public memory is more legitimate. The curators are con- cerned that the increasingly self-conscious contributions—a framed plaque or a sealed letter for example—to the collection are less au- thentic, less powerful than the Purple Hearts and C rations with which the collection began; but these more choreographed forms of giving are also part of the process of nation building that is happening at the Wall. These self-conscious gifts are given as explicit gestures in the mak- ing of a collectivity. People want to get in on the act because the war changed the culture for everybody.[62] There is a lot at stake at this Wall, not only for the veterans and their families but also for every citizen who lost her bearings or her connection to the nation in the wake of the war. "The ideas," writes historian John Bodnar, "and symbols of pub- lic memory attempt to mediate the contradictions of a social system:

ethnic and national, men and women, young and old, professionals and clients, leaders and followers, soldiers and their commanders."[63] This mediation is alive in the multiple public memories being made at the Wall.

The great number of letters written on the stationery of local hotels and on receipts and business cards indicate improvisation and limited preparation time. Some things seem to be offered more spontaneously than others; a wedding ring is something that you are likely to have on your person and something that you are likely to associate with a great deal of value. Some things attest to weeks or months of preparation: embroidered pillows; carefully painted portraits; hand-beaded crosses; plaques decorated with photographs, medals and letters; and combat boots hand carved in wood are labor intensive gifts. Some things establish a direct connection to the war, and some things are obviously left by Girl Scout or Boy Scout troops. Further, some offerings protect themselves from the collection, the increasing number of *sealed* letters and packages is excellent evidence of this. Other things are left at the Wall with, as I have mentioned, notes granting permission for exhibition or preservation in the collection.

A look at a small part of the collection demonstrates the presence of both of these impulses in the collection. The things left at the Wall in November of 1990 make a good sample because Veterans Day is in November and because they provide a strong sense of the tenor of the collection. Although these things, of course, have no statistical meaning for the collection as a whole, they are interesting nonetheless.[64]

Objects Left at the Wall in November of 1990

Notes	77	Notebook	1
Military medals	72	Big glass door	1
Photographs	60	Belt buckle	1
Letters	52	Photo of license plate	1
Flowers with notes	40	C rations	1
Poems	35	Name tag	1
MIA/POW items	34	Booby trap wire	1
Fake flowers	26	U.S. Constitution	1
Flags with notes	16	Artwork	1
Rubbings	15	Toilet paper	1
Military clothing	13	45-rpm record	1

Rocks	12	"Class of '70" sticker	1
Lists of names	11	Handmade buffalo	1
Framed letters, tributes	11	Feather with beads	1
Newspaper clippings	11	Bottle of gin, empty	1
Sealed letters	8	Canteen	1
Cans of beer	7	Deck of cards	1
Cigarettes	6	Australian flag	1
Dog tags	6	Slim Jim	1
Bullets	6	Blue Max information	1
Bibles	6	Marine Corps book	1
Nursing items	6	American flag pillow	1
Hats	6	Yearbook	1
Business cards with notes	6	Round symbol	1
Yellow ribbons	5	"Go Hunting" poster	1
Candles	4	"Read My Lips" sign	1
Military posters	3	Zippo lighter	1
Native American items	2	Chambers Bros album	1
American Legion card	1	Sylvester Pez dispenser	1
Gold leaf	1	"Home from Frag" sign	1
String of beads	1	Agent Orange card	1
St. Christopher medal	1	Ceramic "stuff"	1
19 cents	1	"Learn from History" sign	1
8 cents	1	Framed knitting	1
Marine cup	1	Embryonic warrior	1
Ashes of Army vet	1	Wine cooler	1
Cassette	1	Prayer	1
Ace of hearts	1	Frag	1
Sealed package	1	Marines hymn	1
Soap case	1	Pete & Marine Stewart poster	1
Cross, hand stitched	1	Partially burned Vietnam poster	1
Acorn earring	1	"1 in 55, Survivor Guilt" plaque	1
Stained-glass butterfly	1	Washington state flag	1
Russian flag pin	1	Meal ticket	1
"Benny" sticker	1	Prayer card	1
Pen	1	Cigar	1
Marines 3d trophy	1	Cross	1
Glove with GI names	1	Order form	1
Partially burned flag	1	Soviet Union plaque	1

"Grandma for Peace" sign	1	SP-5	1
Ring	1	Pipe cleaner glasses	1
Brick with name	1	Bamboo and metal cage	1
"Smile" sticker	1	Paper figure	1
Texas flag	1	Child's glove	1
Peace wreath	1	Louisiana flag	1
Lighter	1	Crystal	1
Brown paper turkey	1		

Total number of objects   641

A quick summary of the shape of this piece of the collection illustrates the various collections within the collection. The majority of these items are nonmilitary. There are more objects than written messages. Of the written messages more are spontaneous notes than long, deliberated letters. More photographs are left than long letters. Twenty-eight kinds of things appeared more than once at the wall. That eighty-five kinds of things appeared only once indicates that there is no clear consensus about the kinds of things that should be left at the Wall. The Constitution, the burned flag, the state flags, the peace wreath, the "Grandma for Peace" sign, the pins and the Soviet plaque, the military paraphernalia, the "Learn from History" sign, the "Home from Frag" sign, the dog tags, the Agent Orange card, and the thirty-four POW items are all explicitly political negotiations with the nation.

Together, all of these things are a potent testament to the will of these people to make their mark in this conversation about the war, the bodies, and the nation. These objects form a collection that presents a tremendous challenge to the generic memory of the soldier and to the idea that the changes in the American imagined community wrought by the Vietnam War have been accepted and understood by the members of this community.

THE THINGS

high-heel shoe	*meal ticket*	*19 cents*
Purple Heart	*baseball glove*	*nurse's hat*
booby trap wire	*sealed package*	*POW band*
helmet with peace sign	*peace poster*	*bicycle part*

shot glass	tennis ball	salt shaker
unmarked cassette tape	key chain	photograph
cowboy boots	teddy bear	patch[65]

This wedding ring belonged to a young Viet Cong fighter. He was killed by a Marine unit in the Phu Loc province of South Vietnam in May 1968. I wish I knew more about this young man. I have carried this ring for 18 years and it's time for me to lay it down. This boy is no longer my enemy.

Frederick Garten, Sgt. USMC

—Letter left at the Wall[66]

Leaving something at the Wall is a communicative act, a complicated kind of speech.[67] To offer something at the monument is to imply that the thing has meaning and value beyond its intended function; and yet the particular function of the offered thing gives it the values that are speaking at the Wall. The question of how to understand the things left at the memorial asks us to think about their function and to give credence to their symbolic life. Doing so requires a shift in scholarly thinking about things.

The symbolic lives of things have eluded many scholars interested in using them to reconstruct the details of historical moments. This is, in part, because the symbolic weight of everyday objects has rarely been as powerfully felt as it is at the Wall. A ring or a favorite tea cup might be an important part of a private memory, but until the Vietnam Veterans Memorial was constructed, there had been little room in public memory for this kind of detail. As a result, scholarship in material culture, where one might look for answers to questions about how to understand these things, does not provide a clear model for thinking about the things left at the Wall. Work in material culture falls into two broad but distinct camps. One is interested primarily in theories of interpretation as they might apply to things, and the other is interested in the details of the things themselves. We might call the former "conceptual material culture studies" and the latter "material culture studies."

Thomas Schlereth's *Material Culture Studies in America* is the best anthology of the more material scholarship.[68] This work is drawn from art history, folklore studies, architectural history, and social history. It is primarily concerned with the particular history, construction, function, fabric, design, and use of material objects. It argues that studies of material objects have much to contribute to the project of writing history. It argues, rightly, that things are full of useful information about the everyday lives of their users. Schlereth and others want to discover more details about the origins, production, and histories of things, to make them available as tools for teaching about the details of a place in time; but they do not explore the symbolic work of material things. Borrowing a mission statement from Brook Hindle, Schlereth writes, "The mission (of material culture studies) is a great one. Even the beginnings registered so far are exciting. They point to the fulfillment of the deep-running need of this generation and those to come for a better history of their past which is both true and useful. It will be truer and more useful than present histories precisely because its abstractions will be tied by an intricate web to the real world of material culture."[69] In a sense, this desire on the part of these scholars to connect historical narratives to everyday details echoes the desires of those bringing things to the Wall—a truer, more useful representation of the past, writ large with things. But while this scholarship has produced some amazing stories of histories found in things, it is often so concerned with the physical details of the things that it neglects to usefully place these stories in their cultural contexts.

The more theoretical work comes out of a hybrid of linguistics and anthropology and is principally concerned with structuralism, hermeneutics, and poststructuralism. Christopher Tilley's anthology *Reading Material Culture* tries to define this disciplinary and theoretical merger at the site of material culture by culling applicable insights from the writings of Claude Lévi-Strauss, Paul Ricoeur, Clifford Geertz, Roland Barthes, Jacques Derrida, and Michel Foucault.[70] The anthology is both wonderfully rich and strikingly barren—it is thick with a riot of ideas about signs and systems of signs, but it is almost completely without mention of particular things. This problem robs this scholarship of the details that could give shape to these ideas. Tilley's structuralists are interested in how things might work as a language system, and his poststructuralists are interested, primarily, in decontextualizing the study of things. In the anthology Bjørnar Olsen argues that in Barthes's writing, material culture "became 'decontextualized' (or liberated) from the historical moment of creation, and committed to new readers and the future . . . due to its veritable duration this material text opens itself to infinite readings as it continually confronts new readers in altered

historical situations."[71] This is an inspiring idea, but the work of actually doing readings is as difficult as one might expect—it is the challenge presented by the objects left at the Wall.

There are useful models in Tilley's work and in Schlereth's work.
Things have a weighty specificity because they are imagined and constructed in particular historical contexts, and they have multiple,
changing meanings outside of these contexts because the systems of
signs in which they operate are always changing. However, in the things
at the Wall there is a tension between the context from which they come
and the communicative work they do. Scholarship in material culture
needs to build models for thinking about contexts and systems of signs
together. I am not the first scholar to want to do this work. Anthropologist Grant McCracken was inspired by structuralist and post-
structuralist theoretical principals but frustrated when he tried to apply them to particular objects. He could not fit the shapes of the
buildings he was reading into a subtle, scientific system of signs.[72] His
book *Culture and Consumption* argues that "we need to move beyond
the limitations and banalities that now inhere in the 'clothes as language'
approach."[73] The banalities of this approach include extensive chart-
ing, graphing, and schematizing of the workings of these objects as a
language in order to decode an underlying pattern of meaning. The
problem with these linguistic models for the study of things, as they
have been used, is that the things are overwhelmed by the models used
to study them; it is not that things cannot fulfill the structural requirements of language, but that it is not productive to stuff things too tightly
into the schemes of these language models.[74]

M. M. Bakhtin's simple notion of heteroglossia—the idea that "all utterances are heteroglot in that they are functions of a matrix of forces practically impossible to recoup, therefore impossible to resolve"—is useful here for thinking about how to bring together the two prevailing impulses in studies of material culture.[75] Bakhtin's notion asks us to think about this interpretive work as witnessing and reconstructing the coming together of the matrix of forces—the contextual and the symbolic—that give these utterances at the Wall their particular meanings.

On August 15, 1986, someone left a cardboard box with a bicycle tube for Joseph Cook, whose name is carved into panel 58e.[76] Clearly this utterance is heteroglot. What is the history of a bicycle tube? What is it made of? Who makes it? Why? For whom? Who uses it? For what? What does it tell us about Joseph Cook? What does it tell us about the war? About grief? What does it mean to decontextualize this? What other questions do we need to ask? Surely the bike tube has multiple meanings; how do we get at them? And, what do they mean for those who have survived Joseph Cook?

Things have meaning before they come to the Wall, and at the base of the Wall they are shot through with more meanings. The medals, the wedding ring, the sliding glass door, the Slim Jim, the bullets, boots, baseballs, T-shirts, can openers, coffee cups, Kool Aid, newspaper clippings, books, records, dice, hats, rings, toy elephants, cigars, seashells, crucifixes, key chains, gloves, pine cones, lockets, stuffed rabbits, and toy motorcycles all speak loudly.[77] The work of this book is to puzzle through the possible impulses that brought them to the Wall; this is an effort to think about the symbolic work that these things are doing and to figure out what this symbolic work, as a communication between the citizen and the nation, can teach us about how these Americans imagine the nation and their place in it. The work of making memorials is a good place to begin this exploration.

DISCOVERING
THE MEMORY OF BODIES

A HISTORY OF AMERICAN WAR
MEMORIALS

William S. Hodgson—letter and fishhook
Unknown—letter signed Anna Grove
Richard Shuley—bugle off cap
M. Davis—Thanksgiving book
E. Cunningham—$3.95, comb, and postage stamps
S. R. White—stencil plate and 2 cents
James Wallace—purse and 25 cents
Unknown—inkstand, knife, letter, and 75 cents
A. Calhoun—diary
Unknown—purse and 25 cents
Unknown—soldier's pocket book
Unknown—pipe
L. H. Lee—two combs, diary, and bullet that killed him[1]

This is a list of the precious things found in the pockets of Union soldiers killed at Gettysburg. In the heat of the battle the bodies of the
dead were hastily and randomly buried in shallow graves; a few days
later local patriots decided to reclaim them. They dug up the bodies
and searched them for clues to the soldiers' identities. Using fragments
like those in the list above, the citizens of Gettysburg matched names

to as many bodies as they could and then reburied the Union men with proud grave markers in what would become the Soldiers' National Cemetery. From the things came the names, and from the names came an enduring expression of national unity and pride.

At the Vietnam Veterans Memorial the names of the dead and their precious things are reassembled to make a vastly different kind of memory about war, bodies, and the nation. National pride, the names of the dead, and personal mementos are refigured in the making of the public memory of America's longest war. American memorializers in the 1980s started with the assumption that the names of the dead were the most important part of the commemoration of war. This assumption was shaped by a complicated history of memorial impulses, which began most significantly at Gettysburg in 1863. New traditions created at Gettysburg radically transformed ideas about what to do with the bodies and the memory of the war dead and, in turn, transformed the making of national memory in the United States and Europe. The new memorial practices came at just the moment in which powerful nation-building impulses were developing on both continents. The impulse to remember the individual soldier as an emblem of the nation, in short, came at the moment of the flowering of nationalism. The Wall comes to us out of a rupture of this history.

Until the 1860s, memorial traditions had remained relatively constant since the time of the ancient Egyptians. European and, later, American memorializers, drawing on a limited range of symbolic forms, remembered wars as triumphs of state or divine power, without paying particular attention to ordinary soldiers. The second half of the nineteenth and the greater part of the twentieth centuries witnessed a strong, steady shift away from this unadulterated adulation of centralized power toward the more complicated, textured practice of remembering wars by the sacrifices and lost lives of common fighting men.[2] Articulating the memory of a war came to require articulating the imagined shapes of the individual as a representative of the nation,[3] to require articulating the connections between the heroic individual and the nation. Each of the various shifts of emphasis in memorializing marks a different articulation of the connections between the individual and the nation. The story of making memorials in the twentieth century is, in part, a playing out of the construction of a mass, uniformed individual and of the nation.

When the boys of '63 were exhumed at Gettysburg, there was a practical problem in carrying out this new idea for dealing with the bodies of the dead. During the Civil War, as in virtually all wars before it, the soldiers in the field either did not carry or were not issued any kind of identification because there had been little interest in identifying the bodies of the dead. There are, however, many stories about Civil War soldiers on both sides rigging up homemade identification tags of all sorts—a scrap of leather tied around an ankle or a name and address scrawled on a scrap of paper and shoved into a shoe—stories about these men understanding themselves as worth marking. This lack of dog tags left the exhumers with the task of searching each body for clues about the name and identity to which it had been connected in life. So, in the most literal sense, the impulse to remember the bodies of individual soldiers began with a pilfering of pockets for things.

Why did the people of Gettysburg feel compelled to remember these particular soldiers? Their pockets were likely pilfered because the ideas of the Union and the nation that had inspired them to fight were predicated, in part, on the idea of individual rights and because the dead had been citizens of the nation as well as soldiers in its army. The people of Gettysburg were expressing changing expectations of the nation and new ideas about the value of individual lives and private relationships.

Historians interested in memory and memorializing have pointed to tightening familial and community bonds as possible reasons for these changes.[4] This makes a lot of sense. William Hodgson's letter and fishhook were likely exhumed and catalogued because someone needed to understand the enormous costs of this battle in terms of the individual—the son and the citizen—as well as the nation.

When the soldier is a citizen and the citizen is promised a sacral status, the role of the soldier is necessarily transformed. When a citizen-soldier fights to protect the rights of the people—be they property rights or civil rights—the rhetoric or the idea that inspired him to fight apparently does not evacuate his dead body. But sacrificing a life for the cause of the collective body, for the idea of a government for the people, is problematic, logically. A single monument to Grant or Lincoln could not speak to victory or loss in this ideological framework. In

1863, standing on the battlefield in Gettysburg, Lincoln did not choose to talk about Union ideals of liberty or the economic strength of a united continent. He chose instead to praise the sacrifices of fallen men. He chose to remind his listeners that these sacrifices were greater than the president, his words, and even the nation. This framework makes the loss of the individual a greater sacrifice—rhetorically—and therefore more valuable to remember. Certainly the burial of these soldiers at Gettysburg gave Lincoln the perfect site to articulate the relationships of the individual and the state and the nation. He used it to promise both the nation to the citizen and the citizen to the nation. These Civil War memories "stretched to coincide with a larger network of national pride, militarism, and remembrance" and profoundly changed the history of making memory in America.[5]

The Civil War was the first war in which the bodies of dead soldiers were buried individually. World War I is remembered powerfully by the insistent naming of all those who died. World War II is remembered, in the most literal sense, by monuments that are the spoils of victory: highways, schools, parks, and so on. The memorial to the Vietnam War, a war fought in the name of individual liberty by a generation of Americans whose imagination of their nation did not always stretch to Southeast Asia, is a refiguring of each of these responses. The things in the pockets of Gettysburg's soldiers mark the beginning of the impulse to make strong particular memories of dead soldiers to appease families and to heal the nation, an impulse powerfully expressed at the Vietnam Veterans Memorial.

MAKING CULTURE

rams horns

In the science of archaeology, one of the markers between *Homo sapiens neanderthalensis* and *Homo sapiens* was found in the unearthed grave of a young boy in what is now Siberia. The key to this much celebrated discovery is that the boy was buried with rams horns set on either side of his body. His dead body seems to have had some meaning to his survivors. In the minds of late-twentieth-century scholars, this evidence of ritual or decorative burial signals an awareness of a past, a present, and a future, a future in which there is some value in honoring or remembering the dead; such a conception of time and memory marks one foundation of human culture.[6]

As human memorial practices have become vastly more complicated, the ways in which a culture imagines itself have been writ small in the changing shape of the granite and bronze with which people make promises to the future about the past.[7] The questions that have shaped memorializing reveal the most essential tensions that have shaped the culture; the memorials themselves reveal the responses that have been available. In the late nineteenth and twentieth centuries, the questions that have shaped memorializing have been about bodies and the awkward contradictions of a nationalism predicated on individualism.

Both products of the mid-eighteenth-century revolutions, nationalism, the flourishing of faith in the imagined community of the nation, and individualism, the flourishing of individual self-awareness within the nation, are dependent on each other.[8] This interdependence has informed the work of memorializing in American culture; it has inspired obelisks carved with names, empty cenotaphs, memorial football fields, and dirty combat boots set at the foot of a list of names in black granite.

In the late nineteenth and early twentieth centuries nations were built, in part, on a contract between citizens and the state about the crucial symbolic value of the body of the soldier. The development of nations has been predicated on the willingness of free soldiers to risk their lives for the promise of a sanctified posthumous social position.[9] In mid-nineteenth-century Germany and France, patriotic poetry and songs celebrating the ideal of individual lives made meaningful through the sacred work of fighting for—and risking death for—the nation were tremendously popular, marking the elevated status of the citizen-soldier. As historian George Mosse argues, it was a "willingness to sacrifice themselves on the altar of the fatherland" that young French and German men "hoped would serve to energize their own life and that of the nation."[10] During the American Civil War, for the first time in the history of the United States, common soldiers were buried individually in graves marked with their names. When President Lincoln dedicated the first national battlefield memorial and the soldiers' cemetery at Gettysburg, the nation was celebrated with the memory of the bodies of male citizen-soldiers.

The new social position of these soldiers, both in life and in death, required a new memory of war. Nations promised the soldier a hallowed place in public memory in exchange for his life; nations began, increasingly, to remember war through the heroic contributions of soldiers. As Mosse argues, the "cult of the fallen soldier" after World War I inspired the strong need for remembering the war dead because "each individual soldier who fell in battle had become a person of note, sharing the mission of all the fallen."[11] This first major twentieth-century war, a war that produced unprecedented mass death, is remembered with long lists of names and with monuments for unknown soldiers; the response to the horrors of the scale of violence in this war was an insistent assertion of the memory of uniform, mass sacrifices made for the nation. Following Mosse's logic, historian John Gillis argues that after World War II, the real, material rewards that most white soldiers were able to reap explicitly celebrated their status.

A part of this history, the Vietnam Veterans Memorial was imagined and constructed just as the nation was struggling to overcome a legitimation crisis inspired, in part, by the war it commemorated. More than that of earlier memorials, the design of the Wall, and the traditions upon which the designer drew, foreground the importance of the individual body rather than the nation for which it was sacrificed. This memorial suppresses the symbolism of the nation and disperses it into the aggregate of the names. It is, in part, a national monument to the failure of one imperialist conception of the nation. This memorial does not celebrate the nation. It turns, for its substance, to the names of the dead.

This sacralization of the names is stunningly effective. The Wall is a sacred public space unlike any other in the United States. People visit it with a hushed respect that is different from the noisy chatter with which they approach the Lincoln Memorial or the curious patter with which they tour the National Cathedral. They respond to the names with uncharacteristic reverence, and they participate without embarrassment in the memory being made at the memorial. The memorial seems to eschew national rhetoric, and this effacement of the nation seems to deformalize the public response. It opens up the space for people to claim the memorial as their own with personal and public offerings, and to make themselves part of the process of defining the nation. *How* the definition of the nation is shaped at the Wall and *for whom* are questions the answers to which only time will reveal. But something new has unquestionably been added to the tension of forces that forge national identity, and this study is an inquiry into that new impulse.

The social and political forces that shaped the generation most deeply touched by the Vietnam War created a new community of grief and a troubled relationship, within this community, to the symbolic vocabulary of traditional war memorials. Just as Lincoln needed to turn to the bodies of individual men to remember Gettysburg, the official forgers of the memory of the Vietnam War needed to construct a memory that promised to imagine the costs of the war as no memorial before it had. To do this they combined and refigured all of the memorial impulses of twentieth-century American wars. They built a remarkably complicated memorial, but still they did not find a way to represent all of the conflicting impulses—sorrow, sacrifice, shame, pain, pride, suffering, victory, loss, and genuine confusion about patriotism and the nation—that the Vietnam War produced. So people brought their own memorials to the Wall.

This chapter charts the move from the ancient, heroic monuments to glorious divinities, to the modern memorialization begun in the Civil War period and developed dramatically during World War I. It chronicles a history in which the central memorial trope shifts from glory to sacrifice, a shift especially central to the struggle to remember the Civil War, World War I, and World War II. Finally this chapter explores the ways in which these modern ideas about memorializing were exploded and revised in the Vietnam memorial.

MAKING MEMORIALS

Obelisk of Tuthmosis III
Mound at Marathon
Trajan's Column
Arc de Triomphe

The earliest war memorials were monuments to the erasure of bodies in deference to the power of divine forces and glorious leaders. They were dramatic homages to the victories of gods and kings. The Egyptians built towering obelisks to commemorate the divine powers that blessed their leaders with victory; the Greeks carved great, epic reliefs depicting the mythic battles fought by their heroic leaders; and the Romans, true to their imperial impulses, stole the memorials of their defeated foes and carried them home to Rome.[12]

Art historians who have studied the history of war memorials, Alan Borg and James Curl in particular, have been interested in the formal and symbolic vocabularies with which memorializers have spoken.[13] Because these ancient war memorials did not engage the stories of common soldiers, traditional art history has not paid attention to the fates of their bodies or memories.[14] In fact, the absence of the common soldier in these memorial traditions is an obvious reminder of the soldier's place in the early social systems the memorials commemorated. With the exception of Greek soldiers, whose traditions were not taken up by other Europeans until the twentieth century, virtually all soldiers killed in battle before the Civil War were ignored and abandoned to hastily dug, shallow mass graves. For pre-nineteenth-century memorializers, victory was remembered with celebrations of triumphant deities and leaders.

The Egyptians memorialized with enormous plain rectangular blocks of stone. These obelisks, or God-blocks, were symbols of the potency of the rulers of Egypt. The massive blocks cut from the earth attest to the engineering skills of the Egyptians but were erected as strong reminders of the power of the divinities leading Egypt to victory; they were originally associated with the sun god but came to symbolize the relationship of the rulers of Egypt to all divine powers. After 1479 B.C. some obelisks were carved with the name of a particular victor and the story of the victory. One such obelisk, erected by Tuthmosis III (1479–1525 B.C.), survives in Istanbul. It is carved with the story of the battle but not the story of the fighting men; Egyptian soldiers were not citizen soldiers but hired mercenaries, and the story of the battle was clearly not their story.

For fourth-century Romans it was a matter of pride to steal Egyptian obelisks and ship them back to Rome, and, as Borg argues, it was from Rome that the obelisk entered the Western design vocabulary.[15] The first stolen obelisk still stands, one hundred feet tall, in the Piazza del Popolo in Rome. It is a 235-ton memorial to the conquest of Egypt in 10 B.C., and it established traditions of remembering war that lasted for nearly two thousand years. Another dominant early memorial form —the column—also seems to have originated in Roman thievery and appropriation. Columns are found throughout the Near East dating from 480 B.C., but they were not consistently used as war memorials until they had been transported to Rome.[16] The carefully joined pieces of stone and the shapely carving of the small decorative flourishes on the columns were intended to speak of human mastery over the environment rather than of divine power or state power. Romans popularized the idea of columns as symbols of victory in war and often topped them with statues of victorious leaders. The best known example is Trajan's Column in Rome. (There is a similar column at West Point to commemorate the Civil War dead.)

Triumphal arches were perhaps the most prevalent Roman memorials. Originally, these arches marked significant city entrances; eventually they were used to commemorate particular military victories. The Arch of Titus in Rome, for instance, was built to celebrate victory in Jerusalem in A.D. 70. In 1247 Holy Roman Emperor Frederick II built an enormous memorial arch at Capua, which was much imitated throughout the Middle Ages. As Borg argues, in the nineteenth century, triumphal arches were commonplace. The most famous arch—Paris's Arc de Triomphe—was begun in 1806 to celebrate Napoleon's victories.

The ancient Greeks, in contrast, did not remember wars with these triumphal arches and columns. Instead, they paid special attention to and honored the memory of their war dead. There was a powerful place in Greek ideology for the heroic figure of the fallen soldier; to die on a battlefield was to die an honorable death. A few distinguished leaders were buried in elaborate private tombs, but most soldiers were buried in communal graves called *polyandreia*. These communal graves were decorated with elaborate markers commemorating the glorious sacrifice of the young. The most famous memorial to Greek soldiers is probably the Mound at Marathon, a memorial to the soldiers who fell defending Athens from the Persians in 490 B.C. The mound was built over the bodies of the dead as an enormous testament to their victory.[17] But the mounds, only a few of which remain today, are the exceptions rather than the rule in Greek memorial traditions; a more common practice, and one that has appealed deeply to the twentieth-century imagination, was the inscribing of the names of the war dead on memorial stelae. The earliest such "casualty list" is dated at 465 B.C.[18]

Because this attention to individual soldiers runs counter to the long history of bold memorials to victorious leaders, it is worth speculating about why the Greeks built such a different kind of memory and about why the rest of Europe ignored these traditions until the nineteenth and the twentieth centuries. Certainly, the social position of those who fought is at the heart of this question. A soldier who is a citizen rather than a hired mercenary requires a different kind of memory.

The basic elements of Western memorial architecture are lifted from the Egyptian and Roman rather than Greek traditions: obelisks, columns, and arches make up the great bulk of memorials in Europe and the United States. Historian George Mosse contends that the development of eighteenth-century citizen-soldier armies around the time of the American and French revolutions dramatically reshaped the ideologies and mythologies that surrounded soldiers and thereby the nation.[19] He argues that the army volunteers were powerful myth makers who introduced sacrifice and sacred heroism as the central tropes of memorialization. Mosse maintains that in nationalism, people found individual identities through war, giving individual men a sense of power and presence in a community. This vision of an empowering nation was predicated on the willingness of the eighteenth-century volunteers to fight and on their practice of seeing themselves as martyrs to a cause larger than themselves—the infant nation.[20]

It is at Gettysburg that the relationship of this nationalism, volunteer soldiers, and the work of remembering war boldly rewrote memorial traditions.

The Civil War: Discovering the Memory of Bodies

As we have seen, before the Civil War, American soldier-dead were buried in unmarked mass graves. Monuments remembered battles and heroic leaders but not the individual fallen soldiers. At Valley Forge, where more than three thousand American soldiers died during the winter of 1777–78, there is only one marked grave, the grave of a lieutenant who requested that he remain with his men.[21] The closest thing to a "proper" burial for soldiers came in the 1850s, when a few frontier forts established post cemeteries with individual marked graves. These were not for battle dead, however, but for soldiers who died in accidents or from illness far from home.[22] As late as 1861, at the battle of Manassas, Union and Confederate dead were buried in unmarked mass graves. In that same year, however, the War Department estab-

lished a policy that delegated to officers in command the responsibility for burying dead officers and soldiers; this responsibility included trying to provide "names for a registered headboard to be placed at each soldier's grave." In the following year, the National Cemetery System was established by an act of Congress, and a number of states, including Pennsylvania, passed legislation requiring attention to the bodies of the dead.[23] These policies did not trickle down to military practice immediately. In June of 1863 the Union Army still had no system for burying the dead individually, and headstones were not used. There is no mention of these policies in the writings of the key actors at Gettysburg.[24]

The battle at Gettysburg was a crucial turning point in the war. The Confederate Army was rested from its recent victory in Chancellorsville, but its supplies were running low; the Confederacy desperately needed the one more major victory that General Lee hoped would earn support for his cause from Europe. But the resounding defeat it suffered in Gettysburg changed the momentum of the war. For the Confederacy this loss marked the beginning of the end. Lee had tried to take advantage of the general discomfort in the war-weary North, but his troops lost and provided the Union with a dramatic symbol for a victorious, united nation.

What inspired patriots in 1863 to transform the battleground at Gettysburg into a hallowed burial ground by unearthing and reinterring the decaying bodies of the fallen soldiers? Why at this moment was there a shift in the long history of burying soldiers in mass graves where they lay on the battlefield? In July of 1863 no formal burial parties were organized to put the mass of stinking bodies strewn around the battlefields in the ground. Most Union dead were randomly buried, by their friends, in shallow graves that made "the woods and fields at Gettysburg a hodgepodge burial ground."[25]

As the days wore on, however, the Union bodies became the center of an effort to make the battlefield sacred ground. While the makeshift hospitals, entrepreneurial embalmers, and Union soldiers were busy attending to the injured and the dying, two Gettysburg lawyers and longtime rivals—David Wills and David McConaughy—were getting to the work of making memorials.[26] Pennsylvania Governor Andrew G. Curtin, while in Gettysburg to visit with the wounded, asked Wills to attend to the war dead.[27] Wills wrote the governor soon thereafter requesting a central burial site as a "propriety and actual necessity." Wills was concerned with getting this project moving so as to have a place to bury the "many hundreds who are dying here in the hospitals." In a July 24 letter to the governor he wrote, "Our dead are lying on the fields unburied, (that is, no grave being dug) with small portions of earth dug up alongside of the body and thrown over it. In many instances arms and legs and sometimes heads protrude and my attention has been directed to several places where hogs were actually rooting out the bodies and devouring them."

In the same letter he explained that he had been talking successfully with representatives from New York and Baltimore about the need for a common burial ground—evidence that he was unsure about who was responsible for the bodies—and that he had, in fact, decided on the right place for these burials:

> There is one spot very desirable for this purpose. It is the point on which the desperate attack was made by the Louisiana Brigades on Thursday evening and were finally driven back by the Infantry, assisted with the artillery men, with their handspikes and rammers. It is this spot above all others for the *honorable burial* of the dead who have fallen on those fields.

Wills's emphasis in this last sentence is a clear indication that he imagined his responsibility for "overseeing the removal of the bodies" to stretch beyond a public health function. He understood the task of attending to the bodies to include some gesture of respect towards the individuals who died. He continued in the July 24 letter,

My idea is for Pennsylvania to purchase the ground at once, so as to furnish
a place for the friends of those who are here seeking places for the perma-
nent burial of their fallen ones, to inter them at once, and also to be a place
for the burial of the hundreds who are dying here in the hospitals. The other
States would certainly, through their Legislatures, in co-operation with our
Legislature, contribute towards defraying the expenses of appropriately
arranging and decorating the grounds. . . . The bodies should be arranged,
as far as practicable, on order of Companies, Regiments, Divisions, and
Corps. . . .

Wills was clearly trying to negotiate a number of problems presented
by these bodies. He needed to assure the Pennsylvania governor that
the state would not have to pay for the entire memorial, he needed to
reiterate the importance of respectful burials, and he needed to imagine a plan for organizing the graves that would acknowledge the political and military hierarchies that might need to be remembered along
with the dead.

Wills included in this letter not only these details of place and design and the gruesome description quoted above but also the following plea: "I know the soldiers in the field would feel most grateful for
such a proper mark of respect, on the part of the Chief Executive, for
his fallen comrades, and the multitude of friends of the fallen dead, at
home, would rejoice to know that the bodies of their brave kindred
had been properly cared for by our Governor."[28] This appeal to concerns about morale in the Union Army, which was quite low at this
point, and to concerns about appeasing Northern families who had sacrificed their sons for the Union is important. Wills wanted to assure
the living soldiers that they would get posthumous respect in exchange
for their lives, and he wanted to console the families with the assurance
that their kindred would be cared for "properly." He was also trying to
sell the governor on a possible political advantage: he emphasized that
the governor, who was facing a re-election campaign, would be serving his cause and constituents well with a memorial burial ground.

Wills's lobbying of the governor, thus, took four main tacks. He
stressed the need for honorable burial, the inhuman conditions of the
battlefield, the peace of mind of the families of the fallen, and the
morale of the troops. He seems to have tried several arguments without particular confidence in any one of them: the pleading quality of
the letter suggests that he was not confident that the governor would

be interested in his proposal. His letter is a testament to the evolving, uncertain status of the war dead. Wills was not sure that the need to honor sacrifice or the potential boost to Union morale or the wishes of the family were important enough to merit the trouble of establishing this cemetery.

In any event, some of these arguments did work with Curtin; Wills won the governor's approval. He ran into trouble, however, when he tried to purchase the land for the burial ground. Wills discovered that David McConaughy, the president of Gettysburg's Evergreen Cemetery Association, had already purchased the sections of the battlefield that he, Wills, had described to Curtin. McConaughy sought to revive the ailing financial circumstances of his cemetery by expanding it to include parts of the adjoining battlefield for the burial of the fallen soldiers. Because Wills had the authority of the governor's office at his disposal, he was able to buy the land back from McConaughy by August 17, 1863. On this date Wills wrote to Governor Curtin again, "By virtue of the authority reposed in me by your Excellency, I have invited the co-operation of the several loyal States having soldier-dead on the battlefield around this place, in the noble project of removing their remains from their present exposed and imperfectly buried condition, on the fields for miles around, to a cemetery. . . . the grounds embrace about seventeen acres on Cemetery Hill . . . it is the spot which is specially consecrated to this sacred purpose."[29]

McConaughy was cut out of the development of the soldiers' cemetery, but he did not retire from the commemorative work at hand. He turned his attention to the memorialization of the battlefield itself. Within a few days, McConaughy had purchased large sections of the land on which important battles, including Little Round Top and Big Round Top, had been fought. In an open letter to the people of Gettysburg dated August 19, 1863, he wrote, "Immediately after the Battle of Gettysburg, the thought occurred to me that there could be no more fitting expressive memorial of the heroic valor and signal triumphs of our Army . . . than the battlefield itself, with its natural and artificial defenses preserved and perpetuated in the exact form and condition they presented during the battles. . . . In pursuance of the original purpose I now propose to the patriotic citizen of Pennsylvania to unite with me in the tenure of the sacred grounds of this battlefield."[30]

He went on to propose that these same patriotic citizens pay ten dollars each to buy the rest of the battlefield to preserve it as a historical landmark. The letter is full of rich, sensuous descriptions of the heroic contours of this landscape. He praises the "massive rocks and wonderful stone defenses," "the wooded heights," and the forbidding "granite spur" of the infamous Round Top. McConaughy's proposed formation of a monument association met with great approval in the local paper as a "happy and patriotic conception to commemorate the heroic valor of our national forces in the recent battle."[31]

The Gettysburg Battle-Field Memorial Association was soon formed. Its charter promised to preserve the battlefields in their present condition. The language of the September 5 announcement with which McConaughy publicly declared the intentions of the newly formed Gettysburg Battle-Field Memorial Association was boisterous with new patriotism:

> The Battle-grounds of Gettysburg—the Battle-field of Pennsylvania—the scenes of the only battles fought on the soil of the free North—the Battle-field of this second war of Independence, because the turning battle of the war, from which dates the downfall of the Rebellion—it appeals with mute eloquence to the great loyal heart of the people. To it all eyes turn as to a sacred spot, which should be guarded with religious care, and zealously preserved from disturbance, neglect, or decay, or the wasting of the elements . . . these have become sacred to all who love the republic and delight to honor its brave defenders, whether among its living or its dead.[32]

McConaughy went on to ask, "Shall we not pay a just and grateful tribute to the heroic valor and signal triumphs of our army?" He emphasized the need for "perpetual witness" and "honorable emulation." He called for a "shrine of loyalty and patriotism." He drew here on a new elegiac tradition, and his plea parallels the sentimental language of domesticity to convince the citizens of Gettysburg of the value in his project.

This language reflects subtle differences between McConaughy's vision and Wills's. Wills was asked to address the problem of the bodies and the families; McConaughy was interested in the potential patriotic and economic value of the land. McConaughy described the ways in which the drama of the battle was inscribed in the landscape, and Wills described the valiant fighting of the men to hold the land in which he hoped to have them rest honorably. McConaughy bet on the "sacred grounds," and Wills bet on the fallen soldiers. Apparently,

in the wake of the battle, the memory of the fighting was important enough to the citizens and the governor to accommodate both memorial efforts.

In the months after the battle, neither lawyer knew quite which formulation of patriotic, heroic, or martyred memory would best appeal to his audience. The heroic memorial to and the honorable burial of the fallen at Gettysburg emerged from the competing efforts of the lawyers. Their writings provide an opportunity to witness the rough beginnings of memorial practices that would shape American national identity and public memory for the next century. As historian John Patterson argues, "the process of regathering and identifying the decayed bodies of the fallen men deserves to be recorded as a significant step in the democratization of American experience."[33] The ground became sacred because so many had fallen in an effort to hold it. The sacrifices of the fighting men emerged as the central memorial trope, and the bodies were made the focus of this patriotic memory.[34]

Ninety years earlier, when the "world's most democratic" army fought on the American side of the Revolutionary War, most of the revolutionary volunteers were new immigrants who could find no other way into the social fabric, but their role "contributed to the expansion of the definition of the citizenry and defined participation in armed conflict as part of the normative definition of citizenship."[35] In the years between the Revolutionary War and the Civil War, the American military consisted of state militias, which were intended to be composed completely of able-bodied free white men. They were, in practice, made up of the poor and the recently immigrated. In the immediate pre-Civil-War years 60 percent of all volunteers in state militias were Irish immigrants and another 10 percent came from western Europe.[36] There was little social prestige associated with soldiering, and desertion rates were very high. It is not surprising that the bodies of these soldiers were buried in mass graves.

During the Civil War, recruiting and conscription remained less than completely democratic, even as the work of soldiering began to take on a higher social value. Until March of 1863, the Union Army depended mainly on volunteers, but two years into the war, with awful stories of bloody carnage sweeping through the North, campaigns for new volunteers were not successful. A handful of new state drafts were met with firm opposition, and there were many desertions.[37] The Federal Conscription Act of 1863 responded to these problems with a sharp assertion of federal power, but the conscription act did not demand all Northern bodies equally. It allowed any man to buy a deferment with three hundred dollars (a figure the framers of this law erroneously thought would be within the reach of working men), and it allowed any man to hire another man, presumably for less than three hundred dollars, to serve in his place.[38] So the wealthy who did not want to serve did not serve: 118,000 men hired stand-ins, and 87,000 paid the three hundred dollar deferment fee.[39] Moreover, nearly 160,000 native-born Northerners illegally evaded the draft between 1863 and 1865. As a result, nearly 50 percent of those who served during this period were either foreign-born or poor, and many were both.

Still, the men in the Civil War militias were a more representative, willing group than those who had fought in the Revolution. The great majority of native-born men who served, the other half of the soldiers in the Civil War, were farmers and relatively skilled farm workers.[40] The men who volunteered, or who did not evade the draft, represented a real citizen fighting force: they were fighting for something other than money. The Civil War volunteers and draftees played a crucial role in transforming the memory of the soldier because they were just the kind of army that George Mosse argues was the foundation for twentieth-century nationalism. Their mission was, at least in part, ideological, and they had families waiting for them at home. In spending these lives, the federal government was exacting a high price from its citizenry in exchange for which the nation would have to value the memory of the dead.

This promise of an honored memory did not make all soldiers happy with their lot. Some of the fiercest dissatisfaction surfaced in the New York City draft riots of July 1863. Fueled by a growing sense of pride and frustration among the poor and foreign-born who were asked to fight, hundreds of men (mostly Irish Catholics) raged in the streets of New York for three days. They understood themselves as both threatened by and capable of resisting federal authority. Furious about the terms of the draft, particularly the exemption of freed blacks, these rioters disrupted the daily life of the city so radically that troops fresh from the fighting in Gettysburg had to be shipped in on July 16 to quell the violence, which eventually killed more than a hundred people. While this anger about the inequities of the new military and the surge of racial resentment that would remain a shadow side of American nationhood were not part of the memory of this war, the public indignation of the New York draft rioters was an expression of their unwillingness to participate in a system of conscription that did not treat them fairly. The riots were, in part, an expression of the same conception of the citizen that inspired the people of Gettysburg to give their dead a proper burial.

The cemetery at Gettysburg was also a product of changing middle-class funerary practices. In the immediate prewar years a rapidly growing, increasingly urban, and increasingly prosperous middle class was replacing less standardized, private practices with services for which they could now pay. One of these services was the burial of the dead. Cities needed public burial places, and a handful of professions emerged as a result. In 1831 the poorly named "rural cemetery movement" was initiated with the founding of the Mount Auburn Cemetery in Cambridge, Massachusetts.[41] This cemetery was designed as a park-like space in which to bury the citizens of the increasingly dense city and in which visitors might get relief from the city, commune with nature, and grieve in a sculpted pastoral landscape.[42] By 1861 there were sixty-six such cemeteries in the eastern United States. Northerners were reinventing burial practices to accommodate urban life; the cemeteries were meant to be used by the living as rural sanctuaries from the city and by the dead as a peaceful reward.[43] In Gettysburg, David Wills hired William Saunders, a Scotsman working for the Department of Agriculture, to design the soldiers' cemetery at Gettysburg, because Saunders was a part of the rural cemetery movement.[44] Like the civic-minded Northeasterners who were building rural cemeteries, Wills wanted a carefully choreographed resting place for the dead that would invite a steady stream of visitors.

Saunders brought the ideals of the rural cemetery movement with him to Gettysburg, but he also had to face pressing political questions in the design of the soldiers' cemetery. The first was that the bodies would be grouped by state, and the second was that the states' lots would be carefully mapped so that no state was given prominence over the others. As historian Gary Wills has observed, "by considerable ingenuity in grading the cemetery's incline, and by arranging the graves in great curving ranks, Saunders avoided preferential treatment of states or inequality in the ranks of the fallen."[45] The enormous importance of balancing the position of the states is an indication of the complicated relationship of even the Northern states to the idea of the nation: the graves were organized by state in a semicircle, with each state allotted a section that radiated out from the center. This design foregrounded the individual grave, but its attention to the place of the states also acted as a reminder of the limited acceptance of the idea of the nation. Even as individual bodies were being recognized, the form of the recognition marks an incomplete transition to the cult of the nation.

Lincoln's tribute at Gettysburg, however, completed the transition. His dedication of the battlegrounds and commemoration of the dead are remarkable in their negotiation of the state, the nation, and the body. His address dramatizes the democratizing impulse by making the war dead sacred, and it uses this impulse, in a brilliant rhetorical twist, as a powerful nation-building tool. He remembers the dead by dedicating the field:

> Now we are engaged in a great civil war, testing whether that nation, or any nation so conceived and so dedicated, can long endure. We are met on a great battlefield of that war. We have come to dedicate a portion of that field as a final resting place for those who here gave their lives that that nation might live. It is altogether fitting and proper that we do this.

He celebrates the valor of those who gave their lives, he praises the commemoration of the field on which they fell, and then he retreats, cautioning,

> But in a larger sense we cannot dedicate, we cannot consecrate, we cannot hallow this ground. The brave men living and dead who struggled here

have consecrated it far above our poor power to add or detract. The world will little note nor long remember what we say here but it can never forget what they did here.[46]

"Cannot dedicate," "cannot consecrate," "cannot hallow this ground." The ironies echo around these much consecrated phrases like noisy ghosts. The world has long remembered the men who fell through Lincoln's carefully chosen and obsessively documented nation-forging words. This wise capturing of the emotional heart of the memorial has itself been fantastically memorialized. Not only is the Gettysburg Address a staple of histories of the United States, but it is also the only speech known to have been physically commemorated. In 1915, one year after the last soldiers were finally officially buried, a broad granite monument was erected to the memory of the Gettysburg Address.[47]

Gettysburg, this definitive site for American memory of war, spawned yet another memorial practice. The first Memorial Day was celebrated in Gettysburg in 1868.[48] It was established as a holiday for the remembrance of the "heroic war dead" rather than the war itself. It was heralded with an official order, that read, in part,

> What can aid and do more to assure this result than cherishing tenderly the memory of our heroic war dead who made their breasts a barricade between our country and the foes? Their soldier lives were the reveille of freedom to a race in chains and their deaths a tattoo of rebellious tyranny in arms. We should guard their graves with sacred vigilance—all that the consecrated wealth and taste of the nation can add to their adornment and security is but a fitting tribute to the memory of her slain defenders.[49]

The language of this proclamation and the confidence of its purpose cement the contribution of the battles at Gettysburg in shifting the focus of the memory of war onto the bodies of the fallen soldiers.

World War I: Naming Absence

908,371 British killed
191,652 British missing
1,357,800 French killed
537,000 French missing
116,516 Americans killed
4,500 Americans missing[50]

Memorial practices after Gettysburg further expressed the changing relationships of the bodies of American soldiers, American soil, and the idea of the nation. Thirty-five years after Gettysburg, in 1898, another crucial decision about the bodies of American soldiers was made: the policy of repatriation was initiated. In the midst of the Spanish-American War, civilian morticians were contracted to disinter and identify the bodies of dead American soldiers and prepare them for shipment back to the United States. As the official historian of the National Cemetery System writes, "it was probably the first time in history that a country at war with a foreign power had disinterred its soldiers who died on foreign soil and brought them home to family and friends."[51] This policy, which continues to give families the option of bringing their sons and daughters home, can leave no doubt about the importance of the memory of soldiers in the work of nation building. Spending American bodies on imperial adventures on foreign soil required an especially careful negotiation of the relationship between the citizen and the nation; the bodies had to be treated with particular respect, and families had to know that their sons would eventually come home to rest in the ground for which they died. Bringing these bodies to rest in American soil was, and has remained, essential to the fabric of the imagined nation.

Fifty-five years after Gettysburg, World War I brought further changes to the work of making memory of war. Although there was some interest in practical memorials, the traditional memorial forms—cenotaphs, obelisks, arches, a growing number of soldier-hero statues—were erected throughout Europe in small villages and city centers to mark local and national memories of the war. These traditional forms were, however, reshaped at the sites of the new battlefield memorials, and these reshaped forms have had a lasting impact on Western memorial design. Driven by the sheer numbers of the dead and the ideological void left by the nature of the conflict, memorial commissions—most notably in Britain—turned to the lost bodies and to the names of the dead. Although the burial of the dead at Gettysburg became the centerpiece in the rhetorical articulation of the ideologies inspiring the Civil War and the reforging of the American nation, the hundreds of thousands of bodies missing in French fields were not so easily incorporated into a statement of national purpose or justification of the war. The war started and ended on nearly the same battlefield and killed 8 million men and women. (One French citizen in twenty-eight died in the war.) Even the noisiest patriots were depressed by the grisliness of this war. "It was the job," argues art historian John Harris, "of the architect to put into tangible and symbolic form the sense of loss and tragedy felt by those who survived."[52] From their very first meetings, memorial commissions in Europe spoke of remembering the tragedy of this war as a warning against future wars. This idea was a sharp break from established traditions of memorializing. Obelisks, columns, and bronze statues of proud leaders do not speak of loss. "The bombast of the imperial Roman monuments, of Napoleonic triumphal arches or Prussian victory columns" hardly seemed to speak to the memory of four years in the trenches.[53]

The English designs of Sir Edwin Lutyens, a well-known patriot and an architect with the Imperial War Graves Commission, reflect his training in the Renaissance humanist tradition, which had long drawn on grand granite gestures. But for his battlefield memorial at Ypres Lutyens turned, with many of his peers, from the celebratory to the cautionary, to warnings against war made in the names of the dead.[54] In 1918 Lutyens and his peers began to design what Thomas Laqueur describes as "venues for names."[55]

Sir Reginald Blomfield's Menin Gate, a memorial to the men and women killed at Ypres, used the arch of an existing gateway through which nearly every Allied soldier who fought there had passed, but Blomfield transformed the arch both by covering it with the inscribed names of the dead and by stretching the traditional form of the arch to accommodate all 54,896 names of the missing.[56] The Menin Gate made the names the center of the memorial. The names seemed to be all that these architects found worthy of the task of remembering so much loss, but this use of names was complicated: it both asserted an individual memory and lost that memory in the mass of names. As Thomas Laqueur's essay on memory and naming argues, "a new era of remembrance began: the era of the common soldier's name or its self-conscious and sacralized oblivion."[57]

The central design element of Lutyens's 1927 memorial to the missing at Thiepval is also a listing of names, 73,357 of them. Like Blomfield's memorial, the Thiepval memorial refigures the traditional form of the arch to hold the incredible number of names. This determined emphasis on naming transformed the commemoration of war in Europe after 1919; the names became the substance of the memorials.

While the bodies at Gettysburg were a bridge between the idea of the nation and the status of the individual, the bodies of World War I were lost: literally, in the mud, and, rhetorically, in the scale of the war, and this made it very difficult for memorializers to justify the individual losses for the sake of the nation. Memorializers responded to this difficulty by abstracting the names of the dead. It is not surprising that the battlefield memorials for the missing at Thiepval and Ypres were the most potent and innovative memorials to this war. Twenty names on an obelisk in the middle of a town square articulate the losses of the community with a heavy specificity, but 73,357 names covering columns and expansive vaulted ceilings express incomprehensibility. These veils of names cannot help but call into question the relationship of the individual to the nation. In this way they are a key middle point between the bodies and the things carried to the names at Gettysburg and the names without bodies at the Wall.

The other major memorial contribution of World War I was the memorial to the unknown soldier. Like the Menin Gate and the Thiepval memorial, these memorials reflect the tension between naming bodies, naming absence, and "sacralized oblivion." The first tomb for an unknown soldier, the inspiration of the Reverend David Railton (a chaplain in Flanders), was proposed to Westminster Abbey early in 1920.[58] It was dedicated on November 11, 1920, with the inscription, "An Unknown British Warrior." Because the unknown soldier is one body celebrated for its anonymity, it has been argued that this and the other tombs of unknown soldiers are doing strikingly different memorial work than the Menin Gate and the Thiepval memorial, in which individual names stand in the place of lost bodies. However, both memorial impulses grapple with the scale of lives lost and with the conflictual simultaneous reification and massification of individual losses.

In Europe, both of these memorial efforts, in their turns away from the simpler expressions of the contract between the nation and the citizen at Gettysburg, signaled a failure of national ideology, which was compensated for by this strong but complicated assertion of individual names. American memorializers, who looked to Europe for clues about how to remember so much loss for so little gain, adopted both of the new practices in ways that reflected a crisis of individualism, nationalism, and patriotism similar to that of the Europeans. An unknown soldier was buried in Arlington National Cemetery on Veterans Day in 1921 to mark the memory of all unknown soldiers from World War I. The process for selecting a body to rest in the tomb was remarkably elaborate. Great care was taken to ensure the anonymity of this soldier; all burial records were destroyed, and the coffins of the four bodies from which the unknown soldier was selected were continually shuffled to guarantee that nothing would be known about the body in the tomb. And in November of that same year the soldier, an unidentified soldier exhumed from France's Marne Valley, was placed in an enormous white granite tomb inscribed with the words, "Here rests in honored glory an American soldier known but to God." This inscription is important because it does make a few things known about the unknown soldier—he is honored, he is glorious, and he is American. At the dedication ceremony this soldier was decorated with the Congressional Medal of Honor, the Distinguished Service Cross, and medals from Belgium, England, France, Italy, Romania, Poland, and Czechoslovakia. Hymns were sung promising a "memory hallowed in the Land you loved."[59] Since the dedication ceremony presided over by President Warren Harding, the tomb has been under the guard of United States Army soldiers; this guard establishes the sanctified place of the anonymous soldier's body in American culture.[60] This celebration of the memory of the unknown soldier, the American tomb, like the other tombs for the unknown, is worshipped both for its specificity and for its anonymity. It manages to simultaneously reify and erase the body of the individual soldier.

Most local World War I memorials in the United States, however, did not follow the new European models. They were patriotic, celebratory, and relatively practical.[61] Those who commemorated the war seem to have shared a new determination that the memorials be useful. In 1916 Theodore Roosevelt wrote, "Surely a dead man or woman who is a good man or woman would wish to feel that his or her taking away had become an occasion of real service for the betterment of mankind, rather than to feel that a meaningless pile of stone, no matter how beautiful, had been erected with his or her name upon it in an enclosure crowded with similar piles of stones."[62] The piles of stone that had meant so much to the nation nearly fifty years earlier in Gettysburg were no longer enough to honor individual sacrifices made by

citizens for the nation. This new generation of American memorializers wanted the memory of the fallen to contribute to the "progress of
that civilization they have spent themselves for."[63] In July of 1918 the
cover of *American City* magazine read, "When this war shall have
ended, the American people will wish to build monuments to the men
who have led them to victory. Let them begin, now, by so planning
for the return of peace that the reconstruction period shall be marked
by the greatest era of constructive progress in the public interest—
national, state, county and municipal—that the world has ever seen."[64]

While this broad vision of the constructive possibilities of practical
war memorials was not fully realized until after the next world war,
memorials to World War I were often built as part of civic beautification projects or to provide meeting places and other services for veterans.[65] Inspired by the City Beautiful movement Nashville, Tennessee;
Berkeley, California; Grand Rapids, Michigan; and a handful of other
cities built memorial civic centers and auditoriums, the most functional
of which is in San Francisco, where the Veterans Building, the Opera
House, and the Civic Center were constructed as the three parts of the
city's memorial.[66] The Indiana War Memorial Plaza was also a part of
this particularly American movement to remember World War I with
civic beautification.

After the war, the Bureau of Memorial Buildings proclaimed, "What
shall we give our boys now they are coming back? Nothing is too good
for them. For that reason intelligence must go into the gift. America
should give with her head as well as her heart." This bureau, established in 1919 "to assist in the guidance of the nation-wide movement
to erect community buildings as war memorials," offered detailed instructions for the building of war memorials that would carry American idealism "into practical effect."[67]

World War II: Building the Nation

Memorial Highway
Memorial Bridge
Memorial Auditorium

Richard Nixon, vice president, patriot, and cold warrior, assured his
audience at the 1954 dedication of the Iwo Jima Memorial, "We realize that to retain freedom for ourselves, we must be concerned when

people in other parts of the world may lose theirs. There is no greater challenge to statesmanship than to find a way that such sacrifices as this statue represents are not necessary in the future, and to build the kind of world in which all people can be free, in which nations can be independent, and in which people can live together in peace and friendship."[68] This promise captures the climate in which memorials to World War II were commissioned and imagined. Nixon's rhetoric makes a powerfully forward-looking, preoccupied promise to the present about the future. It both warns against international intervention and celebrates its value. It is about building a new, free world.[69]

Most of the monuments to World War I, both in the United States and in Europe, were barely completed when the second war began, and by the time it was concluded, sentiments about how, what, and why we should remember were changing. Anxieties about the dangers of utilitarian monuments were fading away.[70] Coming out of a long depression and an expensive war overseas, national commissions and local communities expressed more interest in spending money on municipal improvements than in setting ideology in stone. It might be possible to read this waning of interest in inscribing meaning for the culture as a signal of the indifference to or disenchantment with nationalist rhetoric about the war. However, this practical turn in the work of memorializing was an expression of a genuine commitment to the material expectations of postwar nationalism in the United States. The people who wanted memorials did not want to waste time and money on symbolic stone that did not advance the prosperity of a victorious nation. Americans seemed to want to reap the benefits of the free world for which they had sacrificed so much. So they built football fields, playgrounds, and highways and called them war memorials.

The whole country became, in a sense, a living memorial to World War II. In contrast to those who constructed the central memorials to World War I, these memorializers wanted to remember the promises that pulled the country into the fighting rather than the men and women who gave their lives. In 1863 the sacrifices of individual fallen men and women provided the texture for the articulation of a useful nationalism. In 1918 the sacrifices of individual fallen men and women were reified and massified in response to the costs of nationalism. In 1948 these sacrifices were used as a reminder of the importance of enjoy-

ing, maybe even the duty to enjoy, the benefits of free industrial cap-
italism for which 175,000 Americans had died. Dwight D. Eisenhower
wrote, "Here we and all who shall hereafter live in freedom will be re-
minded that to these men and their comrades we owe a debt to be paid
with grateful remembrance of their sacrifice and with the high resolve
that the cause for which they died shall live."

In most cities and small towns, the names of the World War II dead
were added to the World War I memorials, or a second, modest plaque
was added to the memorial gazebo or obelisk in the town square.[71]
When a new local or state memorial was erected, it was in most cases
as much a monument to a forward-looking prosperity as it was a memory of suffering.[72] The new memorials were practical, functional pieces
of the American infrastructure. In the postwar era Americans did not
build cenotaphs and obelisks; they built bridges, highways, and auditoriums. They made better roads for transporting goods. They made
proud performance halls. They built better fields on which their children played football and baseball.

One proponent of these living memorials wrote, "The idea that war
memorials should advance the ideals for which wars are fought is not
new but has grown with the years and has today taken on the force of
popular conviction. That modern war, which mobilizes the entire population and re-creates for emergency periods the functioning community, should end in the reaction of community buildings dedicated
to lasting community and personal rehabilitation—this is indeed an em-
inently appropriate concept."[73]

In 1945 the *Toledo City Journal* conducted a survey of five hundred
towns and cities that concluded, "the determination that the war
memorial shall be useful is an 'outstanding note.'" Responding to the
strong reaction against the aesthetic, that is, the expensive and useless,
the survey assures it readers that "it is reasonably certain that most
memorials erected after this war will be quite different from those built
after other wars."[74] One soldier wrote to the *Saturday Evening Post* to
support the idea of a living memorial. Comparing it with obvious disdain to the Menin Gate he quoted the inscription, "To our heroic dead,
they died that we might live in peace," and argued that it would be better "over the entrance to a slum-children's' playground than on an al-
abaster vase, and any man's service would be prouder to have one small
swing in that playground given his name than all the marble-columned

temples that ever wasted good space, time and money."[75] Another, more succinct expression of this sentiment was printed in a *House Beautiful* article in 1945. It asked the question, "Do you believe your town can afford to build an imposing monument to World War II, while just around the corner children are playing in the streets?"[76]

Joseph Hudnut, professor of architecture at Harvard argued eloquently for a simple, useful living memorial,

> We might let go of all idea of permanence and take something which . . . is for now a symbol that we are trying to build a civilization of free men. . . . Whatever contains and sustains that for which our soldiers fought is a commemoration more eloquent and enduring than the loftiest monument. . . . I am not for Memorial Convention Halls or Memorial Baseball Fields . . . but I am for some act, immediate and unequivocal in every town and village. . . . Build something simple and considered, useful to the community— park, playground, schoolhouse, music hall, theater, library, church accessible to all faiths; not for practical convenience, but for service to the spirit. . . . There are buildings which lift community life out of the business of getting and spending. . . . Not war, for that can never be recorded.[77]

But there were still those who argued that merely calling it a memorial did not guarantee that it would remind people of anything.[78] Paul P. Cret, chairman of the War Memorials Committee of the American Institute of Architects, wrote that the work of memorials is the "perpetuation of the memory of a great man or great event for future generations . . . merely calling them memorials will not make them such."[79]

These memorials did not simply promise a future, they promised a prosperous future. Recreational spaces for children were mentioned in virtually every argument for living memorials. The calls for living memorials, whether they came from self-serving recreation lobbies or earnest philosophers, ring with the phrase "for the next generation." Prosperity, a good life for children, and patriotism became inseparable.

This fierce American determination to move forward is enacted even in one of the national memorials to World War II. The Iwo Jima Memorial, seen in this light, is a powerful bronze image of American soldiers thrusting the flag into the ground, staking their claim. They are planting the flag, in Asian soil, at such an angle that it is propelled forward, and the soldiers themselves—carved from the images of real soldiers (perhaps most importantly for this argument, soldiers who survived the war and returned to the United States to live the lives they fought to protect) in a photograph of an almost actual event—are all frozen together in this moment of forward momentum.[80] It is, as Vice President Nixon promised, a memorial that remembers the conquering future of a superpower rather than the sacred sacrifices of individual men and women. The bodies it remembers are forging the future.

Vietnam: Making and Remaking Memory

Pop Tarts	*cigar*
Bible	*patch*
Northwest Airlines ticket	*"Black House Association" sticker*
army boots with butterfly	*Texas A&M Class of '64 button*
newspaper collage	*photocopy of photograph*
medal with hat	*cross*
crude metal peace sign	*baseball to Henry*[81]

In the same way that the end of World War II engendered the Vietnam War, the World War II memorials—in their connection to people's daily lives—laid the groundwork for the Vietnam Veterans Memorial and the public response that it has inspired. The Wall might even be usefully imagined as a merger, in the new memorial terrain established at Gettysburg, of the World War I and World War II memorial impulses. It carries the existential angst of the absence of meaning beyond names that marks the World War I battlefield memorials, and it carries the commodified, if not the functional, impulses of the World War II memorials. Historian John Gillis gets to the heart of this change when he argues that "The cult of the fallen soldier was replaced by a new emphasis on veterans, who were immensely better treated than any of their predecessors. This time around the promise of a land fit for heroes would not go unfulfilled. The fact that the returning soldiers could actually find a place in the present reduced considerably the pressure to memorialize them."[82]

For the Vietnam veterans, in contrast to the World War II veterans, the intensity of the crisis of finding a place in the culture created—and continues to create—an enormous pressure to make a memory of the war that will heal that radical rupture the war created between so many citizens and the nation. The need for this memory and the difficulty of making it have forced another crucial change in the work of making memory in America.

The Vietnam Veterans Memorial may be the only truly "living," national memorial in the United States. It is alive because it is transformed every day by medals and tennis balls and cans of beer left at its base. The leaving of things at the Wall is partly a product of this long history of memorializing; those who leave things are using the names of the dead to remember enormous individual and national losses. It is also, ultimately, a response to the failure of the memorials that this history has produced. The expectations that inspired the people of Gettysburg to bury the Union dead, that honored veterans of World War I with city centers, and that built a new national infrastructure for those who fought World War II were not diminished after the Vietnam War. These artifacts left at the Wall seem to reassert invisible individual identity, and many seem to speak about finding a voice in national culture; they are certainly negotiating the memory of the war and particular lost lives. To better understand the memorial impulses at work here, we need to understand the context from which these things come. To understand this context we need to turn to the history of American funerary traditions. Where does the impulse to leave these things come from? What can it teach us about the public memory of this war? The third chapter of this book tries to answer these questions.

3

SEASHELL MONUMENTS
AND CITIES FOR THE SILENT
AMERICAN FUNERARY TRADITIONS

The history of Western war memorials in the nineteenth and twentieth centuries has been shaped by growing attention to individual lost lives. Public memorials increasingly remember pivotal moments in the life of the nation with celebrations of individual sacrifice. The history of American war memorials has been defined by an increasing emphasis on the sacrificial citizen-soldiers as emblems of the nation. The transformation of the individual citizen's status has forced the shapes of public memorials to change and in so doing has changed the symbolic makeup of the nation.

While the remembrance of citizen-soldiers was changing, there were equally powerful changes in the work of marking the deaths of ordinary citizens. First, civilian funerary practices were beginning to emphasize the importance of the secular community and its past in the process of remembering death. Americans began to build "cities for the silent" that shifted the responsibility for public grief from the church to the city and, sometimes, to the nation. Nineteenth-century civic leaders used the burial of the dead to assert and foster a newly emerging historical consciousness, one that they hoped would inspire patriotism and build community. Second, the importance of caring for the bodies of the dead and the resulting popularity of embalming marked both a move toward the professionalization of death ways and a fetishizing of the memory of bodies. Finally, outside of the broad influence of these Anglo-American traditions, many other traditions emphasizing the particular afterlife of the dead, rather than their relationship to national or professional communities, have survived and evolved. Beyond the edges of white middle-class America, funerary traditions have thrived entirely unaffected by nineteenth-century secular cemeteries. African, Mexican, and later Italian and Chinese Americans, and many other ethnic Americans have remembered the dead with specific, personal memorials laid out on grave sites. They have adorned graves with the familiar objects of daily life—photographs, broken dishes, and children's toys—in an effort to keep their relationships to the dead alive, and to help the spirits of the dead move through the liminal place between death and the afterlife.

Mainstream American funerary traditions have been shaped by secular impulses to improve public life and the status of the nation with beautifully landscaped cemeteries, but scattered but flourishing alternative burial practices have been powerfully influenced by religious traditions that give the living responsibility for the bodies and the spirits of the dead. Whereas the mainstream tradition has been shaped by distinctly forward-looking civic-mindedness and the rise of professional funeral directors and embalmers, these popular traditions are based on a theology that understands the past and the present to be seamlessly connected, a theology that encourages mourners to sustain an active memory of the dead. These contrasting memorial practices imagine different purposes for remembering the past. At their inception, the largely Protestant mainstream traditions sought to remember the lives of Americans collectively as parts of a proud new community; the other traditions, which are frequently Catholic, seek to sustain the memory of a specific person to guarantee his or her transition into the next world. It is the confluence of and conflicts between these memorial impulses that shape the response of so many Americans to the Wall; the failure of the nation-building cemetery or the embalmed body to speak to the losses evoked at the Vietnam Veterans Memorial has drawn these more individuated traditions into the work of American public memory.

The impulse to use public memorials to privilege the memory of the individual as an emblem for the nation, the impulse to use the dead to assert the past of the community, and the impulse to use things to negotiate the liminal position of the dead meet at the Vietnam memorial. People have responded to the individuated memory that the Wall

makes with a new memorial impulse—leaving something at the Wall
is an act of negotiating each of these relationships—between the dead
and the nation, the dead and the past, and the dead and the living—
in the face of a changing social and political universe. This chapter will
explore the development of American funerary traditions, which are
an essential part of the cultural knowledge that people bring to the
drama at the Vietnam Veterans Memorial.

MAKING CIVIL MEMORY

*It is desired that places of business be closed on the afternoon
of the 24th and that household cares be laid aside, that all
may devote the afternoon to the solemnities of the occasion.
Free carriages will be found on the north and west public
square for the accommodation of ladies and gentlemen
as far as practicable [sic] free.*

—Broadsheet published by the Oak Ridge Cemetery, May 24, 1860

On May 24, 1860, in Springfield, Illinois, the local cemetery board issued this invitation to the dedication of Springfield's newly completed
"city of the dead."[1] On the day of the dedication, Abraham Lincoln, a
few months away from the presidency and three years away from de-
livering the Gettysburg Address, sat on a podium at the Oak Ridge
Cemetery listening as his friend Mayor James C. Conkling proudly sang
the praises of his city's newest cultural institution.[2] Conkling spoke of
his great hope that "when the heart, wounded and crushed amidst the
extending elements of a cold and selfish world has lost its elastic power,
when the last pulse has beaten, the last sigh has heaved, the last groan
has been uttered, when man has run his allotted courses and fulfilled
his destiny on earth . . . here the remains of his mortal nature may secure a refuge from the fierce storms and conflicts of life."[3] Conkling's
dramatic rhetoric is full of familiar nineteenth-century references to
the home as a haven from a heartless world; in his dedication a final
resting place is conceived of as a home. He elevates the status of what
had previously been called a graveyard to a "sacred enclosure for the
last demands of frail humanity," the cemetery.[4]

The Oak Ridge Cemetery was Springfield's contribution to a rapidly
expanding rural cemetery movement. Named for its desire to move

cemeteries outside of urban centers, this movement championed the value of a parklike resting place for the dead that would take the living away from the distractions of urban life. New York's Greenwood, Philadelphia's Laurel Hill, and Boston's Mount Auburn, the original rural cemetery, were joined by at least sixty-six other rural cemeteries between 1831 and 1861.[5] The Mount Auburn Cemetery marks a change in the practice of burying civilians, a change as significant as the transformation of war memorials engendered by Gettysburg. While the impulse at Gettysburg was to replace mass graves with memories of individual soldiers, the impulse at Mount Auburn was to have individual graves serve civic functions for the living. Both cemeteries were part of the development of a national dialogue in which the dead became a key site for the articulation of ideals about the nation.

The construction of these new cemeteries was stimulated by the confluence of expanding urban populations (especially the growing national bourgeoisie), increasing interest in horticulture and landscape architecture, a thickening web of urban improvements, a growing impulse in religious liberalism to focus on the soothing, curative qualities of nature, and an increasing interest in the value of public monuments. This last factor, the concern about the need for public monuments in the new nation, was especially important. When physician and botanist Dr. Jacob Bigelow and Chairman of the Massachusetts Board of Internal Improvements Nathan Hale joined forces to respond to the unsightly and unsanitary condition of Boston's scattered graveyards, their principal interests were civic improvement and civic enlightenment. They wanted to create a beautiful park in which to bury the citizens of Boston, one that would become a proud landmark on a par with the campus of Harvard University. They intended it to compete with newly constructed public monuments in Washington, Baltimore, and other cities.[6] The cemetery was planned, as historian Blanche Linden-Ward has argued, by civic leaders who "considered a cemetery, even more than patriotic monuments in public places, representative of the high culture of the city and the nation." The dedication speech given at Mount Auburn, like that at Oak Ridge, fairly rang with lofty ideals about the potential for uplift in a serene, gently landscaped city for the dead. It promised that the cemetery would sustain a memory of the past by "honoring the deceased, cultivating the civilizing emotion of melancholy,

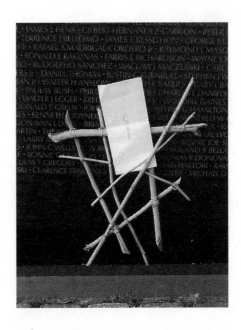

teaching moral lessons, and fostering a sense of the present and the future."[7] "Our cemeteries," proposed well-known jurist Joseph Story in his lengthy oration, "rightly selected, and properly arranged, may be made subservient to some of the highest purposes of religion and human duty."[8]

This new emphasis on the need for monuments and formalized community memory reflected the Brahmin class's growing sense of its own importance and the value of its public culture. Foreign visitors to the United States in the early nineteenth century were beginning, as Linden-Ward puts it, "to remind Americans that their lack of common culture and sense of history could shorten the republic's longevity."[9] The French had been busy building monuments since the first days after their revolution, but Americans had not.[10] At the same time, because many of the members of Boston's emerging Brahmin class had come to the city from rural areas, they had no particular place to be buried themselves.[11] Their concern about remembering the dead not only was part of the development of a historical consciousness but also was directly connected to their developing sense of importance as individuals and as a class.

Before the rural cemetery movement took hold, Protestant New Englanders were buried in their local churchyards or burial commons without a lot of pomp. In the seventeenth century, "the material forms of [New England] burial places epitomized the harshness of their theology."[12] Churchyards were not often visited, nor were they well-maintained. The most common tombstone inscription, *Memento Mori*, usually inscribed on plain gray slate, was intended as a reminder of the finality of death and of the certain trials awaiting the unredeemed. Because redemption was not something that one could hope to find in the final hours of life or at any time after death, it was also a grim reminder of the close participation in the life of the church required by the doctrine of predestination. These barren graveyards were in no way intended to comfort the living; their social function was to remind passersby of "the insignificance of the earthly past" and the finality of death.[13]

This admonition was not, however, expressed universally in the young republic. As early as 1683 Minister Samuel Willard encouraged his parishioners to "embalm the memory of Saints," to build and cherish the memories of important men in their communities. As Linden-Ward argues, "memory of the exemplary individual—the 'Saint' or later the secular 'Great Man'—functioned in the same didactic way as Winthrop's concept of the 'city on a hill,' to perpetuate notions of community ordained by Providence." There was, for example, a sense that despite the theological importance of warnings about death, new generations would benefit from the memory of the secular struggles of the nation's founders to establish the nation. Willard was "yearning for new material forms of remembrance capable of inspiring retrospection and resolve."[14] So, although these commemorations did not actually materialize for more than a century, even the first inclinations toward the public memory of individual lives had a decidedly civic function.

Although eighteenth-century ideas about death were shifted away from Calvinist fears of damnation toward a more forgiving, emotional response to loss, burial practices did not change dramatically in response to the flowering of melancholy, except in the elaboration of headstone decorations within churchyards. The subtle changes in the headstones were, however, significant.[15] The gray slate that had been commonly used was increasingly replaced by newly available white marble. The willow-and-urn motif became a popular stela decoration.[16] *Memento Mori* was replaced by the far more gentle and particular phrase "in memory of." While the elegies of the "graveyard poets" stressed "the depths of melancholy," the material culture of the burial grounds themselves was slowly softening this harsh position.[17] A more secular commemoration of individual deaths as part of the life cycle was slowly beginning to emerge. Thomas Gray's tremendously popular "Elegy Written in a Country Churchyard" (1750), a gentle musing on the cycles of the days and of the seasons, worries about the neglect of the memory of the "rude forefathers of the hamlet."

This softening of death produced a new interest in public memorials, a development most visible in the history of George Washington's grave site at Mount Vernon. Immediately after he died, in 1799, George Washington was buried in a simple tomb in a native oak grove in the gardens of his Virginia home on the Potomac. The garden surrounding this plain structure, although hardly the lavishly landscaped English garden to which he had aspired, was much discussed as a beautiful and romantic tribute to the "immortal spirit" of the first president. But although in 1799 the *idea* of a proud, marked burial for the president was clearly articulated, the *material* form of the memory did not live up to the ideal. By the 1820s the tomb had fallen victim to the dwindling fortunes of the Washington family; it was a shabby ruin and the subject of much debate.[18] In 1831, just as the rural cemetery movement was beginning to form, the newly organized Mount Vernon Ladies' Association of the Union replaced the original tomb with a brick vault and a new marble cenotaph decorated with an eagle, stars and stripes, and the word "Washington."[19] And while the association's most glorious contribution to the developing interest in public memorials was its impulse to recreate a prouder site for Washington's body, they, like the association of Southern women who would oversee the burial of Confederate soldiers at Gettysburg, set the tone for future work in the forging of the public memory of the nation. Like their male counterparts in Boston, these women established a precedent for the synthesis of civic volunteerism, well-landscaped burial grounds, and reliance on nation-building iconography in the burial of the dead.

As Linden-Ward argues, "secular memory, whether personal and inspired by affective individualism, or community in the name of new patriotism—could be enshrined in material terms with monuments and with funerary associations." On the occasion of the 1850 dedication of the Magnolia Cemetery in Charleston, South Carolina, cemeterian Charles Fraiser declared, "To the dead . . . in our own beloved country, we owe, not only the foundations of the great fabric of our liberties, but those lessons of wisdom, justice and moderation, upon the observance of which alone can depend its stability." At Mount Auburn, secular memory was made with carefully sculpted "natural" beauty and artful monuments intended to "render the lessons of history tangible and to inspire the sentiment of patriotism." The 116-acre hillside cemetery was laced with gravel pathways and avenues named after trees and flowers. These avenues were lined with family plots, in which slate headstones were forbidden. The monuments functioned, in the words of jurist Joseph Story, to demonstrate to the living "our destiny and duty." These monuments, often the same type of columns, cenotaphs, and obelisks used to memorialize war, were carved with genealogies and patriotic signs intended to create a "sense of historical continuity, a feeling of social roots."[20] And although Mount Auburn had initially urged stylistic restraint and Yankee simplicity in the building of monuments, the heavy symbolic burden they bore and their intimate association with familial pride inspired a wide array of elaborately sculpted monuments.[21] The sculptors of these monuments drew primarily on Greek and Egyptian themes to assert memory for the sake of the community.[22]

The rhetoric of the cemetery dedications encouraged a reserved emotionalism. One of the ideals of the parks was to "make the living forget the trials of death in contemplation of the present beauty on our earth." The rural cemetery movement aspired to create cemeteries to serve the grieving; its proponents imagined that the tranquillity and serenity of strolling the lanes of the cemetery with companions in sorrow would ease the pain of this final separation. The movement transformed burial markers in America from reminders of the fact of death to remembrances of the past.[23] As the language of their dedications implies, these cemeteries were meant to build a foundation for the memory of the nation. The introduction of a shared past in the ideal of these cemeteries created "a sentimental imagining of a continuing relationship between the living and the dead, but one effected only through depriving the dead of their specific identity."[24]

In this context, a flag or a carnation carried to an individual grave site as traditional acknowledgment of a life sacrificed for the nation makes some sense. It is a modest tribute to a particular kind of contribution that American cemeteries were built to remember.

EMBALMING NATIONAL MEMORY

Abraham Lincoln may die,
but the principles embalmed in his blood will live forever.

—Words printed on a sign held up
as the president's body passed through Erie, Pennsylvania

The story of the "afterlife" of Abraham Lincoln's body demonstrates quite clearly how funerary practices were recast by changes in the theology and the business of death. The story of the burial of President Lincoln's body is clearly not typical, but it dramatizes, in literally larger-than-life terms, essential themes in the development of twentieth-century private funerary traditions.[25]

Even before he was dead, President Lincoln was conscripted for one final service to the nation. As he lay dying, a great argument raged among his closest advisors, including John Hay and Secretary of War Edwin Stanton, about what should be done with his body.[26] Mary Todd Lincoln was unceremoniously ushered away from her husband's side by these statesmen, who did not appreciate her strong show of emotion. As she was physically removed from the process of his death she said, "I have given my husband to die," and indeed she had.[27] She came very close to losing him in death, as she had lost his dying, when Stanton and others protested her desire to bury him in Springfield. In the complicated political climate of the time, they considered the recently established Arlington National Cemetery a more fittingly distinguished and visible resting place for this Union-saving President, but social mores emphasizing the importance of burying families together carried the day. It was decided that he would be buried with his son in his hometown cemetery, Oak Ridge. Before his return to Springfield, however, his body was to make one final nation-building tour, under the direction of Stanton.

On April 15, 1865, after an autopsy by Surgeon General Joseph K. Barnes, undertaker Harry P. Cattell of Brown and Alexander embalmed the president's body in the White House.[28] The science of chemical embalming experienced a tremendous rise in popularity during the Civil War, and this rise demonstrates (as do the handmade dog tags) the new importance given to the bodies of family members sacrificed for the nation and the new value placed on the individual soldier.[29] For

the first time, families wanted the bodies of their sons returned home.[30] Until the 1860s most Americans had relied on simple refrigeration for the preservation of bodies; corpse coolers and cooling boards were simple, if grotesque, technologies for keeping bodies on ice. However, these techniques were not practical for returning soldiers from battlefields to their hometowns on hot, crowded trains. So, there was a surge in the development of chemical technologies.[31] Before the war, embalming had been used only for anatomical research, but as the trade advertisements from this period make clear, it quickly became an important mechanism for reuniting families torn apart by the war.[32] Embalmers, responding to the new expectations of both medical science and the body, promised families perfectly preserved bodies, "both internal and external."[33]

Employing the newly developed techniques for preserving lifeless bodies, Cattell provided Stanton with a presidential body that could be seen, admired, and lionized by American citizens one last time. The secretary of war organized a mobile sixteen-day public funeral for the president. A slow-moving train carried the president from Washington to Springfield via Baltimore, Harrisburg, Philadelphia, New York City, West Point, Albany, Buffalo, Cleveland, Columbus, Indianapolis, and Chicago. Lincoln became a fantastic advertisement for the miracles of embalming. In every city the train was greeted by thousands of spectators and mourners, tolling bells, exploding fireworks, genuine fear and grief, and intense interest in the condition of the president's body. Although most reports tried to be respectful of the president, it is clear that by the time he arrived in Buffalo his body was deteriorating: his skin was sagging, his color went from gray to green, and his railroad car was thick with the smell of decaying flesh.[34]

Lincoln's body was used by his advisors as a visible emblem of the resilience of the body of the nation. During his sixteen-day journey, the President was disconnected from his domestic family and offered up to his national family. His advisors, in their efforts to suspend the corruption of the national body, used his body as a substitute for the bodies of lost sons and as a symbol of all the sacrifices made to save the Union. Literally, he was paraded across the country as an emblem of the survival of the national body.[35] His embalmed body was like the uniformed, identified body of the national soldier.

Lincoln's physical body was buried on May 4, 1865, in a family plot. He was laid to rest in a public cemetery designed to improve the local standard of living by increasing sanitation and providing a public space for private contemplation; like the many soldiers carried home on trains, Lincoln was brought back to rest in his family's private plot in a public cemetery.[36] He was buried with one son and would eventually be joined by Mary Todd Lincoln and two more sons. He came to rest there with a resounding finality. The physical body was turned over, by his domestic family and the national family, to the perpetual care of his local cemetery professionals and monument builders.

All of the crucial changes in American funerary practices are connected to the turning over of private care for the dead to specialized professionals. As many historians and anthropologists have stressed, nineteenth- and twentieth-century cemetery and funerary traditions in the United States are often more closely connected to shared ideas about how to run a good business than about shared understanding of the meaning of death. Most studies of American funerary traditions start with an ironic mixture of apology for the morbidity of the subject and surprise at the distance that Americans want to keep between themselves and the subject of death; the studies often complain that the businesslike character of American funerary practices produces mourning—at least public mourning—that leaves mourners grossly dependent on euphemisms and professionals to keep them protected from the dead.[37] Writing bitterly about a businessman too caught up in the concerns of the market to notice a passing funeral procession, poet Lydia Howard Sigourney asked, "Poise Ye?, in the rigid scales / of calculation, the fond bosom's wealth?" Historian Ann Douglas begins her crucial discussion of mourning in Victorian America with this biting critique of the failure of the world of commerce to understand the importance of the funeral. She writes, "Sigourney's implicit point is that the private rituals of mourning should outweigh the public demands of business, that the claims of home and church should count for more than the imperatives of the market place."[38] What Sigourney could not have known is that commerce was about to take a tremendous, profitable interest in the funerary that would eventually displace women in the work of burying the dead: the growth of the funerary industries effectively removed caring for the dead from the realm of home work (and, therefore, of women's work) by placing the responsibility in the hands of "chemists and physicians and . . . undertakers."[39]

Like Mary Todd Lincoln grieving for the loss of the death of her husband, grieving Americans transfer their grief to be processed cleanly for the good of both the community and the business of death, but it is important to note here that this transfer is neither complete nor a very good reflection of how people actually experience private grief. Historian LeRoy Bowman has argued strenuously that the idea that "the external aspects of a funeral have any but the most superficial relation to deep sorrow is a groundless assumption,"[40] and he is right. People undoubtedly experience grief that is untouched by funeral directors and mass-produced coffins. The experiences of the grieving are far more complicated than the simple procedures for the burial of the dead can reflect, and the American funeral as it has evolved does not provide a place for the expression of the kind of sorrow he imagines people to have felt.[41] Still, while Americans have not been entirely at the mercy of the managers of the business of death, it is true that once they can afford to, they have preferred to turn this work over to people in the business.

The growth of national interest in professional associations in the 1880s profoundly affected the business of burying the dead. In the first years of the decade, the National Funeral Directors Association, the Coffin Manufacturers Association, the National Burial Case Association, and more than twenty state funeral-directors associations were formed.[42] In 1882, at the Michigan Funeral Directors Association's first annual meeting, Charles Conklin proposed that they drop the term "undertaker" in favor of the more highbrow "funeral director."[43] Funeral directors replaced family members and ministers in organizing rites of burial; bodies were embalmed by specially trained chemists; and coffins were mass produced and shipped all over the country. Funerary professionals were working to build the corporate body, and although this work is a more subtle kind of nation building, these funeral directors, like the founders of Mount Auburn, were working at building standard, national, corporate funerary practices. By the 1930s they had largely succeeded.

One of the last battles they fought was to standardize headstones and monuments within the cemetery. Around the turn of the century, the newly organized associations of funeral directors and cemeterians expressed a good deal of concern about the problem of individuals who wanted elaborate, celebratory monuments erected at the grave sites of loved ones. In 1895 one prominent cemetery manager protested that such monuments intrude on the landscape of the cemetery, "add nothing to a man's reputation, and do not prolong his memory; the endowment of a bed in a hospital . . . is far better than the usual structure of stone."[44] Cemeteries developed strict regulations and have continued to discourage too much individuation in stone. The cemeterians wanted to streamline their work by requiring clean, uniform grave sites and taking control of the burial out of the hands of the bereaved.

The standard funeral—which has remained largely unchanged from the 1930s to the 1990s—begins with death in a hospital and transportation of the body to a funeral home. There the body is embalmed, dressed, and made up; this process is usually followed by a viewing of the body and a funeral service in the church of the deceased or at the funeral home. The service is most often followed by a smaller burial service at the cemetery. It is not until the body is buried that there is, in this standard funeral, a place for the participation of the grieving; often mourners decorate graves with flowers and with flags. The grieving, of course, experience uncontrollable, unpredictable, and unnamable emotions, which are a part of even the most streamlined and professionalized funerals. Yet that there is little ritualized space for the expression of this range of emotions in many funerals is an interesting and complicated legacy of the impulse of early American memorializers to build civic rather than particular memory. Like the war memorials, these burial practices abstracted the body and de-individuated

the dead, making a public memory of an orderly nation rather than a
riotous life.

OTHER FUNERARY TRADITIONS:
GRAVE GOODS AND PLASTIC PUMPKINS

cups and saucers	flashlight	cigar boxes
false teeth	salt and pepper shakers	spoons
medicine bottles	piggy bank	tomato cans
knives	toys	bric-a-brac statues
dolls head	toilet tank	bottles[45]
	clocks	

The impulse to standardize and professionalize the work of burying the
dead was not, however, universal. Traditions unaffected by Anglo-
Protestantism, professionalism, and middle-class aspirations have
thrived outside of the Northeast. African Americans, Chinese Americans, Mexican Americans, Italian Americans, and Native Americans,
among others, have funerary traditions shaped by different cultural
needs and forces. These traditions provide an essential part of the vocabulary with which people speak at the Vietnam Veterans Memorial,
and they seem, in fact, prefigurative of the response to the Wall. Common to all of these traditions and to the offerings at the Wall is the theme
of an active, ongoing relationship between the living and the dead. Such
relationships are predicated on the belief that the living must help the
dead to negotiate the liminal space between death and the afterlife.
The traditions based on this belief are an important part of changes in
public memory because they are the traditions of so many of the men
and women who fought in the Vietnam War and because the status of
those killed in this war was also liminal. Like the people grieving at the
Wall, these Americans use the things that populate their everyday lives
to negotiate the position of their dead.

Writing about the distinction between Latin American cemeteries
and most American cemeteries, writer John Matturri articulates a key
distinction precisely: "The Latin cemeteries . . . acted to elicit thoughts
of particularized ongoing relations between the living and the dead,
whereas North American cemeteries encouraged at most a vague sentimental attachment to the deceased." He quotes historian Ray F.

Wyrick's argument that "their ideal seems to be to try to keep alive the fame or the wealth of those who have died, whereas ours is to make the living forget the trial of the death in contemplation of the present beauty of our earth."[46]

Mainstream cemeteries in the United States have been shaped, at least in part, by the theological, national, and professional transformations described above; these cemeteries have been constructed as proud parks for the preservation of the memory of an American past. Among American funerary traditions outside the mainstream, the common thread is that they imagine death to be a less circumscribed process, a process in which the living play an active role and in which the particularized memories of the dead are central. "Death," writes Robert Hertz, "does not confine itself to ending the visible bodily life of an individual; it also destroys the social being grafted upon the physical individual and to whom the collective consciousness attributed great dignity and importance."[47] This conception of death requires a more complicated response. For many Americans death is neither a threat to the unredeemed nor a site for the celebration of patriotism; instead it is part of the process of movement through a spiritual world in which the living have a responsibility to help the dead. This relationship is expressed, materially, in offerings tucked inside coffins and left at grave sites.

Although they share an interest in sustaining relationships to the dead, the various traditions are not, however, homologous; they have quite different histories. Research exploring these traditions is limited, but enough work has been done for some compelling patterns to emerge.[48] Postemancipation and early-twentieth-century African Americans in rural areas had elaborate traditions of grave decoration that used broken cups and broken seashells to articulate a final message to the dead. Early-twentieth-century Navajo and Zuni made sacred offerings at grave sites. Italian Americans, and other American Catholics, have traditionally perpetuated the memory of the dead through prayer and memorial iconography that ranges from formal photographs to Connie Francis records. Mexican American traditions of offerings and elaborate, beautiful grave decoration are still vital in many communities.

Many African Americans have marked their graves with gifts. Graves in rural African American graveyards have often been decorated with a dense covering of offerings. These offerings are so far from what researchers in the field have expected to find in cemeteries that anthropologists from the University of South Carolina initially missed a local graveyard and concluded that "there didn't appear to be anything there other than some late nineteenth-century and twentieth-century junk scattered throughout the area."[49] That junk turned out to be just the kind of treasure they were after. These graves and graves in South Carolina, Georgia, Texas, Kentucky, Alabama, Mississippi, and other sites throughout the South were elaborately decorated with broken seashells and personal items belonging to the deceased. According to art historian John Michael Vlach, these things included "pottery, pressed glass, cups, saucers, bowls, clocks, salt and pepper shakers, medicine bottles, spoons, pitchers, oyster shells, conch shells, white pebbles, toys, dolls' heads, bric-a-brac, light bulbs, tureens, flashlights, soap dishes, false teeth, syrup jugs, spectacles, hand lotion, cigar boxes, piggy banks, gun locks, razors, knives, tomato cans, flower pots, marbles, bits of plaster, and toilet tanks." Vlach understands the leaving of these things as emerging from the belief that ancestors might return to take a favorite thing, or the last thing that they used in life—a cup or a pitcher. He argues that the things are left by the living to placate the dead, to keep them happy, and to keep them from returning. He quotes one Georgia woman as saying, "I don't guess you don't be bothered much by the spirits if you give 'em a good funeral and put the things what belong to 'em on top of the grave."[50] In Vlach's telling, this woman's husband affirmed her observation by saying that the spirit needed things the "same as the man." The problem, in this case, was a matter of guiding the dead away from the impulse to return to the realm of the living. The things act as strong communication with the dead. They are often broken at the grave to send a particular message: here are your things, they are broken, this is no longer your world.

Glasses, vases, bottles, pitchers, and other household items that are likely to have been touched by or used to comfort the dying are commonly used as grave decorations in African American cemeteries. This form of grave decoration has been traced to burial customs in West and Central Africa.[51] People left artifacts that had some real, direct, physical connection to the dead, but in most cases these things were broken before they were left on the graves. Vlach cites an explanation given by Rosa Sallins of Harris Neck, Georgia, who said, "You break the dishes so that the chain will be broke. . . . You see, the person is dead and if you don't break the things, then the others in the family will die too."[52] So, in a sense this tradition is also about protecting the living from the dead. It is about continuing to negotiate, to interact with the dead in the grieving process. In these communities, the dead require continued attention, even after they are buried.

Seashells and bits of plaster and enamelware are often used to cover graves. Shells are common grave decorations throughout Africa; Vlach connects these shells and the bits of plaster and white china to Congo region traditions associating death with whiteness and with water. He writes, "it is believed in lower Zaire that deceased ancestors become white creatures called *bukulu*, who inhabit villages of the dead located under river beds or lake bottoms; they may return from this underworld to mingle with the living without being seen."[53] Seashells are obviously associated with water and river beds. Set on a grave, they are icons of the liminal status of the dead.

Graves are also decorated with other, miscellaneous material possessions of everyday life. Clocks are a very common element in African American grave decoration. Vlach observes that they are often set at twelve to mark the start of the judgment day, or they are set to the hour at which the person died.[54] They stand as a reminder to the dead and to survivors. Other things, such as the letters, cards, coins, and crosses, have traditionally expressed an impulse to help the dead find their way. Even from the limited evidence available about particular grave sites, it is easy to see individual personalities take shape in the offering of spectacles, a cigar box, salt and pepper shakers, and a piggy bank.

Vlach follows these traditions in the United States into the 1930s, but there has been little scholarly work to chart their more recent incarnations.[55] It is quite likely that after 1920, as more African Americans moved to urban areas and joined the middle class, they buried their loved ones in managed cemeteries in increasing numbers. Nevertheless, communication between the living and the dead through the giving of things has not disappeared even in the face of complaints from frustrated funerary professionals.

In 1986 the minister at the AME Mt. Zion Church in Detroit, Michigan, reported having seen "wedding rings, mementos, photographs, whiskey bottles, books, clothing, flowers, money and a 'real rabbit's foot'" left in caskets. Another Baptist minister reported "flowers, crosses, Bibles, and jewelry left in caskets." A Lutheran minister had "seen flowers, toys, rings, Bibles, and pictures left in caskets."[56] A recent study of contemporary African American mortuary practices illustrates the continuing importance of speaking to the dead with material objects. The research of anthropologist Karen Krepps in African American funerals and cemeteries in southeastern Michigan finds that the leaving of artifacts on grave sites and in coffins is still a part of many African American funerals. In Michigan, African Americans commonly bury jewelry and other personal treasures in the coffin with the body, despite the fact that mortuary professionals actively discourage this practice. Managers of African American cemeteries also discourage grave decoration, by means of printed guidelines for the bereaved, but people continue to write letters to the deceased at the address of the cemetery and leave bottles of liquor, birthday and Easter and Christmas cards, and other miscellaneous offerings in the path of lawn mowers. These offerings are evidence of a still vital association between the dead and their precious things. The leaving of things, it would seem, still does important symbolic work in mediating between the living and the dead.

The central distinction between contemporary practices and the turn-of-the century practices is that in the North in the 1980s, the things left with the dead are left in coffins more often than at grave sites. This is an important distinction, but determining its significance will require more thorough research. It may well be that urban African Americans brought the traditions inside, literally inside the coffin, to protect the things and the dead from disruption by vandals.[57] There may be some connection to African traditions involving the burial of coins, and other items that might be required for the journey into the next world, with the dead. Archaeologists have found coins and other valuables in the coffins of African Americans buried in a turn-of-the-century Philadelphia graveyard.[58] There is much that we do not know here, but it is clear that there continue to be powerful traditions in African American culture that ask the living to appease and aid the dead with things. Certainly, the impulse to use the completed memory of the dead as a civilizing, nation-building tool has not been absorbed by all African Americans.

The same is true in Italian American culture. In the Roman Catholic tradition, practices have been shaped by a sense of responsibility for keeping the memory of the dead alive. Catholics' belief in purgatory—

which creates the possibility that a loved one might spend a year or
more in a liminal state between heaven and hell—inspires this responsibility. The prayers and good works of the living "can facilitate
this passage [into heaven], and, in establishing the opportunity and obli-
gation to intercede into the fate of the dead, purgatory established . . .
'a mutual economy of salvation.'" Like the processes of death described
by Robert Hertz, this mutual economy of salvation conceives of death
as a process rather than a discrete event. It requires the living to memorialize the dead in ways that have conflicted with the ideals of cemeterians in the United States. Not only do traditional Italian Americans
leave out a plate of spaghetti on the anniversary of a death and place
memorial advertisements in local papers on All Souls' Day, they also
place a high value on creating a grave site that marks a particularized
memory of the dead. This is accomplished with extensive floral decorations, greeting cards, photographs, "wedding announcements, religious articles, and holiday decorations."[59] Photographs have been particularly important in the memorialization of Italian Americans. Affixed
to grave markers and set on graves, these photographs sustain the presence of the dead. These photographs are often mixed with religious
iconography and everyday objects. Crucifixes, rosary beads, and medals
of saints are potent religious icons, and they are often left on graves in
the Italian American sections of cemeteries.[60] All of these things work
to keep the grief alive, to make a particular memory, and to aid the journey of the dead. These practices have survived through three generations of immigrants, who continue to want particular, personalized grave
markers; these practices have also inspired generations of tension between cemeterians and Italian Americans.[61]

Many twentieth-century Mexican American Catholics also have
lively, dynamic relationships to the dead. In the Southwest, Mexican
Americans often honor the dead with elaborate grave decorations; they
maintain ongoing communication through the things left on graves.[62]
Research in this area is limited, but one close study of San Fernando
Cemetery in San Antonio, Texas, illustrates the potency of the continuing connection between the living and the dead. In many twentieth-
century American cemeteries, "the economics of perpetual care over-
ride local or individual attitudes toward death and mourning, and
twentieth-century urban cemeteries tend toward visual uniformity."[63]

The San Fernando Cemetery is an exception to this rule because it is in a racially segregated part of the city. In this distinctly non-Anglo cemetery mourners break the visual uniformity with plastic pumpkins, balloons, Easter baskets, Christmas trees, food, coins, greeting cards, miniature toys, tea sets, cans of beer, and more. On religious and secular holidays the cemetery is packed with the cars and trucks of family members coming to decorate graves; anniversaries and birthdays are also often observed. The grave markers are generally modest and the lawns are carefully groomed. Yet the elaborate collections of handmade and mass-produced offerings laid out on the graves distinguish this cemetery. The work that these tokens do seems clear; they are "a means of continuing to incorporate the deceased within the lives of the surviving family members."[64] They are part of Catholic traditions that require the living to sustain a memory of the dead to help them negotiate the passage out of purgatory. They imagine a connection between the living and the dead that is radically different from the traditions of the white Protestant middle class; they suggest a more fluid understanding of death and an active role of mourners in the mechanisms of death.[65]

Of course, not all Americans are immersed in Protestant traditions, and traditions everywhere are influenced by the mixing of cultures. Some of these "living traditions" have commingled and cross-pollinated. In 1969, in an Alabama-Coushatta Indian graveyard in Polk County, Texas, cultural geographer Terry Jordan noticed "a pair of dark glasses, an empty bottle of after-shave lotion, a toy car, a safety razor, and a conch shell" on the grave of a recently deceased man. A few feet away the grave of a white child "served as a table for a miniature tea set."[66] Jordan found another example—in Bowie County, Texas—of graves in a white cemetery that had been elongated to accommodate an enormous collection of decorations, which included toys, furniture, vases, and other pottery. Like African Americans, German Americans and Mexican Americans in Texas commonly use shells as grave decorations.[67] There are graves of Texas Germans buried in the 1920s that look very much like graves of South Carolina African Americans buried in the 1890s. Amerindian traditions in the southeastern United States involve burial mounds decorated with engraved river mussel shells.[68] Scots-Irish residents of Texas have traditions involving leaving "dishes,

pipes, and stones" on graves, which might either be connected to ancient Scottish traditions or have been picked up from other Texans.

Grave decorations from many regions and traditions mix in these
rural Texas counties, where African Americans and Mexican Americans and Irish Americans and German Americans have been buried
side by side for generations without the regulations of professional
cemeterians. The funerary practices of these various cultures share
enough common ground to suggest a sensibility that extends into the
broader population. Despite important differences, these grave decorations all suggest a relationship of the past to the dead that runs contrary to mainstream funerary traditions. They imply a relationship between the living and the dead that is shaped by the unfinished nature
of death and by the guidance, or sometimes warnings, that the living
give to the dead. In other words, they suggest that part of the process
of death is the active participation of the living in finding a stable resting place for the dead, and they concomitantly imagine each dead person as specific, concrete, and particular.

The grave decorations at San Fernando Cemetery are deeply suggestive of what is happening at the Wall. It is difficult, if not impossible, to directly link these traditions of grave and coffin decoration to
the leaving of things at the Wall; the things left at the Wall are not exactly like the things left in these cemeteries. Yet if we can imagine that
the disrupted social position of those who died in the Vietnam War is
like the liminal position of the dead in these communities, then we
might imagine that the things left for them do similar symbolic work.
These traditions outside of the mainstream may have provided a model
for the work of grieving this war, especially for those who inherited these
traditions.

The classic memorial traditions of the Civil War depended on the
notions of the body and the community in dominant funerary practices.
Both the memorial traditions and the funerary practices are being
rewritten at the Vietnam Veterans Memorial. The belief, held by various groups, in an ongoing, vital, material relationship between the living and the dead has transformed the way in which the cross and the
photograph and the beer and the coffee cup and the record and the
pumpkin and the seashell and the piggy bank left at the Wall are understood. The politicians who waged the Vietnam War called on Americans outside of the white middle class to fight and die; the families of

these men and women have drawn on funerary traditions outside of the mainstream to remember their losses. They have brought and continue to bring their vital relationships to the dead to the Wall, and in so doing they have transformed the making of American public memory.

OFFERINGS AT THE WALL

fishing rod	*"Proud Vet's Wife" T-shirt*
Honda hat	*teddy bear*
rock, "left by Jewish couple"	*ribbons*
bag of bar-b-qued meat	*poem*
notes	*photos of helicopter*
"magnificent bastards" lighter	*Hank Williams Jr. tape*
baby photo	*painting*
mess kit with knife	*two shot glasses*[69]
votive candle	

Writing about the Wall as a site of public memory, historian John Bodnar concludes that "by the latter part of the twentieth century public memory remains a product of elite manipulation, symbolic interaction and contested discourse."[70] But this does not quite ring true. The teddy bear and the "magnificent bastards" lighter are interjections in a contested discourse about symbolic interaction, but they are hardly entirely products of elite manipulation. The votive candle and the Honda hat are part of a truly public memory. Like so many historians and critics who have written about the memorial, Bodnar does not consider the things. His lack of attention to the powerful concrete vernacular response to the Wall—in this essential element of the commemoration there—allows him to miss a strong, multivocal, contradictory, unsolicited public response.

This book started with a question about what it means to leave a medal at the Vietnam Veterans Memorial. So far, in answer to this question, I have argued that the absence of a clearly stated government position on the war in the design of the memorial tacitly asked people to respond to the memorial with their own interpretations. I have argued that the design of this memorial comes out of a history of memorial design that has been driven by the problem of representing individual sacrifice in the name of an imagined national community. In departing from that tradition, I have argued, the Wall makes a place for pri-

vate grief and powerful resentment and a whole range of funerary practices based on the idea of an active relation between the living and the
dead to seep into the crack in civic and patriotic tradition. I have also,
now, proposed that many funerary traditions outside the American
mainstream, informed by this belief in a relationship between the living and the dead, have offered a model for the new relationship between grieving and citizenry and the nation.

It is in its compelling symbolic attraction and popularity as a central part of the tourist—which is to say, pilgrimage—experience in
Washington that the Wall and the practices that have grown around
it are so important. At the very center of nation building and national
memory, the meaning of the war and the uncertain, liminal, contested
status of the dead and the meaning of the sacrifices of citizen-soldiers
are being redefined, and so therefore—in ways that are perhaps still
unpredictable—is the idea of the nation that monumental and memorial Washington is intended to convey. The architecture of Capitol Hill
and Pennsylvania Avenue has a finished quality. It aims to mean, to
inspire, and to impress, but the Wall remains open like the fresh wound
of the war itself.

THE THINGS

REMEMBERING BODIES
AND REMAKING THE NATION

dog tags, Smith, R. L.
tobacco pouch with tobacco
field jacket, USMC with letter
baby picture from son Roy
cassette tape
funeral card in frame
Mack truck hat with MACV pin
letter on hotel stationary
Confederate ace of spades
bag of rice
clipping on casualties
note re Agent Orange, and photo
photo of couple at table
Styrofoam Bible
note with check, "this check is to be used . . . love, Mom"
wedding invitation to Capt. Norman R. Kidd
from his daughter
picture of J.F.K. on prayer card attached to
"Impeach Nixon" pin[1]

Barnett, my brother, our skin was not the same but our
hearts were. I've missed you soul brother. Travel in peace.
You are in good company with our brothers
McFarland and Lloyd.
This ten pack is on me. I've come to have
one last smooth one with you.

—Letter left at the Wall[2]

This man bringing beer to the Wall for his friend Barnett is doing something that is both obvious and complicated. It is obvious in that he is bringing a gift for his friend. It is complicated in that his friend has been dead for twenty years, and he is bringing the beer to a national memorial bearing his friend's name.

As I demonstrated in the last chapter, there are American funerary traditions, particularly among African Americans, Mexican Americans, and Italian Americans, that involve speaking to the spirits of the dead with gifts and grave decorations. Although the leap from the grave to a national memorial is new, it is impossible to imagine that the impulse to decorate the Wall has not been shaped by these funerary traditions. After all, this war was fought by conscripts from just the communities in which these traditions thrive: as Vietnam General S. L. A. Marshall commented, "in the average rifle company, the strength was 50% composed of Negroes, Southwestern Mexicans, Puerto Ricans, Guamanians, Nisei, and so on . . . but a real cross section of American youth? Almost never."[3] It would be natural for people to draw on these popular tools for negotiating with the dead to remember the war. In addition, even those who do not come from this tradition have probably seen or heard about this practice. Bricoleurs in the most literal sense, these memorializers are scraping together a memory with the tools at hand. The result is a new mode of public commemoration.

I have argued that the historical context into which these traditions have been inserted—the intensity of disagreement over the war and the ways in which this memorial's design breaks from commemorative traditions—has unintentionally triggered this participatory response. It is as if the still lively controversy about the Vietnam War keeps the dead alive; it will not let them rest, and therefore it inspires a tactile, insistent response from mourners. This uncertainty about the meaning of the war and of dying in it seems to keep the living coming back to speak to the dead.

The liminal, contested place of the war in the culture disrupts the expectation that dead soldiers will be remembered as heroes. Remember that returning veterans found themselves emblems of everything that seemed to be wrong with the nation, rather than emblems of the heroic body of the nation. In the first five years after the official end of the war, more than fifty-eight thousand Vietnam veterans committed suicide; there were more veterans who took their own lives than there were soldiers killed in combat.[4] Thirty thousand Vietnam veterans were in American prisons in 1980, and more than 2 million veterans were suffering from the effects of Agent Orange.[5] The popular image of the Vietnam veterans was that of a "drug-crazed, gun-toting, and violence-prone individual unable to adjust to civilized society." At the same time, these veterans "grew profoundly distrustful of the government that had sent them to fight and deeply resentful of the nation's seeming ingratitude for their sacrifices."[6] As Fred Downs, a much decorated veteran, explains, "a historical paradox was occurring in that Americans began to hate war, and Americans didn't know how to separate the strong feelings that they had against Vietnam and the war and the soldiers who were sent. There was no common denominator of patriotism. The Nam soldier got caught in the crossfire. If war is wrong, and that war in particular was wrong, the soldier was wrong for fighting it."[7] There was no common denominator of patriotism because the fundamental terms of patriotism had been disrupted. This disruption was clearly incredibly painful for many, many veterans, but it was not and is not a problem just for veterans and their families. After the Vietnam War, the instability of the social position of the soldier marked a national crisis of identity and, therefore, of memory.

Understanding this historical context—a crisis of national discourse into which popular traditions of grieving are inserted—helps to clarify the meanings in the offerings themselves. Seen in this light, each object is part of a conversation about the nation. Each object is a response to the problem of patriotism in the wake of the war. Each object is caught up in the symbolic negotiations of the shape of the nation at the Wall.

David Guynes, the collection's curator, has written, "we can think of the objects' meanings as stored, latent by virtue of their being left where they were, as accumulations. The fabric of their own pasts is being undone, exposed publicly, in the same way the country as a whole may be in the process of weaving a new concept of itself to replace the old."[8] This insight, the idea that the meaning of the objects taken together obscures, in a sense, the meanings of the particular objects, is an important starting place for thinking about the things. The difficulty of assigning specific meanings to individual objects left at the Wall is further compounded by the sheer number of people, objects, personal motivations, and possible interpretations. Nevertheless, citizens leaving things at the Wall are making their own memorials, and, as the lists that follow demonstrate, this memorial work is not a coordinated effort with a clearly articulated vision. It is the unsolicited work of people whose lives and sense of place in the culture have been disrupted by the war.

Divining the meanings in these memorials—individually and as they speak together—is difficult because there is no shorthand for reading the meanings of everyday objects used to make memory in national public spaces. There is no shorthand because there is no history of speaking with things in public places. Yet it seems crazy not to try to think about the specific meanings these objects carry, if only because thinking about their meaning might, at the very least, serve as a way of drawing out the terms of the conversation about the nation that they produce.

GIVING GIFTS

59 cents from Doug Magruder	*41 cents and a note of thanks*
braided lock of hair	*code of conduct card*
ace of diamonds	*flag pins, Desert Storm plaque*
beer can, sausage, and smokes	*two Bud cans, letters, Gary Harthren*
medal with case	*"Vietnam Remembered" sticker*[9]
jacket with note in pocket	

What rule of legality and self-interest, in societies . . . compels
the gift that has been received to be obligatorily reciprocated?
What power resides in the object given that causes its
recipient to pay it back?

—Marcel Mauss, The Gift

You received gifts from me; they were accepted.
But you don't understand how to think about the dead.
The smell of winter apples, of hoarfrost, and of linen.
There are nothing but gifts on this poor, poor Earth.

—Czeslaw Milosz, *Unattainable Earth*

All of the things left at the Wall are, in some way, gifts. It is as a gift—an offering in an economy of exchange—that each thing enters the conversation about the war and the losses. Like bringing a beer to a friend on the Wall, giving a gift is both a simple exchange and a deeply implicated social act. Gift giving holds communities and cultures together. Gifts are given to make, affirm, and uphold social bonds. They also mark differences, assert power, and create dependence.

In his seminal essay on gifts and gift giving Marcel Mauss argues that gift exchange is central to the life of preindustrial communities. He argues that a gift is always a part of a larger system of exchange; there is no such thing as a purely motivated gift or a gift for which reciprocation is not expected. Giving a gift creates mutual responsibility. All gifts, he contends, are part of a crucial economy in which "the whole society can be described by the catalogue of transfers that map all the obligations between its members."[10] In his vision of these "total social phenomena," he maintains that "all kinds of institutions are given expression at one and the same time—religious, juridical, and moral which relate to both politics and the family; likewise the economic ones." The total social world, he argues, is shaped by codes of exchange, and all of the rules of the culture are expressed in gift exchange. Given things carry enormous, particular symbolic weight. They map the connections between the giver and the receiver.[11] This thinking about gifts opens up the possibility that gifts not only express the social world but also help communities to negotiate it. Gifts, in Mauss's understanding, describe and map out social obligations. The exchange of gifts marks social boundaries and shapes social relationships.

In the aftermath of the Vietnam War, these codes of exchange broke down. Angered and disgusted by the dishonesty with which the war was waged and with its loss, most Americans wanted nothing to do with Vietnam veterans or the memory of Americans killed in Vietnam. In 1975, when the war seemed, finally, to be over, there was no groundswell of affection and admiration for those who fought. The country entered a state of "self-conscious collective amnesia" in which the war disappeared from public political debate and from newspapers and televisions. The Memorial Day and Veterans Day holidays that had, since the Civil War, regularized the celebration of the memory of soldiers were hardly observed.[12] This social breakdown created an enduring crisis about the memory of the soldiers and therefore about the foundation of the nation. The Vietnam Veterans Memorial is a response to this crisis. It was conceived as a place for veterans and the dead to be given the respect and honor that were, according to these essential social codes, their due. The builders of this memorial wanted to reconstruct the community that had been shattered by this broken promise. They wanted to keep the promise, belatedly, in some form; they wanted to "heal the nation" by restoring a proper memory of the soldiers.

People carrying their things to the Wall are answering, and asking, questions about society's obligations to its soldiers. After other recent wars, bringing flags to the grave sites of soldiers on official memorial holidays was an important part of paying homage to fallen soldiers for their sacrifice; the flags marked an honored memory of the dead and were a reminder of the debt that nation owed to its soldiers. This debt was not paid after Vietnam, and bringing a medal or a lock of hair or 59 cents or a political sticker to the Vietnam Veterans Memorial is an intervention in the public crisis of memory spurred by the nation's failure to pay it. The giving of these gifts is a powerful symbolic response to this betrayal; all of the medals and money and fetishized pieces of bodies and political iconography, taken together, are a palimpsestic collective negotiation about the problem of the memory of the deaths and the war.

THE THINGS

Bud can at 3w
walnuts
driver's license
bottle of Olde English aftershave lotion
ace of spades
Sunne S. Robinson's business card with "New Jersey
Cosmetology Association Remembers"
funeral card for Airborne Ranger John Bradman
black baseball cap with gold bars
pamphlet, "Did God Go AWOL in Vietnam?"
student's pencil bag
bumper sticker with dog tags attached
note in cryptic language
cigarette
rubbings
card, "Smile, Jesus Loves You"
fruit cocktail at 21w, 41w, 44e, 30w, 56e, 18e, 66e, 32e
dog tags[13]

Guys stuck the aces of spades in their helmet bands, they
picked relics off an enemy they'd killed, a little transfer of

*power; they carried around five pound Bibles from home,
crosses, St. Christophers, mezuzahs, locks of hair, girlfriends'
underwear, snaps of their families, their wives, their dogs,
their cows, their cars, pictures of John Kennedy, Lyndon
Johnson, Martin Luther King, Huey Newton, Che Guevara,
the Beatles, Jimi Hendrix, wiggier than cargo cultists. One
man was carrying an oatmeal cookie through his tour,
wrapped up in foil and plastic and three pairs of socks.*

—Michael Herr, *Dispatches*

In *Dispatches*, his memoir about the war, Michael Herr describes a kind
of "flip religion" that the soldiers he knew developed around their
things. In his story about remembering the war, "The Things They Carried," Vietnam veteran Tim O'Brien also writes about a special, superstitious relationship between the soldiers he knew and their things.[14]
He writes about how they differentiated and protected themselves with
the things they carried. One guy carried his girlfriend's panty hose
around his neck, another a generous supply of pot, another an inces-
santly thumbed photograph of his girlfriend, another an extra round
of ammunition, another a stone that he thought would bring him good
luck, and another his father's Bible. In the story, the things become so
important to these men because the things are all that the soldiers have
to remind themselves that they are not simply replaceable grunts. Far
from home, in a crazy situation that they could not control, these soldiers identified themselves and established their bearings with their
special things. They hoped the powers in the things would keep them
alive. The things were markers against the threat of the erasure of the
individual soldier in the mass of conscripted men.

The things set at the Wall serve a similar function. They mark some
kind of particularity in response to the problem of the memory of the
soldiers; they are markers against the threat of the erasure of the memory of the war and its soldiers. They are insistently working to recast the
soldiers' identities and to reestablish the veteran's place in the culture.

A random list of things left at the Wall begins to evoke the terms of
these negotiations: a copy of *War and Peace*, a pair of medic's scissors,
a Ukrainian flag and a leg brace, a package of papers from a course entitled "Vietnam in Film," a yarn hank, a note about a vet who died of
AIDS, a handful of seashells, a pair of lacy red panties, a Zippo lighter, a
copy of *Steppenwolf*, a brass pipe, a can of turkey loaf, a St. Christopher

medal, a green elephant, a "We're Not 'Fonda Jane'" sticker, a Martin Luther King Jr. postcard, a champagne bottle and three glasses, a high school reunion program, a photo of two caskets, a "Femme Vietnam" pin, a Vietnamese medal, a child's painting, a Father's Day card, a petosky stone, an origami bird, a pack of Lucky Strikes, a child's sock, a fishing rod, a votive candle, a hockey puck, a pack of baseball cards, a Hank Williams Jr. tape, a rock "left by a Jewish couple," a diploma from Pennsylvania College, a "Khe-Sahn Vets" banner with a photo of Mick Jagger, a stick of antiperspirant, a pair of shot glasses full of bourbon, a trumpet, a Puerto Rican flag, a stained-glass window reading "Matthew F. Sharpnack, 1947–1967," a television set, an eagle feather, a can of tennis balls, a bayonet, a 1966 nickel, a wallet (with photographs, credit cards, identification, and money), a Mickey Mouse Club hat, a driver's license, a T. S. Eliot poem, a pack of Pop Tarts, an airline ticket, a flight suit, a bag of dirt from the grave of Donald Candler in a Royal Crown bag, a bronze star, a hospital ID bracelet, a pack of matches, a note written on toilet paper, a stuffed dog, a sealed envelope addressed to "unknown soldier," a cookie in the shape of a cornhusk, a clipping about Daniel Moore, a poem, a plastic money key chain, a package of Kool-Aid, a Statler Brothers record, a ring, a tissue with a lipstick imprint on it, an Agent Orange poster, a photocopied photograph in a frame with note reading "football star," a half-burned flag, a winter army jacket, a penny, one pair of new Nike running shoes at each of eight different panels, a Chinese paper fan, an animal bone, a good conduct medal with a letter from President Bush to Michael Brennan, a woman's handkerchief, a papier-mâché rifle, a USAF watch that belonged to D. Wrobleski left by his nephew, a framed photograph of a Mrs. Johnson's fifth-grade class, an urn with the remains of Army veteran Martin Ranko, an envelope with two death notification letters, a license plate, a wedding band, a bottle of shampoo, a gun clip, a rubber duck with three safety pins, and on and on.

This is an overwhelming list. It demonstrates the unsolicited, wild range of memorial impulses that ordinary citizens bring to the Wall. And it is painful testimony to the intensity with which people have experienced the crisis of public memory in the wake of the Vietnam War. Some of these things make sense intuitively as gestures of friendship (a beer) or of protest (a burned flag), but most of the things left at the Wall are open to a wide spectrum of interpretive possibilities. Why bring a television set to a national memorial? Why leave a bag of dirt from the grave of a veteran? Why a penny? Why the Nikes? Why a diploma? I have argued that things are interventions in a crisis of public memory and that the range of things left at the Wall makes it difficult to map out the work of particular interventions. Furthermore, some of the things are, of course, deeply private and we can only guess at what they try to commemorate.

In spite of these difficulties, the following categories in the things do draw out the particular questions that are being negotiated. Studying the logs of objects left at the memorial, looking for clues about how to understand them, I was in turns overwhelmed by the volume of things, pulled into the interpretive possibilities with which each object is riddled, and compelled by five broad, and insistently overlapping, categories of objects that emerged. The great majority of objects mark specific individual memories, some speak to the problems of patriotism or community, some are negotiations between the living and the dead, some work to establish a community of veterans, and some make explicit political speech. Certainly, these are pretty rough categories, but they are also useful. They help to clarify what is at stake in the memorials people are making.

What follows is a kind of map—based on these categories—for understanding some of the things. This map is illustrated with a few interpretations, which are suggestive and provisional rather than definitive simply because I cannot know what was in the mind of each person carrying each object. The exploration of these categories that follows demonstrates that many, many people carrying things to the Wall are

working to come to terms with particular losses *and* with their troubled patriotism. This seemingly simple idea may be a lot to conclude from cans of beer and worn-out sweatshirts, but thinking about the kinds of things people leave and the act of leaving things make the work that people are doing with their offerings difficult *not* to see.

The first category, the memorials to specific individuals, is, perhaps, the easiest kind of offering to identify and the most difficult to assign meaning to. A hockey puck, a stuffed dog, a pack of baseball cards, a fishing rod, a business card, a can of tennis balls, and a trumpet have no obvious connections to the war. These things stand as a memory of what someone liked, or what they did; they are carried to the Wall to make a specific memory of loss; they assert the value of making that memory. A bottle of Olde English aftershave is just the kind of gift that seems likely to have been left in memory of a particular soldier. The aftershave was probably left for someone who wore it; it builds a specific memory. The failure to, or the impossibility of, making a real memory of all of these lost lives inspired someone to mark this singular memory: this is what he smelled like, it is worth remembering.

Some objects reassert the fact of a particular death. John Frederic Bradman's name is carved on panel 13w, line 26. In 1990 someone brought to the Wall a funeral card from his funeral. The card restates the fact of his twenty-year-old death. It might have been left to demonstrate to him that he had been well taken care of; it might have been intended to keep the public memory of this death alive. Nearly every day the fact of a death is restated in this way. Literally hundreds of newspaper clippings about the funerals of these men are carried to the Wall and left there to be read.[15] Certainly, the funeral card and the clippings work to keep the memory of these soldiers alive. They are like Sunne S. Robinson's business card, which promises, in a note scrawled on the back, that the "New Jersey Cosmetology Association Remembers." Of course, what is remembered here is not entirely clear. There are two Robinsons on this panel;[16] the card could refer to one of them or it could be trying to make a broader memory. In either case, it is a simple promise, a promise that Sunne Robinson needed to make real, and public, by writing it down and setting it at the Wall.

The objects in the second category, objects that speak to issues of community and patriotism, are caught in a tension between affirming and renouncing the Wall, the war, the dead, and the nation. Because the Wall does not celebrate the war and because it mourns enormous losses, leaving an emblem of patriotism or a marker of membership in American community at the memorial is a complicated symbolic act. A dog tag and a medal are all examples of this complicated exchange. By removing these things from their contexts, the mourners at the Wall disrupt the functions of the things and raise questions about their meanings.

The dog tags illustrate my point most clearly. Dog tags were first issued in England at the turn of the century because the British army had, following the example set by Americans at Gettysburg, started to identify and bury its dead soldiers.[17] Dog tags are contradictory symbolically because they represent the tension between celebrating the individual identities of soldiers and replacing those individual identities with a serial number. So the dog tag is itself a powerful emblem of the evolving relationship between the nation and the individual. The tags quite literally represent the expectation that a body sent to war will be reclaimed, returned, reinterred, and remembered. Leaving a dog tag at the Wall marks a need to speak to the problem of the identity of the soldier whose name is punched into the metal; at the memorial, dog tags emphasize the displacement of the soldier's body and identity and the deep confusion caused by the instability of the meaning of the war.

Dog tags started to appear at the Wall in 1982 and have continued to be set against the granite at a regular rate: at least once a week someone leaves a pair of tags. Sometimes they have come together in organized protest; more than forty dog tags were left in one day in protest of U.S. policies in Central America.[18] They were left in a calculated effort to represent the potential deaths—the potential bodilessness—of American soldiers if these policies created another Vietnam. It was a smart, systematic reminder of the price of a war without public support.

But most dog tags come to the Wall one by one. The connection between the dog tag and the body is obvious. This connection comes out of a particular historical moment in which a new relationship of the mass citizen and the nation was being forged. So turning the dog tags of a dead son back in at the Wall marks an explicit rejection of these terms.

Most of the dog tags did not belong to a person named on the Wall. The majority, maybe as many as 80 percent, of the dog tags left at the Wall belonged to surviving veterans and were probably placed there by the veterans themselves.[19] These tags do not echo a name already on the Wall; instead they add a new name. These new names are a different kind of intervention in the crisis of memory. They unofficially introduce the surviving veteran into the conversation; they establish a link between the status of the dead soldiers and the status of the living soldiers. They make it clear that it is not only the dead but also the survivors that are being mourned.[20] You might leave your dog tags because you don't understand what it means to survive this war. You might leave your dog tags because you want to reject your generic military identity. You might leave them because you want to leave behind the body that fought. You might leave them because your grief or your service needs to be remembered. You might leave them because you don't understand why you survived. You might leave them because you feel as though you did not survive. Leaving a dog tag at the Wall uses a literal token of citizenship to make an explicit assertion of the memory of a particular loss at the same time that it lays open a series of questions about patriotism.

A Purple Heart left at the Wall does some of the same work. Leaving a medal both attests to and calls into question its value. It might be left as a high honor for a fallen friend or as a demonstration of how little value the honor has. Some medals are left for the explicit purpose of renouncing their value—in 1986 more than seventy medals were left in one afternoon as a protest of U.S. policies in Central America.[21] Some medals are left to honor the dead; Bernie Triano, a veteran from New

Jersey, left his Purple Heart to let his friends know that "they are not forgotten."[22] Medals awarded to veterans in other wars have been saved on mantels and in top drawers; giving a medal up is an indication that the giver sees it as an ambivalent emblem, or that the giver sees the memory of the soldiers in jeopardy and is inspired to act.

The third category of objects people offer are those that are mediations between the living and the dead. All of the objects left at the Wall are gifts, and I have argued that, as such, they all mediate between the living and the dead; but some do so more explicitly than others. A can of beer, a Slim Jim, and a pair of nursing pads offered at the Wall all seem to share the possibility that they are offered as gestures meant for the dead. Cans of beer show up all the time at the Wall. Budweiser is a particularly popular brand. What kind of gift is a can of Bud? "Budweiser/King of Beers," which comes in a red, white, and blue aluminum can, is a popular, cheap domestic beer, and during the war it was supplied to American soldiers in Vietnam by Anheuser-Busch. Using slogans like "This Bud's for you" and "Proud to be your Bud," its advertisers have sold it for decades as a hallmark of male friendship, as a reward given from one man to another for a job well done.[23] These slogans, like the slogans of military recruiting offices, "I Want You" and "Proud to Serve," render the mass-produced soldier both common and a "King."

Like the beer left for Barnett, many cans of beer get left with notes that illuminate the intentions of their bearers. A letter left with a bottle of Colt 45 reads: "Hey Bro—here's the beer I owe—24 years later. You were right. I did make it back to the world. Great seeing you again, I'll be along soon. Thanx, Sarge."[24] In this case the beer is an explicit expression of gratitude to a fallen friend, and it fulfills a decades-old promise. Another note left with a beer, on April 4, 1989, reads, "Sorry Greg, I named my kid after you and here's the beer that we would have drunk." One of the most striking and often lamented difficulties of returning to the "world" for Vietnam veterans was the contrast between the remarkable intensity of the bonds among soldiers in combat and the lack of any kind of community into which they might return. A can of Budweiser or a bottle of Colt 45 brought to the Wall is a gift that speaks clearly to the problem of what is owed to the dead. It also speaks to the absence of a place in the culture for the living veterans. In this way, a beer at the Wall is a simple intervention in the problem of the memory of the Vietnam soldier. It rewards sacrifice and confirms the connection between the living and the dead.

A Slim Jim, the skinny little metal device made for breaking into locked cars, was carried to the Wall in 1990. It is a valuable, hard-to-come-by tool. There are a handful of symbolic resonances that might be attached to a Slim Jim at the memorial. It might be making a memory about a stolen life, or it might be a metaphor for unlocking the seamless listing of the memorial, or it might be a reference to a habit of stealing cars. In any case, it is an evocative, keenly particular kind of memorial to make. It did not come with a note or a name attached, but it manages to give an anonymous name a distinct memory. It is a reminder of the need of the giver to mediate the liminal status of the dead; like prayers for a soul in purgatory, the Slim Jim helps the living to unlock, to release, the dead.

The Wall inspired the leaving of a pair of nursing pads in the fall of 1986.[25] They may have been left as a reminder of the labor this war cost the mothers of the dead: "I fed him from my own breast for this?" They might represent a yearning for physical contact with a lost son. They might also be a reminder that most of those who died in the war were, at nineteen, still boys. The stolen child leaves the breasts overfull and leaking. The pads might also be gifts from a mother whose child lost a father in the war. They may serve as an introduction—a physical connection between her body and their child. In any case there is a shocking intimacy in the gesture. It is a reminder of the costs of the war; it makes a sensual, bodily memory that speaks to a different kind of connection to the dead.

A fourth category of things that get left at the Wall encompasses objects left as tokens of the shared experiences of veterans. Like the characters in O'Brien's fiction and Herr's memoir, many soldiers in Vietnam were superstitious about various things.[26] If you died in Vietnam you were said to have drawn an ace of spades. Leaving an ace of spades at the memorial restates the fact of a death and suggests a shared understanding of what the death meant. The p-38 can opener and other pieces of equipment issued to common soldiers are symbols of the war. There were other things that took on particular meanings in Vietnam; Zippo lighters and Pez candy dispensers are, for many veterans, emblematic of days spent in Vietnam.[27] These things show up at the Wall

as markers of the experience and as a kind of private communication between the living and the dead vets.

The cans of fruit cocktail left one each at eight panels make a tremendous memorial to a community of veterans. They are surely left in reference to the C rations of fruit cocktail that these men shared in Vietnam. In combat situations or in the middle of days of endless boredom, a can of sweet, neatly diced fruit could be a heavenly gift. The gift of a can of fruit cocktail makes a very particular memory, one that is not quite like some of the others: the memory seems sweet, and it is not charged with questions about masculinity. It also tries to remember a community within the community of the dead at the Wall. It marks a particular collective memory.

Finally, the fifth category of objects are those that make some kind of explicit political speech. Campaign buttons, bumper stickers, placards left after rallies on the Mall, Agent Orange T-shirts, and, of course, the POW/MIA coffee mugs all seem to be responding to the Wall as a site for public debate.

All of the objects left at the Wall make amazing individuated memories, and the rough patterns into which many of them fall tacitly reveal a desire to renegotiate the disrupted relationship between citizens, soldiers, and the nation. People who choose to come to make memory at the Wall bring a mass of individuated memories that provisionally coalesce into a collective statement of the problems of the memory of the war. Together, they do not take a definitive position, but they do draw the boundaries of the problems of memory. They insistently make truly individuated memories of the dead that assert the particularity of the lives lost, and they repeat a deeply felt desire—in the form of concern about community and the liminal position of the dead and the need to remember individuals and the value of traditional emblems of patriotism and the ongoing life of political debates around the war.

In a long careful argument about commemoration at the close of the "American century," historian John Gillis writes about an antimonument movement which he believes is democratizing memory. He argues, "its advocates reject the notion of memory sites and want to deritualize and dematerialize remembering so that it becomes more a part of everyday life, thus closing the gap between the past and the present, between memory and history." The implication of this argument is that the everydayness of this new memory moves people past an engagement with the nation. He writes, "the reality is that the nation is no longer the site or frame of memory for most people, and therefore national history is no longer a proper measure of what people really know about their pasts."[28] This statement does not describe what happens at the Wall; the Vietnam Veterans Memorial Collection is a reminder of the potency of the nation in the imaginations of grievers at the Wall.

Certainly for visitors to the Vietnam Veterans Memorial, the nation is an important part of the framework with which they understand their own pasts and their futures. Americans making memory with their things are too intensely involved in negotiations with the nation to have abandoned it; they are trying to recover a usable idea of the nation in the face of the betrayals and contradictions of Vietnam. People are not carrying their cans of beer and baby pictures and locks of hair to cemeteries where those who died in this war are buried; they are responding to a shared crisis in a public place. Americans coming to the Wall have not forsaken the idea of the nation; they are struggling to salvage it and its place in their identities. They are not simply expressing the antiwar movement's rage or the hawks' pride; they are participating in a struggle of politically diverse, ordinary citizens to make a memory of the war that will allow them to reclaim their place in the culture. These things do not mark the death of the nation or patriotism; on the contrary they mark a tremendous effort to reconstitute the nation and the citizen's faith in it.

"YOU ARE NOT FORGOTTEN"

MOURNING FOR AMERICA

Humankind cannot bear very much reality.
—T. S. Eliot

white bear with ribbon
pile of buttons, Sony Walkman and earphones
white lollipop with stand
POW bracelet
yellow painted stake with black cloth ribbon
rosary
"Proposition One Voter:
Initiative for Nuclear disarmament" sticker
sock with note from USMC
John Christopher Robertson in plastic bag
18 flags
Danang hat
phone number of Ralph G. (636–9535)
and number of Keith Armtrout
registration verification for Timothy P. Hartican
can of Pepsi, pack of Pall Malls,
pack of Life Savers, blueberry muffin
St. Francis medal
purple rock[1]

One of the central metaphors of *The Deer Hunter*, the movie that inspired Jan Scruggs's campaign for a Vietnam memorial,[2] is that the veterans returning to the small Pennsylvania community found themselves prisoners to a profound social displacement that echoed their imprisonment in Southeast Asia. The movie ends with the young members of this community mourning the death of one of the veterans by singing "God Bless America." Sitting around a table after the funeral of their former POW and AWOL friend, unable to speak, they find in the patriotic hymn something to say to each other about the death.[3] As literary critic Rick Berg argues, it "is not an attempt to reiterate the shoddy values of a hollow patriotism. . . . what we see is a community shattered by Vietnam, trying to express a deeply rooted nationalism, with all its ironies and contradictions."[4] The Wall was meant to belatedly acknowledge the contributions, and the confused social position, of living veterans in this context. As an effort to help veterans get back into the changed world they left to serve in Vietnam, the Wall has opened up a public space for debate about what it meant to fight in, and come home from, this war; thousands of ordinary people have carried their own memorials to be a part of the memory negotiated at the Wall.

The memorial was intended to help veterans find a place for themselves in the culture; to do this it needed to release veterans from a social purgatory shaped by the war and by enormous changes on the home front after the war. The veterans may have imagined themselves swaggering war heroes, but they came home to find themselves hated; they came home to the antiwar movement, the civil rights movement, the beginnings of the sexual revolution, "long hair, short skirts, and high prices."[5] All of these things changed the fabric of American patriotism. But the Wall did not explicitly try to repair the tattered patriotism with which vets (and their families) came to terms with the war. It certainly did not try to justify the causes for which they were sent to fight. At the dedication Scruggs, a master of understatement, told reporters, "too bad it wasn't a simple war . . . then we could put up a heroic statue of a couple of Marines and leave it at that."[6] The organizers of the memorial project wanted an acknowledgment of the pain wrought by this war, but they felt they could not use the old symbolic framework to understand the complicated problems of this grief.

As I have argued, the things left at the Wall constitute more than just a response to the tragedy of lost lives, although this function is obviously central; beyond grieving for the dead, the Wall inspires people to grieve the loss of patriotism, nationalism, and community in the wake of the Vietnam War. The things left there represent a kind of complicated countermemorial; they embody the desire for a nation that

can reconcile the ideal of sacrifice and the contingent fate of Vietnam veterans.[7]

This mourning for the nation takes place in all of the things left at the Wall, but it is most explicit, or at least easiest to see, in the POW/MIA offerings. T-shirts, ID bracelets, coffee mugs, and bumper stickers referring to POWs and MIAs make an unprecedented public intervention in the interpretation of the war and of the military's place in the culture. Even so, the meaning of the objects is not always self-evident. Many of them are simultaneously affirmed and renounced by their presence at the Wall. Leaving your Purple Heart, for instance, might be a high tribute to a fellow soldier or an expression of disdain for the honor and the body that granted it; leaving a POW baseball cap reasserts the memory of the possible suffering of Americans abandoned in Vietnam, and it retires the memory to a storage site in suburban D.C. There is an active tension in the symbolic meanings of these things. But unlike the other offerings at the Wall, the POW/MIA things are designed, produced, and sold as part of an organized effort to make and maintain a particular memory of the war.

Since 1982, tremendous attention has been paid to the POWs and the MIAs, whose names are carved in the Wall along with those of the known dead.[8] For millions of Americans, the POWs and MIAs have become a focus for the rage, heartbreak, disillusionment, and disgust with the nation brought on by the Vietnam War. According to a 1991 *Wall Street Journal*/NBC News poll, "69% of the American people believe that U.S. prisoners of war are still being held in Southeast Asia, nearly twenty years after the United States called its troops home." This is an amazing figure, but the phenomenon did not begin in 1991; since 1969, the POW/MIA myth has had enough public support to inspire numerous military and Congressional investigations and seemingly endless promises from politicians.[9]

Although endless debates have raged about numbers, lists, classifications, sightings, and ill-fated "reconnaissance missions," little has been written about why so many Americans believe that the Vietnamese are still holding live American soldiers.[10] The central metaphor in the rhetoric of the POW activists is that while there is one American prisoner in Southeast Asia, all of America is held hostage. The movement's slogan, "You Are Not Forgotten," speaks to the POW and the citizen alike. The POW/MIA movement has provided millions of people with a community in which to renegotiate their relationship to the nation. It has given a legitimate, acceptable shape to rage and displacement that is directly connected to the war, and also, perhaps more important, it has given shape and focus to other griefs connected to the changing social landscape that Americans have faced since war. The POW/MIA memory rewrites the roles of the central characters in the war such that the Vietnamese become the victimizers and the Americans become the victims. This revised narrative is manifest at the Wall in the shape of thousands of stainless steel bracelets and black T-shirts, the material emblems of commitment to the POW/MIAs.

Just as leaving a Purple Heart at the memorial can both affirm and renounce its symbolic value, the POW commemoration has at its heart both a feeling of loss and a resentment toward what has been lost. The POW/MIA movement understands the war in terms of the failure of the United States government to stand by its soldiers; its rage at the government is expressed in the name of patriotism. The POW movement rewrites the history of the war with the memory of Americans as victims; it has developed a populist, antistatist, nationalist position with which to try to come to terms with the war. It is a political movement inspired by the crisis of memory that keeps the war alive.

This chapter explores the POW/MIA artifacts left at the Wall as one response to the threats the legacy of the war has held for patriotism, the military, and the place of the war hero in the culture. The people who come to the Wall are not only claiming the national monument as their own but also taking responsibility for making a memory of the war themselves; they are forging a history of the war and its legacy at the Wall. The POW/MIA commodities, sold by dedicated veterans just a few feet from the Wall, provide one carefully calculated response to the crisis of memory caused by the war. In the collection of things left at the Wall, there is an enormous depth of experience, and there are thousands of radically individuated memories of the war; the POW/MIA things are part of a concerted effort to organize and shape these memories into a celebration of the sacrifices of veterans and a condemnation of the government's treatment of its citizens. These things serve two functions particularly; they act as a reminder of the strength of will with which ordinary Americans want to have faith in the nation, and they act as a reminder of the intensity of private emotion invested in the other things. The POW/MIA movement literally hands out emblems of a particular position about the memory of the war. The fact that so many people choose to leave their own symbolic gestures is a testament to the need they feel to make particular, individual memorials. The fact that both kinds of negotiations have continued at the Wall is a testament to the need to explore new possibilities for the shape of the nation and the shape of the soldier.

The friends and families of the men and women killed in Vietnam, and millions of other Americans whose lives have been shaped by the war, have not been constrained either by a state position on the war or by mainstream American memorial traditions in their responses to the Wall. And while they have fought to make a wide range of memories of the war, many have used the memory of "our men who are still over there rotting in bamboo cages" as a solution to the problem of salvaging patriotism. They have put forth the restless, not-dead soldiers as a powerful and troubling emblem for the restless dead. The missing (and those who feel imprisoned at home) have been symbolically—but not literally—reclaimed and lionized. The POW/MIA things keep alive the hope that this war might still be won, keep alive the idea of the war hero, keep alive the virtues of being a Gold Star Mother, keep alive the dignity of "American fighting men," and keep alive the hope that all the sacrifices of the war were not made in vain. They also sustain an image of the Vietnamese as cruel and inhuman, which might make the horrors of the war more palatable for reinterpretation.[11] And yet they do this "patriotic" work in angry opposition to the American regime.

The story of the tenth anniversary celebration at the Wall illustrates the role of the POW/MIA issue in the life of the memorial and demonstrates the insistent restlessness of all of the interpretive frameworks brought to the Wall. The events of this day are a strong reminder that there is no consensus or closure about the meanings of the war or the place of the veterans in the culture, even after ten years of intense grieving at the Wall. The war is still restless and the battles over its meaning continue.

THE TENTH ANNIVERSARY

Congressional Medal of Honor	*toys*
framed photographs	*letters*
worn military uniforms	*POW bracelets*
assorted medals and insignia	*MIA flags*
Agent Orange T-shirts	*many, many wreaths*[12]

The ceremony on November 11, 1992, to mark the tenth anniversary of the Vietnam Veterans Memorial was a deeply schizophrenic public event. It did not celebrate what we might expect a Veterans Day in Washington to celebrate. There were no clear codes about what it meant to be a vet, to be patriotic, to stand by your nation, or to support your nation's soldiers. There was more rage at the government than pride expressed, and there was virtually no consensus about how to rebuild the idea of the vet or the idea of the nation.

In the program for the events of the day there is a quotation from former President Gerald Ford that reads,

> There is something very special about the Wall. The long tragic conflict in Vietnam was different from any military conflict in the history of America. Vast public differences on US government policy dominated the news media. It was not a typical period in America's history. The Wall, during its 10 years, has created a constructive sentiment of reconciliation among those diverse views.

In the same program Senator John Warner writes,

> For 10 years, the Wall had reflected and validated the entire spectrum of human emotions. Rage, desperation, pride, joy, comfort, understanding, hate have all commingled among those who have approached this Wall. I hope that all those who visit this memorial will reach a peace with the past and a secure healing for the future, just as those immortalized on this Wall have found an everlasting peace.

The spectrum of emotions expressed in these statements was evident at the ceremony to celebrate the work of the Wall, but clearly visitors to the memorial had not made peace with the past. The dead have not found everlasting peace, because the living have found a site for the expression of an unruly, contradictory, unsteady mix of powerful emotions and political positions; in responding to the liminal position of the dead, they have kept the war alive.

The festivities started at 8:30 A.M. with a slightly bedraggled mass of marchers moving past the imposing architecture of the Treasury building and the National Archives. Parading along wide and empty sidewalks in the shadow of the limestone architecture along Constitution Avenue, the veterans seemed to illustrate the great divide between the soldiers and the institutions that sent them to fight. The marchers spanned a broad spectrum of decorum and postures; there were equal numbers turned out in crisply pressed uniforms, well-worn fatigues, and casual civilian dress. They walked through the nearly deserted streets of the capital in loose groups under state names or political affiliations. Twenty or more Vietnamese men marched together carrying a banner reading "Vietnamese Prisoner of War Association." Most, but certainly not all, of the marchers were white men.

These veterans expressed a wide range of responses to their roles as parading military men and women. The messages with which they marked themselves were pointed and contradictory. The march was certainly, in part, patriotic, with plenty of American flags flying. Yet there was also a palpable anger at the United States government illustrated by paraphernalia that cut against the usual codes of a military parade.[13] Almost as many vets were wearing black and white POW T-shirts and orange and black Agent Orange baseball caps as were wearing green fatigues. Vets irate about the imagined fates of POWs and MIAs and the Veterans Administration's failure to recognize the toxic effects of Agent Orange carried enormous flags—flags that required nearly forty people to carry them along the parade route. Smaller black and white POW/MIA flags were everywhere.

The POW flag bears a stark black and white silhouette of a man with his head bent slightly to reveal a watchtower and a strip of barbed wire behind him; under it are the words "You Are Not Forgotten." Carrying this flag in a Veterans Day parade was a show of solidarity with Americans imagined to be still trapped in Vietnam; a protest of all the pain the war continues to cause; a protest against the loss of the war; a protest against the government for its failure to be responsible for the men and women asked to serve in Vietnam; a statement of pride in being a veteran; an assertion that veterans should be treated with respect; and, finally, a metaphor for the many vets who have never been able to come home themselves. Carrying a POW flag in this parade asserts for the carrier a complicated relationship to patriotism. It makes protest around the war possible without disavowing the war or the nation—it creates a pro-war, pro-vet, antigovernment patriotism.

Carrying an Agent Orange flag in a Veterans Day parade is a more direct protest of United States policies, but it is still not necessarily a protest against the war. It marks a conflicted patriotism that has surfaced in mistrust of both the government and antiwar sentiment. The T-shirts reading "Agent Orange did what the VC and the NVA couldn't do!" and the ravaged skin of the vets wearing them testified harshly to both the power of the toxin and the burning memory of the losses of the war. Agent Orange metaphorically speaks to the poisoning of American masculinity by the American government.[14]

After the parade, men and woman of several generations gathered at the Wall in Gore-Tex raincoats and plastic ponchos waiting for the official ceremony to begin. Some were not identifying their connection to the war with their clothing, and some looked almost like fans at a rock concert with POW T-shirts, jackets, bracelets, and flags. Jan Scruggs began the ceremony by saying that it was a tradition at the Wall to do things informally. Standing with a casual slump, he said that he liked to start events at the Wall by asking the people gathered to take a few minutes to introduce themselves to each other. It was a remarkable gesture; it made the event simultaneously more relaxed and more solemn. He made the event simultaneously more relaxed and more solemn, more human and more sacred. He articulated implicitly the importance of this community in making the monument what it is.

This community, however, was by no means cohesive. The incongruous collection of musicians performing that afternoon exemplified the oddly unsettled flavor of the event. New Age music was blasted over the PA system before Britt Small and Festival, a former Las Vegas show band (dressed very much like a former Las Vegas show band), played patriotic favorites with tremendous passion. They were followed by a quiet, understated acoustic performance by Country Joe McDonald, who was followed by a bagpiper and a sharp, brassy military band.[15] The assembled veterans and others responded to these various talents, styles, and political markers with unvaried enthusiasm and acceptance.

This same uncritical, enthusiastic reception greeted nearly all of the wildly divergent speakers. The speakers at the memorial celebration were a striking mixture of dignitaries and ordinary people.[16] They shared virtually no consensus about how to understand the war or the responsibilities of veterans. Two daughters of servicemen stood on the same platform, spoke about the same general subject, and received essentially the same response. They could not, however, have been further apart. Pamela Handrahan's father has been listed as missing in action for more than twenty years. Handrahan never knew her father but has been very involved in the movement to bring him home. A graduate of a small Christian college, she has spent her adult life traveling the country as a crusader for MIAs and POWs. Blonde, wearing a red dress and pearls, she spoke in a clear, cheerful voice about the plight of MIAs and POWs and their families. She made an impassioned plea for the need to bring these brave warriors home. She read a long, sentimental poem written by the son of another MIA asking for a chance to meet "daddy." A few minutes later Anni Booth Elias stood defiantly in jeans and a fatigue jacket; she introduced herself as a Sioux and the daughter of a man who was killed in a senseless, brutal war inspired by ignorance and greed and managed by thoughtless, clumsy bureaucrats. Elias's preacherlike cadence and her biting refrain ("But who am I to tell you this?") were a deep, pulling challenge to her audience. She told the crowd of veterans that their war was criminal and murderous, and she asked them to challenge her authority; but like Handrahan's sweet praise, Elias's bitter critique was received with eager applause and nodding heads.

Given this disparity in rhetoric and belief, it is surprising that there were not more complaints from the crowd. There were only two loud suggestions of dissent that day. One came from a man who yelled, as Al Gore began to speak, "Bill Clinton was a draft dodger." Gore looked in the direction of the voice and continued without further interruption. A few minutes later, however, just beyond this ceremony, when the wreaths had been laid down and the bands had stopped playing, there was another, more powerful—vigilante—response. A few feet from the model for the Vietnam Women's Memorial, which had been show-

ered with hundreds of green bills throughout the long day and had been
a rallying point in a number of the speeches, an effigy of Jane Fonda
had been erected. Like a lost scarecrow, on a pole in the middle of the
Mall, there stood a sweatshirt and sweatpants stuffed with newspaper,
scrawled with "Hanoi Jane," and topped with a Styrofoam head wearing a brown wig stuck with a Vietcong flag. Six or seven men in fatigues
stood around the figure. As people started to pour away from the Wall,
one of these men broke open his butane lighter, bent over the figure,
poured the lighter fluid between its legs, and struck a match to set it
on fire. It was the act of a few men, but it seemed like a hard promise
that not all of the pieces of patriotism were up for grabs for all vets.
The government may have been wrong, and some vets may have acted
vilely, but the woman who chastised American men fighting in Vietnam
would not go unpunished.[17]

Throughout the course of the day people walked along the Wall and
left hats, bracelets, bottles, combat boots, photographs, and much else.
One of the last messages, in fact, to come over the PA system that day
was an excited announcement that someone during the ceremony had
left a Congressional Medal of Honor at the Wall.[18] Like the POW/MIA
and Agent Orange flags, the artifacts left at the Wall are a means of
forging a bridge across the ever widening gulf between patriotic nationalism and the rage inspired in veterans and their communities by
the disregard with which the federal government treated them.
Through the missives they leave at the Wall, these communities struggle to protest the inaction of the United States government without
aligning themselves with antiwar or even antigovernment positions.[19]

THE RAGE FOR A NEW PATRIOTISM AND THE POW/MIA MOVEMENT

bracelet inscribed "Lieutenant-Colonel Charles Ervin Shelton"
bracelet inscribed "Captain James Grace"
bracelet inscribed "Colonel Nick Rowe"
bracelet inscribed "Master Sergeant Jacob Mercer"
bracelet inscribed "Sergeant Mel Holland"
bracelet inscribed "Sergeant Peter Cressman"

Like the war itself, the POW/MIA issue refuses to die. It has been, since
1969, terribly tangled and impossible to contain. Complicated by political maneuvering, high standards of accountability, the problems of

covert warfare, and the inflamed passions of millions of Americans whose patriotism and imagination of their nation were shattered by the war, the issue has sustained intense interest and remained unresolved for twenty-five years.[20]

The first American POWs in Vietnam were five Air Force men captured in 1954, before the United States government had officially announced its involvement in Southeast Asia. By 1961 eight Americans were classified as missing in action. In 1964, an officer serving as "combat advisor" became America's first *official* prisoner of the war.[21] During the next five years, as the war heated up, the number of POWs and MIAs steadily increased, but the POW/MIA issue was not yet a major public concern. It was not until 1969, when President Richard Nixon decided to launch a "go public" campaign on the issue, that it became a focal point for emotions related to the war.

Five days into his presidency, Nixon introduced the POW/MIA issue at the Paris peace talks with North Vietnam.[22] On May 19, 1969, he kicked off a domestic campaign to "marshal public opinion" for the support of American men held against their will in Vietnam. For Nixon, the issue served two purposes. It created a rallying point to counter the antiwar movement at home, and it gave him leverage in the peace talks that he would have otherwise not had. It worked stunningly on both fronts. In 1970, Nixon announced, "as long as there are American POWs—and there are 1,600 Americans in North Vietnamese jails under very difficult circumstances at the present time—as long as there are American POWs in North Vietnam we will have to maintain a residual force in South Vietnam."[23] At the negotiating table this issue bought his administration four years of stalling (in which to try to reach the impossible "peace with honor"); at home it made his supporters more visible—between 1969 and 1973, 50 million Americans bought POW/MIA bumper stickers—and, in the end, his use of the POWs saved the United States $4.5 billion in war reparations. In the process, he effectively inverted the strategy of the war of attrition by initiating a shift in emphasis from enemy body counts to counts of missing bodies. Throughout the war American officials worked very hard to emphasize the number of enemy deaths and to deemphasize the number of American deaths. By emphasizing the bodies of missing Americans, he opened up an issue that touched many Americans very deeply and would eventually spin out of his control.

President Nixon repeatedly described the POW question as a humanitarian rather than a political issue, but one of his first efforts in the go public campaign made political use of the families of the missing. He declared November 9 a "National Day of Prayer for US Prisoners of War in Vietnam." Richard Capen, Nixon's assistant secretary of defense, traveled across the country visiting forty-five groups of families of missing men, laying the foundation for the organization of the National League of Families of Prisoners of War in Southeast Asia. In May of 1969 the League, as it is known to POW activists, was founded by Sybil Stockdale, the wife of the highest ranking POW in Vietnam.[24] Stockdale held the first meeting at the Coronado Naval Officers' Club in San Diego. Within a year she was the star POW wife at Senator Robert Dole's Constitution Hall POW/MIA Ball, and her League was gathering national attention daily. Its membership was limited to the immediate families of POWs and MIAs. They supported each other and kept a national focus on the "men in bamboo cages."

Another rally point for the issue was VIVA, the Victory in Vietnam Association. This student-faculty group, founded in 1967 as a counterpoint to the antiwar movement, aspired to "support and encourage our American servicemen, wherever they might be involved in a struggle against aggression, and most specifically at this time in Vietnam, and to educate students and others to the scope and significance of our American commitment to freedom by organizing affiliate chapters of VIVA on university campuses throughout the United States."[25]

The group changed its name in 1969, in the face of ever dimmer chances of a "victory" in Vietnam, to Voices in Vital America, and changed its focus in 1970, when it took on the POW/MIA issue. VIVA contributed the movement's most successful campaign tool—the bracelets. In 1969, right-wing talk show host Robert Dorman suggested to VIVA director Carol Bates that she sell bracelets inscribed with the names of POW/MIAs to raise money and public awareness. The bracelets were officially introduced in May 9, 1970, at a Salute to the Armed Forces Ball, where "Governor Ronald Reagan was the keynote speaker, Bob Hope and Martha Raye were made co-chairs of the bracelet campaign, H. Ross Perot was named Man of the Year, and Mrs. Perot ceremoniously accepted the first bracelet." These copper bracelets were the product of determined work to keep old-fashioned, Bob Hope–style patriotism alive in the face of an ever widening credibility gap. And there was a constituency for them; by 1972 VIVA had sold 5,000 bracelets, and by 1973 the bracelets had made $7,388,088 for a thriving VIVA.[26]

In 1973, however, when the North Vietnamese and the Pathet Lao released 591 POWs in accordance with the Paris Peace Accords, the issue and the movement were transformed.[27] In the spring of 1973, the Department of Defense collapsed the POW and MIA and KIA/BNR (killed in action/body not returned) classifications.[28] This unusual move sealed the fate of the issue. In previous wars these categories of unaccounted for military bodies were officially distinct and logically acceptable. A prisoner of war was a someone known to be held by the enemy. Missing in action was a classification for a person whose fate was not known. KIA/BNR was the designation for a person known to be dead, but whose body was, in the circumstances of the war, unrecoverable. A total of 78,750 Americans were unaccounted for at the end of World War II; in other words, there were 78,750 MIAs. After the Vietnam War, 2,273 Americans might conceivably—with generous accounting all around—have been unaccounted for; in other words, there were 2,273 MIAs, POWs, and KIA/BNRs after the Vietnam War. Of these unaccounted for bodies 1,101 would have been classified as KIA/BNR in any other war. So, after Vietnam there were a total of 1,172 MIAs *and* POWs.[29] Given the conditions in which this war was waged, this is a remarkably low number; it is a testament to the extent of control that the Pentagon exerted over conscripted bodies—dead or alive.

Even though the three categories had been collapsed into one, the Department of Defense continued to keep an internal list of men it considered to be POWs. After the release of the 591 POWs in 1973 (dubbed Operation Homecoming), all but fifty-three men on the Department of Defense's POW list had either been released or reported to have died in captivity. Over the next three years, "intensive analysis of these remaining cases resolved all but a handful."[30] After twenty years of fighting all but fifty-three bodies were fully accounted for. Despite the fact that Vietnam and Laos actually released fifteen more prisoners than the United States had demanded, for Nixon and his successors the long process of numbering and renumbering and demanding the release of and denying the existence of remaining POW/MIAs had begun. For the League and VIVA, new missions were defined. Both organizations had been formed to provide a counterpoint to the antiwar movement, but with the official end of the war, they needed to recast their goals.

The POWs who did come home were greeted with tremendous fanfare. As historian Alexander Kendrick has argued, "the inner meaning of Operation Homecoming, if it could have been realized by those who were part of it, was that they had returned to a different country, made so to a large extent by the war and its impact."[31] The changed country has kept the POW/MIA issue alive for the last twenty years. Members of the League and VIVA have been compelled by their desire to hold onto their prewar patriotism to demand that the United States government keep President Nixon's promise not to let one American body go unaccounted for, one American loss go unexplained. These organizations and the millions of Americans who have supported them have been fighting to salvage something of that prewar America from the Vietnam War.

For many the POW issue provided, just as Nixon had hoped, a new framework with which they could understand the war. However, the activists were zealous beyond Nixon's expectations, and they failed to cease and desist when he announced that all POWs had been returned in 1973. The issue has continued to grow and thrive beyond Nixon's wildest expectations, for, rather than disappearing, the problems that he hoped it would address intensified after the war.

The turning point for these organizations came at the 1974 national convention of the League in Omaha. There the bracelet-rich VIVA made a $20,000 contribution and effectively transformed the League into an "agency for militant proselytizing of the faith that Americans

were still being held captive in Indochina." VIVA members wanted into the League, which had always limited its members to the families of the missing; the radical VIVA contingent managed to change the by-laws to add "a new interpretation to include self-proclaimed 'adoptive' family members."[32] After the release in 1973, the members who actually were family to missing men and women either had their father or husband or son home or wanted, for the most part, to put all the pain and the waiting behind them and get on with their lives. The new, adoptive members were people for whom the POW/MIA issue was a pressing political and social issue. They turned against the flailing Nixon administration and remained hostile to every administration until the election of Ronald Reagan.

These new members cultivated the faith that all the governments were lying and that American men were suffering at the hands of evil communists. Bracelets, T-shirts, and bumper stickers continued to sell in great volume after 1973, and in 1989 the League made $932,344 on the bracelets and other consciousness-raising commodities.[33] VIVA and the League continued to lobby Congress for action in Vietnam.[34] Despite conclusive government report after conclusive government report stating in no uncertain terms that there was no good reason to believe that MIAs and POWs were still being held against their will in Vietnam, people have continued to believe. They have offered enormous rewards, up to $2.4 million, for any living POWs, and in the process have inspired an industry of manufactured photographs and sightings. VIVA and the League were later joined by the American Defense Foundation, the Skyhook II project, and Operation Rescue; with the help of the federal government, these five organizations kept the memory of American POWs alive through the 1980s.[35]

The end of the war presented a problem for Nixon and the POW issue. When Operation Homecoming brought 591 American military men home, the president's interests were in conflict; if he took the position that there were no remaining POWs he would have to pay reparations, and if he took the position that there were still American POWs in Southeast Asia, he would appear to have failed at every turn in Vietnam. As a result, Nixon's official policy, which has been followed by every President since, was to maintain that there were no *known* prisoners of war still being held in Southeast Asia. However, no President has been willing to put the highly charged political issue to rest. Despite year after year of fruitless Congressional and military investigations, official policies have maintained that there might be unknown POWs, and every administration has promised to investigate all leads and has shown compassion for the suffering families.

In 1982, Bo Gritz, a mercenary to whom no scriptwriter could have given a better name, involved Ronald Reagan, Clint Eastwood, and William Shatner in a rescue mission. There are many stories about sightings and aborted rescue missions, but this one is worth repeating here because it connects official policy and the influence of Hollywood in keeping the issue alive in the 1980s so vividly. Eastwood and Shatner put up the money (in exchange for the movie rights), and Reagan was put on call in the event that POWs were located. Reagan promised

Bo Gritz that if Gritz found American POWs in Laos, he would "start World War III to get them out." Gritz was to cross into Laos to search a suspected camp. He elected himself to carry out the mission because "both Teddy Roosevelt and John Wayne are dead."[36] Despite this bravado, Gritz's plans were foiled when he was ambushed by anticommunist Laotians at the border. Needless to say, no POWs were seen or returned.

If POWs were not coming back in the flesh, they were certainly coming home in droves on the big screen in the 1980s. *Uncommon Valor, Missing in Action, First Blood, Rambo: First Blood II, Rambo III*, the six-film *MIA Hunter* series, and a handful of other Hollywood movies made between 1982 and 1987 all recast the story of the Vietnam war. In the Hollywood version of the war, the lone, renegade American hero who bucks a system controlled by corrupt bureaucrats goes back to 'Nam and, in most cases single-handedly, finally wins the war. These movies rewrite the history of the war by making the Americans the victims and, after some serious adversity, the victors.[37] In some cases, the story boils down to good Americans in Vietnam fighting bad Americans in Washington, literally writing the Vietnamese out of the story. This logic follows the logic of the POW movement, which cast the real threat to American soldiers as bad government bureaucrats.

The popularity of these movies, particularly the Rambo movies, was felt at the Wall. In the years after these movies came out, the Park Service had to stop supplying paper and pencils for rubbings of the name John Rambo, which is carved into line 126 of panel 16w.[38] The steady interest in the POW issue has had a far more dramatic impact on the life of the memorial in other forms. Almost immediately after the dedication of the Wall, the POW/MIA issue surfaced as a constant presence at the memorial. Veterans associated with the movement put up canvas tents and established a 24-hour-a-day, 365-day-a-year, combination vigil and "flea market."

The vigil started on Christmas Eve 1982. Two tents were set up, one on either side of the Wall. In front of both tents, a handful of tables were set out and covered with T-shirts, bracelets, books, baseball caps, bumper stickers, posters, and pamphlets, all emblazoned with POW images and all for sale. Since 1982, there have always been petitions to be signed making demands of the governments in Hanoi and in

Washington. The tents flank the Wall; you cannot get to the memorial without walking past this array of consumer goods and political passions. Ted Sampley, a highly decorated veteran who makes his living selling POW souvenirs at the memorial, refers to the vigil as "the last firebase."[39]

Although Sampley describes the veterans holding vigil as "dissident," arguing that they "have every right in the world to be there, fly the flag, and put out . . . literature," the organizers of the memorial have been unhappy with the vigil.[40] Jan Scruggs objects to the commercialization of the memorial. He has fought with the Park Service because he believes "the money changers have to be chased from the temple," and he continues to complain that the Wall "has become the goose that lays the golden eggs. . . . It's Kmart on the Mall. . . . It's everything the memorial is not supposed to be."[41] He attacks the POW "money changers" because they are turning a profit on sacred ground. He is right, but while the Wall may be a sacred place, it is unlike other sacred places because the ideas or icons to be worshipped are so clearly up for grabs. In other words, this temple has inspired these money changers as part of the work of struggling with the memory of the nation to be celebrated. So the vigilant peddlers continue to hawk their wares and shape the memory of the war.[42] The things they sell are gifts, like the other things set at the base of the Wall, only they are part of an organized and commercialized effort to negotiate the meanings of the war. They are, therefore, a more insistent, and easier to decipher, expression of the kind of symbolic negotiating that happens on the Mall.

POW BRACELETS AND THE FORGING OF A NEW NATIONAL IDENTITY

bracelet inscribed "Mel Holland"
bamboo cage
poem, "The Vigil," to John Gallagher
"Where Is Major Victor J. Apodaca Jr.?" poster
"Not Forgotten" coffee mug

bracelet inscribed "Albert Fransen"
MIA bracelet with wishbone
bamboo crosses
bracelet inscribed "Larry Van Renselaar"[43]

The POW/MIA bracelets are like dog tags for those who were not conscripted. For five dollars any visitor to the memorial can buy a memory of the injustices of the war; she can participate, she can express her rage about the deaths, and she can blame the government without forsaking the soldiers or the nation. The bracelets started to appear at the base of the Wall as soon as the vets holding vigil began to sell them at their makeshift shops. Since the mid-1980s they have been collecting at the Wall daily; by 1988, the bracelets were showing up at the base of the Wall at the rate of about five or six a week. There are hundreds of the bracelets in the storage cabinets of the Vietnam Veterans Memorial collection; by 1986, more POW/MIA bracelets had been left at the Wall than any other object.[44] When you consider that leaving anything at the Wall is a surprising break with national memorial traditions, it is remarkable that so many bracelets have been left. However, when you also consider that these bracelets are sold fifty feet from the Wall day and night all year round, and that they are made for the explicit purpose of making a particular memory of the war, it is actually surprising that more bracelets are not set at the base of the memorial.

The bracelets were initially intended to provide pro-war college students and faculty with a marker of their position and to serve as a galvanizing symbol. The bracelets were meant to be worn: to mark the wearer, just as dog tags mark a soldier, as part of an organized fighting force and to make Richard Nixon's "silent majority" of Americans supporting the Vietnam War visible. They were imagined as constant reminders of the pain suffered by American men in Southeast Asia; they were intended to raise consciousness and inspire activism. They were conceived as tangible symbols to sustain this memory. After the war, however, the symbolic resonance of the bracelets changed. They marked their wearers as pro-soldier, pro-American, antigovernment activists for whom the war was still vital. They marked their wearers as citizens enraged with the failures of the nation and unwilling to concede defeat.

What does it mean to leave a bracelet at the memorial twenty years after the end of the war? Leaving a bracelet at the Wall is not the same as wearing it. Leaving it turns the work of oppositional memory over to the public audience of the Wall. Leaving a bracelet marks the Wall, not the leaver. The left bracelet reminds other visitors to the Wall of the plight of the POW; it affirms the work of the movement, and it renounces the inactivity of the government without dishonoring the soldiers. It also guarantees that the owner of the bracelet is not wearing it and therefore is not carrying the memory with her.

Because these bracelets have been produced to make a particular political memory, leaving one at the Wall enters, repeatedly, the position of the movement in the conversation at the Wall. Because these bracelets are mass produced and sold right there at the memorial, leaving a bracelet does not mark a particular memory of the war in the way that a pair of nursing pads or a picture of a beloved Trans Am does. It enters the position of the movement into the conversation of many independent voices; it provides a unifying emblem for some mourners at the Wall. The vigilant vets at the memorial are selling visitors a framework in which to understand the war with the offerings to leave at the Wall; they are trying to gain support for their cause, and they are working to organize the response at the Wall. The veterans holding vigil are supplying one ready answer for people who come to grieve at the memorial; this answer requires believing that the government lies, that Americans have been fooled, that the possibility of winning the war still exists, and that it is the responsibility of patriotic citizens to fight this battle for the soul of the nation.

The bracelets are not the only emblems of this position. The veterans also sell bumper stickers, coffee mugs, posters, T-shirts, flags, and other POW/MIA memorabilia. Nearly all of these things are printed with the image from the POW flag and the words, "You Are Not Forgotten."[45] A T-shirt reads "Hanoi: Release Our POWs Now!" A coffee mug reads "Operation Triumph: When one American is not worth the effort to be found, we as Americans have lost." The implication of this message is that Americans have not yet lost and that they might win. Together these slogans reimagine the history of the war to reclaim the place of the soldiers, the military, and the social position of these men by insisting that the war could still be won. This response reflects a strangely conflicted patriotism.

The promise "You Are Not Forgotten," implicitly and explicitly made with every POW/MIA offering at the Wall, is a complicated one. Of course the "you" is the American POW imagined to be languishing in Laos or Cambodia, but the slogan also resonates with the sense of many veterans that the country has been desperate to forget the war and the veterans who served. This phrase is a response to the liminal position of Vietnam veterans. It promises to keep the memory of their sacrifices alive, and it promises to change their social position by finally winning the war.

THE ONGOING WORK OF MAKING MEMORY AT THE WALL

bottle of Jack Daniels	*ring with letter*
Purple Heart and Bronze Star	*baseball*
photo album	*ace of spades*
flint knife wrapped in animal skin	*USMC T-shirt*
straw hat with flower	*pie*[46]

The POW/MIA artifacts assert a particular, charged kind of memory at the Wall. They are important for this project because they are so prevalent in the collection; because they provide so clear an example of offerings that strike a common chord; because they demonstrate the tenor of the social and political contortionism—like that of the anti-statist nationalism—expressed at the memorial; and because they serve as a strong contrast to the other things left at the Wall. The POW/MIA objects are a reminder of how truly remarkable are the other, more independent, individuated memories and the other, less tightly bound refrains that echo through the objects at the memorial.

The gifts that repeat the names of the fallen and, in their busy tensions around affirming and renouncing the nation, sustain the texture of the lives of the dead in the deeply restless memory of this war. Things that seem so explicitly individual and personal—a straw hat or a flint knife—taken together share (not in spite of but because of their individual nature) the hollow, lonely grief of particular losses. The notes that begin, "I didn't know anyone who died but . . . ," the letters framed to be read by other visitors to the Wall, and the identical gifts left by groups of school children or Boy Scouts are all expressions, of various intensities, of the desire to be part of the community that lives around the memorial. They seem to speak to a sense of loss of community or, at the very least, to the desire to forge a community. The emblems of patriotism frequently left at the Wall evoke a riot of related ideas about the responsibility of the nation to the citizen and the citizen to the nation. The cost of every life spent in the war is made present by a pair of dog tags, an old shoe, a photograph, a can of C ration fruit, or a bicycle fender.[47]

When they speak together, in these rough paths I cut through the collection, and when they speak alone, the things left at the Wall make a lot of noise. They constitute a remarkable conversation. It is a conversation about the shape of the nation, the status of the citizen, and the problem of patriotism. It is a conversation about the impossibility of loss, the deaths of sons, and the births of granddaughters. It is a conversation about war stories of all kinds—combat stories, love stories, and survival stories. It is a conversation about places and placelessness, and homes and homelessness. It is impassioned and unfinished, and it gives us tremendous opportunity to witness the process of ordinary Americans struggling to make meanings of, to make sense of, the Vietnam War and all of its difficult and complicated legacies.

child's painting	*red panties*	*Zippo lighter*
seashells	*petosky stone*	*origami bird*
Lucky Strikes	*diploma*	*Puerto Rican flag*
eagle feather	*cornhusk*	*cookie*
stuffed dog	*poem*	*key chain*
tissue with lipstick		

PUBLIC MEMORY AT THE END OF THE AMERICAN CENTURY

The new memorial practices that have emerged at the Vietnam Veterans Memorial seem to be contagious. Or perhaps it would be more accurate to say that the desire of so many individuals to speak, without invitation, to the problem of failed real and symbolic vocabularies of citizenship—or, simply, to speak about wrenching public and private pain—has not been limited either to the memorial or to the pain and confusion wrought by the war. The need to make sense of the culture, to create communities for understanding loss is widely felt.

The AIDS quilt draws explicitly on the public response to the Wall. It is an organized, and wildly successful, attempt to express a wide range of emotions and to create a community for grieving and for coming to terms with devastating loss. Most of the other walls and makeshift memorials that echo the Vietnam memorial are, however, not the work of any organization. The wall erected in South Central Los Angeles following the violence in the wake of the Rodney King verdict did not, as was reported in the papers, seem to have a spokesperson interested in drawing connections with the Wall in Washington; but the names, on brown plastic nameplates familiar from banks and offices, of those injured were put together on a wall; and people in the community responded by carrying things to its base. When Malice Green was beaten to death by two Detroit police officers, a local artist painted a mural on a wall near the place where Green was killed. His larger-than-life portrait of Green became not only a community gathering place but a site to which people carried offerings. When young Polly Klass was kidnapped and murdered, a memorial sprung up not in front of her parents' house or at her grave but on the shoulder of Highway 101, where her body was found, outside of her hometown, Petaluma, California. For weeks, people stopped by the side of the road and left offerings. After Susan Smith drowned her two children in a lake near Union, South Carolina, televisions across the country were filled by images of the toys and wreaths and photographs and flowers and letters and crosses and prayer cards and many, many other things left on the banks of the lake. In Oklahoma City, where the bombing of the Federal Building killed and maimed workers and their children, offerings began to collect outside the chain-link fences around the rubble before the dust had settled.[1] In the first year after the bombing more than a million objects were carried to (and stuffed into) these fences.[2]

   This is a terrible, ugly list of violent deaths, but it is not a hopeless list. It would be an odd place to end this book, which is essentially a hopeful one, if I did not see in the unmediated communities gathering in the places described above and at the Wall the potent desire to understand these shared griefs and an unwillingness to let these varied tragedies go unremarked. Very different communities facing very different kinds of losses are sharing not only the impulse to make meaning about these losses with things in public places but also the populist impulse to do it themselves. Officially sanctioned and well-organized memorial commissions are certainly still at work trying to forge monuments to help us come to grips with some of our shared wounds, but many, many people seem to want—maybe they even feel compelled— to do the work themselves, to be a part of these fertile pockets of conversation. We need to keep listening in.

high-heel shoe	meal ticket	19 cents
Purple Heart	baseball glove	nurse's hat
booby trap wire	sealed package	POW band
helmet with peace sign	peace poster	bicycle part
shot glass	tennis ball	salt shaker
unmarked cassette tape	key chain	photograph
cowboy boots	teddy bear	patch[3]

NOTES

CHAPTER 1. MAKING A MEMORY OF WAR

1. In April 1971 one thousand members of Vietnam Veterans Against the War camped out on the Mall and protested the war by giving their medals back at the White House and on Capitol Hill. See Todd Gitlin, *The Sixties: Years of Hope, Days of Rage* (New York: Bantam, 1987), 418.

2. The first offering at the Wall was a Purple Heart laid in the memorial's concrete foundation during the summer of 1982. See Jan Scruggs and Joel Swerdlow, *To Heal a Nation: The Vietnam Veterans Memorial* (New York: Harper and Row, 1985), 124. Scruggs's book is an impassioned retelling of the story of the building of the memorial from Scruggs's perspective. It is lavishly illustrated with photographs and includes a list of all fifty-eight thousand names on the Wall. This book and several interviews with Duery Felton and David Guynes at the Vietnam Veterans Memorial Collection have been particularly helpful in my reconstruction of the story of the building of the Wall.

3. Scruggs and Swerdlow, *To Heal a Nation*, 159.

4. These things were left at the Wall in November 1990. All of the things left at the Wall are recorded in the Vietnam Veterans Memorial Collection (VVMC) log books. These log books are my primary source for information about the contents of the collection. Each group of objects taken from the Wall to the VVMC storage building is given an accession number (those cited here are Accessions 474–83). Because the date on which an object was left is not always available and would not be easy to trace, throughout this book things will be cited with an approximate date and an accession number or group of accession numbers.

5. Laura Palmer, *Shrapnel in the Heart: Letters and Remembrances from the Vietnam Veterans Memorial* (New York: Vintage Books, 1987), 27.

6. James Mayo, *War Memorials as Political Landscape* (New York: Praeger, 1989), 13.

7. It is this fractured meaning that has inspired scholars to think about this war as the first postmodern war. Nevertheless, it is important to remember that the world wars were not without their own struggles with fractured bodies

and meanings, and the impulse of visitors to the Wall to try to reconstruct these fractured meanings is not necessarily a postmodern impulse.

8. Scruggs and Swerdlow, *To Heal a Nation*, 8.

9. A precious detail in Scruggs's account is his description of a brunch at Warner's Georgetown home hosted by his lovely, pink-robed wife, Elizabeth Taylor. The brunch raised $40,000 from defense contractors (ibid., 21).

10. Scruggs contends that many veterans were particularly affected by all of the patriotic fanfare surrounding the return of American hostages from Iran on January 20, 1981—the day of Ronald Reagan's first inauguration. The success of Reagan's attempts to rebuild American patriotism was, for Scruggs and his peers, a bitter reminder of the recognition they did not get. Scruggs and Swerdlow, *To Heal a Nation*, 56.

11. Their explicit rejection of public funds was unusual, but the practice of building memorials with public contributions was not. Most Civil War memorials were built with private funds, and the planned Korean War Memorial has been funded by private contributions; but these funding decisions were never considered political. See Michael Kammen, *The Mystic Chords of Memory: The Transformation of Tradition in American Culture* (New York: Knopf, 1991); and the Korean War Memorial Fact Sheet, published in 1984 by the American Battle Monuments Commission.

12. Scruggs and Swerdlow, *To Heal a Nation*, 20.

13. According to Scruggs, McGovern's name on the letterhead cost the fund many contributions in the days before the design was selected. It is likely, however, that after the design was selected his name became an advantage rather than a liability. Scruggs and Swerdlow, *To Heal a Nation*, 24.

14. This statistic does not hold true for the entire campaign. H. Ross Perot and the American Legion both made contributions of nearly $2 million (Scruggs and Swerdlow, *To Heal a Nation*, 24). But, it is worth including because it demonstrates the desire of the VVMF's organizers to see the memorial built with the money of ordinary citizens rather than that of the federal government or a corporate sponsor.

15. The Confederate monuments scattered across the South are the obvious exception. They do not, however, seem to have influenced Maya Lin's design. They are largely figural and heroic. For more discussion of confederate monuments, see Kammen, *Mystic Chords of Memory*, and Bettie A. C. Emerson, *Historic Southern Monuments* (New York: Neale Publishing, 1911). Jerry L. Strait, *Vietnam War Memorials: An Illustrated Reference to Veteran's Tributes throughout the United States* (Jefferson, N.C.: McFarland, 1988), is a great guide to all the American Vietnam War memorials, most of which are bronze plaques.

16. The process of getting approval from the Fine Arts Commission has proved to be the undoing of many memorial projects in Washington, D.C. Both

the memorial to the Korean War—a war that cost the United States nearly as many lives as the Vietnam War—and the Franklin D. Roosevelt memorial had Congressional approval for years but were not easily or quickly approved by the commission. The Korean War memorial was authorized in 1986, and the design was selected in 1989; but it took the designers three years and many serious compromises to get the Fine Arts Commission's approval.

17. Scruggs and Swerdlow, *To Heal a Nation*, 51.

18. The panel included Paul Spreiregen, Pietro Belluschi, Harry Weese, Garret Ecklbo, Hideo Sasaki, Richard Hunt, Constantino Nivola, James Rosati, and Grady Clay. They brought with them a number of complicated political perspectives; some of these judges were veterans of both world wars and some were refugees from fascism.

19. Scruggs and Swerdlow, *To Heal a Nation*, 62.

20. Lydia Fish, *The Last Firebase: A Guide to the Vietnam Veterans Memorial* (Shippensburg, Penn.: White Mane Publishing, 1987), 3.

21. Scruggs and Swerdlow, *To Heal a Nation*, 65.

22. Ibid., 63.

23. A great deal has been written about the Wall and its design. A good introductory bibliography would include Charles Griswold, "The Vietnam Veterans Memorial and the Washington Mall: Philosophical Thoughts on Political Iconography," *Critical Inquiry* 12 (summer 1986): 689; Sonja Foss, "Ambiguity as Persuasion: The Vietnam Veterans Memorial," *Communication Quarterly* 34 (summer 1986): 326–40; Christopher Buckley, "The Wall," *Esquire*, September 1985, 65–73; William Hubbard, "A Meaning for Monuments," *Public Interest* 74 (winter 1984): 17–30; Fish, *The Last Firebase*; and "Vietnam Memorial: America Remembers," *National Geographic*, May 1985, 557.

24. Eventually two inscriptions were added: "In honor of the men and women of the Armed Forces of the United States who served in the Vietnam War. The names of those who gave their lives and those who remain missing are inscribed in the order they were taken from us" and "Our nation remembers the courage, sacrifice, and devotion to duty and country of its Vietnam veterans. This memorial was built with private contributions from the American people." Lin felt strongly that her memorial should not include a flag.

It is worth noting here that a wall carved with the names, at the same scale, of all of the Vietnamese who died in the war would be sixty-nine times the size of this memorial. It would likely stretch the distance between the Washington and Lincoln monuments. "Harper's Index," *Harper's*, March 1991, 15.

25. Richard Nixon requested that his own grave be marked with black granite from the same quarry that produced the panels for the Wall.

26. The frequency with which veterans relate their expectations of the war with references to John Wayne or other war-movie heroes is startling. See Mark

Baker, *Nam: The Vietnam War in the Words of the Men and Women Who Fought There* (New York: Berkley, 1981); Ron Kovic, *Born on the Fourth of July* (New York: McGraw-Hill, 1976); and Philip Caputo, *A Rumor of War* (New York: Ballantine, 1977), for a few powerful examples of this.

27. This tension between the mass and the individual is central to the place of this monument in the history of war memorials. I will explore this tension in greater detail in the second chapter.

28. Vandalism at the Wall is unusual, but in March 1994, these indexes were ripped from their casings and burned.

29. I suspect that many visitors who go to the Wall without a particular name in mind flip through the index in search of family names. I was startled to discover that the only Hass to die in the war was killed on my first birthday, June 21, 1966.

30. Tom Carhart, "Insulting Vietnam Vets," *New York Times*, October 24, 1981.

31. It is worth noting that not one of the many journalistic and scholarly discussions of the monument that I have read ever mentions the female imagery in the monument. The phallic Washington Monument is often raised as a point of comparison, but the opposition that interests me is never explicit.

32. Scruggs and Swerdlow, *To Heal a Nation*, 84. Webb resigned in protest after the design was selected. His fear, as it turns out, was quite well founded.

33. Carhart, "Insulting Vietnam Vets," 23. Carhart's sculpture of an officer lifting the dead body of a GI to the heavens was not selected. See Wolf Von Eckardt, "The Vietnam Veterans Memorial in Washington" (unpublished, 1986), for an interesting survey of responses to the Wall in the popular press.

34. This a truly rich statement. For more about the ways in which Jane Fonda functions as a highly gendered symbol at the Wall see my discussion in chapter 5 of the burning of an effigy of Jane Fonda.

35. "Stop That Monument" (editorial), *National Review*, September 18, 1981, 1064.; Henry Hyde, quoted in Von Eckardt, "The Vietnam Veterans Memorial in Washington," 9.

36. Scruggs and Swerdlow, *To Heal a Nation*, 86.

37. See Arthur C. Danto, "The Vietnam Veterans Memorial," *The Nation*, August 31, 1985, 152–55; Shirley Neilson Blum, "The National Vietnam War Memorial," *Arts Magazine*, December 1984, 124–28; Tom Morganthau, "Honoring Vietnam Veterans—At Last," *Newsweek*, November 22, 1982, 80–86; and "Vietnam Memorial: America Remembers."

38. Scruggs and Swerdlow, *To Heal a Nation*, 24. Kilpatrick championed the memorial in April 1980 with a call to his readers to contribute to the fund.

39. Ibid., 85.

40. Ibid.

41. Of course Watt is an emblem of the early Reagan presidency. His in-

sistence that the Vietnam Veterans Memorial needed to make a clear assertion of noble sacrifice for the nation is just one of the many ironies that shaped
his career. See Haynes Johnson, *Sleepwalking through History: America in
the Reagan Years* (New York: Anchor, 1991), 180.

42. Hart is an interesting figure. Although he was roughly the same age as
the VVMF veterans, he belonged to an earlier generation of artists. He, in
fact, got his start as an a apprentice to Felix de Weldon, the sculptor of the
Iwo Jima Memorial. Although Hart was gassed by the federal government
while protesting the Vietnam War, he was appalled by the ambiguity of Lin's
design and was determined to see his own work on the Mall. Scruggs and
Swerdlow, *To Heal a Nation*, 49.

43. Ibid., 88.

44. The third man's race is intentionally ambiguous. Hart says this figure
"could be Hispanic or Asian American." None of the figures are modeled on
real people—let alone veterans of this war. See Fish, *The Last Firebase*, 14.
Hart's sculpture has been praised for its attention to the details of the Vietnam-era uniforms and equipment. However, as Duery Felton pointed out,
the band of bullets sculpted in great detail across the body of the racially ambiguous figure is upside down—so that the bullets are pointing toward his
head. According to Felton, wearing the band this way is a suicidal mistake few
vets would be proud to have made.

45. The Vietnam Women's Memorial is not only an important part of the
story of the life of the Wall but also the result of a hard fought symbolic battle about the place of the memory of women in American culture, a battle
that deserves a detailed, thoughtful study of its own. For an excellent retelling
of the fight to build the women's memorial, see Karal Ann Marling and John
Wetenhall, "The Sexual Politics of Memory: The Vietnam Women's Memorial Project and 'the Wall,'" *Prospects* 14 (1989): 341–72.

46. Goodacre's original designs were twice rejected by the Fine Arts
Commission.

47. Both Maya Lin and J. Carter Brown, the chairman of the Fine Arts
Commission, were fiercely opposed to the women's memorial for this reason.

48. These associations have buried the dead, built tombs, and raised the
money for, arbitrated the content of, and thereby shaped the meanings of
war memorials since the beginning of the nineteenth century. See Wallace
Evan Davies, *Patriotism on Parade: The Story of Veterans' and Hereditary
Organizations in America, 1783–1900* (Cambridge: Harvard University Press,
1955).

49. Scruggs and Swerdlow, *To Heal a Nation*, 133. In his book Scruggs
seems to both admire and dislike Maya Lin. He tries to strike a pleasant tone
about her, but he is not entirely successful. When he introduced her at the
tenth anniversary celebration, eight years after the writing of his book, his feel-

ings for Lin seemed to have changed: he talked about their friendship and broke into tears.

50. Maya Ying Lin, "Design Competition: Winning Designer's Statement" (Washington, D.C.: Vietnam Veterans Memorial Fund, 1982).

51. Palmer, *Shrapnel in the Heart,* 25.

52. Glen's note also provides insight about why people leave lists of names already on the Wall. The names are already there; why repeat them? Because they need to be remembered together to represent someone's particular experience.

53. Palmer, *Shrapnel in the Heart,* 21.

54. Much of the pre-1984 collection did not survive a series of moves and reorganizations.

55. David Guynes, conversation with author, Lanham, Md., February 27, 1991.

56. The things are immaculately preserved, but because the cataloguing has just begun, there have been no quantitative studies of the things in the collection. The best information is in the volunteer's log books and in the heads of Felton and Guynes. They know this collection well: they have worked with all of the objects; they have spent long hours tracking obscure references in military insignia; they have talked extensively with those leaving objects; and they regularly confer with the Park Service volunteers who spend their days watching the Wall and its visitors. Nevertheless, they will continually remind you that they can only speak from impressions and recollections.

57. Duery Felton, a Vietnam veteran, has complained that reporters are always going after him as he shows them the collection; he says that they are forever trying to make him cry and that their doing so disgusts him.

58. For example Susan Walker, "The Vietnam Veterans Memorial and MARS Dedicated to Keeping the Memories Alive," *Stars and Stripes,* January 15, 1990, 9; Mike McIntyre, "Gifts of Grief," *San Diego Union,* May 14, 1989, D4–6; "Bittersweet Vietnam Memorial Collection," *USA Weekend,* November 10, 1989; Toby Thompson, "Night Watch: Communing with the Names on the Wall," *Washingtonian Magazine,* November 1988, 176; Laura Palmer, "The Wall: The Inexplicable Undertow of the Vietnam Veterans Memorial Draws Visitors in Search of Solace," *GQ,* July 1987, 138–66; Larry McDonnell, "America's Wailing Wall: Mementos Left There Give Life to New Museum," *Asbury Park Press,* October 5, 1986, F15.

59. The quotes in the text are from McDonnell, "America's Wailing Wall," F15; Palmer, "The Wall," 138–66; and McIntyre, "Gifts of Grief," D4–6.

60. Of course, this dichotomy is not completely clear-cut; there are many things which might fall into both categories.

61. David Guynes, conversations with author, Lanham, Md., February 1991, June 1992, November 1992.

62. This collection of inauthentic things could understandably be frus-

trating for veterans: when they finally get some recognition, everybody and his brother wants to claim a part of it. There is a famous letter to Ann Landers that gets at this problem and has been left at the Wall many times over the years. The letter, from a mother "Forever Sad in Madison, WI," complains that well-meaning friends and relatives are always sending her pictures and rubbings of her son's name on the Wall. This Gold Star Mother cannot understand why these people would want to remind her of this great tragedy in her life. But when the friends get to the Wall, they feel its power and want to participate somehow. So they take a picture or a rubbing and get in on the act.

63. John Bodnar, "Public Memory in an American City: Commemoration in Cleveland," in *Commemorations: The Politics of National Identity*, ed. John Gillis (Princeton: Princeton University Press, 1994), 75.

64. During the period of November 10–14, there is a dramatic rise in the number of things left, but there is no real change in the kind of things left. Information supplied by Guynes and Felton, from the Park Service logs for November of 1990. VVMC, Accessions 474, 476, 483.

65. This is a sampling of things left at the Wall in the fall of 1988. VVMC, Accessions 371–91.

66. Palmer, *Shrapnel in the Heart*, 184.

67. Garten's letter was left at the Wall in May 1986. It was a common practice for American soldiers to cut off the fingers of dead Vietcong fighters in order to steal their wedding bands.

68. Thomas Schlereth, ed., *Material Culture Studies in America* (Nashville, Tenn.: AASLH, 1982), 42. Schlereth does a fine job of culling these essays from the disparate wanderings of the field. He reconstructs the field in the following "paradigm dramas": the age of collecting (1876–1948); the age of description (1948–1965); and the age of analysis (1965–). McClung E. Fleming's model for artifact study is a popular guide for many scholars. It states in clear language the procedures of the current paradigm. These are worth exploring, and even testing on an object. In brief, Fleming argues that every object has five essential elements: history, material, construction, design, and function. Studying these five elements in four phases—identification, evaluation, cultural analysis, and interpretation—should yield a rich understanding of the object. See McClung E. Fleming, "Artifact Study: A Proposed Model," *Winterthur Portfolio* 9 (June 1974): 153–73.

69. Schlereth, *Material Culture Studies*, 75.

70. Christopher Tilley, *Reading Material Culture* (Oxford: Basil Blackwell, 1989).

71. Ibid., 199.

72. Grant McCracken, *Culture and Consumption: New Approaches to the Symbolic Character of Goods and Activities* (Bloomington: University of Indiana Press, 1988), 69.

73. Ibid., 89.

74. As Claude Lévi-Strauss writes, "If a little structuralism leads away from the concrete, a lot of structuralism leads back to it" (*Structural Anthropology* 2, trans. M. Layton [London: Penguin, 1977], 115).

75. M. M. Bakhtin, *The Dialogic Imagination*, ed. Michael Holquist, trans. Caryl Emerson and Michael Holquist (Austin: University of Texas Press, 1981), 428.

76. VVMC, Accession 268.

77. These things are pulled from the list of objects left at the Wall in the third week of October in 1988. VVMC, Accession 384.

CHAPTER 2. DISCOVERING THE MEMORY OF BODIES

1. John S. Patterson, "A Patriotic Landscape: Gettysburg, 1863–1913," *Prospects* 7 (1982): 319. Patterson's article about the American obsession with this battlefield is a useful starting point for thinking about the battle and the place.

2. The use of "men" here, instead of "soldiers" or "men and women," is not intended to leave out those few women who were able by sheer dint of will to fight in or serve in the early American armed forces; rather, it is intended as a reminder of who was able to fight.

3. Benedict Anderson's work on nationalism, *Imagined Communities: Reflections on the Origin and Spread of Nationalism* (London: Verso, 1983), informs, in broad strokes, my analysis of the imagined nation and nationalism. I was influenced also by George Mosse's argument, in *Fallen Soldiers: Reshaping the Memory of the World Wars* (New York: Oxford University Press, 1990), that volunteer soldiers were central to the development of imagined nations. This idea is explored more closely later in this chapter.

4. Historians have offered portrait photography and sentimental nineteenth-century domestic novels as physical evidence for the tightening of these bonds. Harlan Unrau, in *Administrative History: Gettysburg National Military Park and Gettysburg National Cemetery, Pennsylvania* (Denver: National Park Service, 1991), and others who have written about the memorials at Gettysburg have made broad references to these possible causes, but no scholar has fully developed an argument on this question.

5. Michael Kammen, *Mystic Chords of Memory: The Transformation of Tradition in American Culture* (New York: Knopf, 1991), 105. Kammen's argument about public memory in America begins with a helpful discussion of the popular response to the Civil War.

6. Brian M. Fagan, *The Great Journey* (London: Thames and Hudson, 1987), 69. There is a growing field of scholarship on the practice and meaning of memorialization. See Kammen, *Mystic Chords of Memory*; John R. Gillis, ed., *Commemorations: The Politics of National Identity* (Princeton:

Princeton University Press, 1994); John E. Bodnar, *Remaking America: Public Memory, Commemoration, and Patriotism in the Twentieth Century* (Princeton: Princeton University Press, 1992); and Edward Linenthal, *Sacred Ground: Americans and Their Battlefields* (Chicago: University of Illinois Press, 1991).

7. Using Raymond Williams's popular definitions of big *C* and small *c* culture, I am writing here about small *c* culture, the broad spectrum of human social relations. I do not imagine Raymond's definitions to be either "organic" or stable, but they are a useful shorthand for shared real and imagined social connections. See Raymond Williams, *Culture and Society, 1780–1950* (New York: Columbia University Press, 1983), xviii.

8. I am borrowing here from Émile Durkheim and Mary Douglas. See Mary Douglas, "No Free Gifts," forward to *The Gift*, by Marcel Mauss, trans. W. D. Hall (New York: Norton, 1990).

9. I am referring here to the development of the nationalism in the arguments of George Mosse (*Fallen Soldiers*) and others.

10. Ibid., 22.

11. Ibid., 99.

12. It is important not to see these developments as evolutionary or necessarily progressive. It is beyond the scope of this project to detail the cultural shifts behind these changes in memorialization.

13. Alan Borg, *War Memorials: From Antiquity to the Present* (London: Leo Cooper, 1991); James Curl, *A Celebration of Death: An Introduction to Some of the Buildings, Monuments, and Settings of Funerary Architecture in the Western European Tradition* (London: Constable, 1980). Borg's work is a detailed, dense chronological study of memorials throughout time, whereas Curl's work concentrates on the nineteenth and twentieth centuries.

14. There is another strain of war memorial traditions that I do not address here. The Mesopotamians developed a pictographic tradition, which was translated in the Middle Ages from representations of heroic leaders to images of mourning friends and family. From this tradition the sculptural form is thought to have evolved. Borg argues that this transformation is marked by the tomb of Holy Roman Emperor Maximilian I, in which his family is represented by full-size sculptures. From this tradition came larger-than-life figural sculptures. Although there are parallels in these two strains of memorializing, for the purposes of my argument I am not retelling the latter story. Borg provides a good overview and a good bibliography. See Borg, *War Memorials*, 23–32.

15. Ibid.

16. Ibid., 5.

17. According them respect or social status has not been the sole impetus for burying the dead; bodies strewn on an abandoned battlefield almost surely

mean disease, plague or cholera, for the local inhabitants, especially on small islands. The well-justified fear of disease led to the practice, in many instances, of burning the bodies of the dead and inspired the need to bury the bodies as quickly as possible.

18. Robert Garland, *The Greek Way of Death* (London: Duckworth, 1985), 90.

19. Mosse, *Fallen Soldiers*. It is important to mention that the casualties of the French Revolution were buried in unmarked mass graves; this practice was likely due both to the complicated issues of citizenship in this civil war and to the fact that this war was part of the early development of the nation and the citizen as we have come to know them in the twentieth century.

20. The increasing numbers of literate soldiers in these early national wars produced a new literature of war that Mosse, in *Fallen Soldiers*, argues is responsible for the spread of the myth of the war experience.

21. Marking the graves of officers was not a new practice; nor was the disregard of the common soldiers. At the end of Shakespeare's *Henry V* the list of the battle casualties reads, "Edward the Duke of York, the Earl of Suffolk, Sir Richard Ketly, Davy Gam, esquire; None else of name"(*Henry V*, act 4, scene 8, lines 102–104).

22. These frontier cemeteries mark the very beginnings of a national cemetery system and a hint of a shift in ideas about the bodies of soldiers, but this development was not a widespread, war-related phenomenon. A July 17, 1862, omnibus act of Congress declared that "the President of the United States shall have power . . . to purchase cemetery grounds . . . to be used as a national cemetery for the soldiers who shall die in the service of the country" (*U.S. Statutes at Large* 13 [1861–63], 596).

23. Dean W. Holt, *American Military Cemeteries: A Comprehensive Illustrated Guide to the Hallowed Grounds of the United States, Including Cemeteries Overseas* (Jefferson, N.C.: McFarland, 1992), 2. Neither Holt nor any of the other scholars who have written on the history of the American military cemeteries have devoted any attention to the logic or ideologies behind these new policies.

24. Kathleen Georg Harrison, Gettysburg National Park historian, telephone conversation with author, July 27, 1993.

25. Jack McLaughlin, *Gettysburg: The Long Encampment* (New York: Appleton-Century, 1963), 182. The iconic photographs of bloated bodies through which we have seen the battle at Gettysburg seem, to a late twentieth-century eye, to memorialize the bodies of the fallen heroes. (These photographs were originally published in *Gardner's Photographic Sketch Book of the War* [1868]. See James Horan, *Timothy H. O'Sullivan: America's Forgotten Photographer* [New York: Doubleday, 1966]; and Alan Trachtenberg, *Reading American Photographs: Images as History, Mathew Brady to Walker Evans*

[New York: Hill and Wang, 1989]). In fact, most of the bodies in these images were Confederate soldiers available to be photographed by Timothy H. O'Sullivan's time-consuming technology because they were left out in the open. Eventually the temporary hospitals asked for a punishment detail of erstwhile Union soldiers to cover them with a thin layer of dirt to keep the smell down. (Kathleen Georg Harrison, "This Grand National Enterprise," Special Collections, Gettysburg National Military Park, Gettysburg, Pennsylvania.) These Confederate soldiers were not exhumed and reburied until almost ten years later when an organization of Southern women rallied to return nearly three thousand of their boys to the Southern soil of Richmond, Virginia, in the 1870s. The Daughters of the Confederacy buried three thousand of the fallen at Gettysburg in the Hollywood Cemetery. See Bettie A. C. Emerson, *Historic Southern Monuments* (New York: Neale Publishing, 1911); and Charles Wilson, *Baptized in Blood: The Religion of the Lost Cause, 1865–1920* (Athens: University of Georgia Press, 1980). The role of women's organizations in tending to the bodies of the dead is an interesting counterpart to the development of embalming and the masculinization of death ways: as the bodies were turned over to male professionals, women's associations were forming to build monuments to preserve the memory of the work of the soldiers.

26. The embalmers were serving the dead soldiers' families, who came by train from all over to claim their sons. This familial interest in reclaiming the dead was not new, but in the past it had been predominately a practice of families of officers rather than enlisted men (Kathleen Georg Harrison, Gettysburg National Park historian, conversation with author, Gettysburg National Military Park, July 20, 1993). Harrison's research on the lives of Wills and McConaughy indicates that they were not friendly. They were both members of the boards of various civic organizations in Gettysburg, but according to the public records, they never once served on the same board.

27. Although there has been much contention among historians over the question of who actually is the founder of the Soldiers' National Cemetery, and how these decisions were made in the days following the battle, much remains uncertain. No one knows, for example, exactly what Curtin asked Wills to do (Harrison, conversation with author, July 20, 1993).

28. David Wills, letter to Andrew Curtin, July 24, 1863, quoted in Unrau, *Administrative History*, 4, 5, 7. Gettysburg historian Kathleen Georg Harrison is deeply suspicious of this account. She is convinced that Wills boldly exaggerated the state of the battlefield to compel Curtin to take action. She contends that both Wills and McConaughy were less than honest in their attempts to secure their positions as memorializers of the battle (Harrison, conversation with author, July 20, 1993).

29. David Wills, letter to Andrew Curtin, August 17, 1863, quoted in Unrau, *Administrative History*, 7.

30. David McConaughy, letter to Ingersoll & others, August 19, 1863, quoted in Unrau, *Administrative History*, 5.

31. Ibid.

32. David McConaughy, announcement of September 5, 1863, quoted in ibid., 9.

33. Patterson, "A Patriotic Landscape," 319.

34. Identifying the bodies, at a cost of $1.59 each, was gory and revealing. Wills wrote, "the bodies in unmarked graves have been identified in various ways . . . sometimes by letters, by papers, receipts, certificates, diaries, memorandum books, photographs, marks on the clothing, belts, or cartridge boxes" (Wills, quoted in Unrau, *Administrative History*, 11). These things became important—they marked the identities of the soldiers, and these identities were important in the arguments of Wills and McConaughy because the soldiers were both brave citizens and cherished sons.

35. David Segal, *Recruiting for Uncle Sam: Citizenship and Military Manpower Policy* (Lawrence: University Press of Kansas, 1989), 3.

36. Sue E. Berryman, *Who Serves? The Persistent Myth of the Underclass Army* (Boulder, Colo: Westview Press, 1988), 32.

37. Iver Bernstein, *The New York City Draft Riots: Their Significance for American Society and Politics in the Age of the Civil War* (New York: Oxford University Press, 1990), 7.

38. Ibid., 9.

39. Berryman, *Who Serves?* 33–34.

40. Ibid.

41. This movement was poorly named because it was an urban phenomenon rather than a rural development. See chapter 3 for a more detailed discussion of Mount Auburn and the rural cemetery movement.

42. See chapter 3 for an elaborated discussion of these funerary traditions.

43. James T. Farrell, *Inventing the American Way of Death: The Development of the Modern Cemetery, 1830–1920* (Philadelphia: Temple University Press, 1980). Farrell's work is a useful, broad study of nineteenth-century traditions.

44. Gary Wills, *Lincoln at Gettysburg: The Words That Remade America* (New York: Simon and Schuster, 1992), 23.

45. Ibid., 22.

46. Abraham Lincoln, "Gettysburg Address," delivered at the Soldiers' National Cemetery dedication on November 19, 1863.

47. In fact, these words are memorialized in stone in two sacred American public spaces—the Gettysburg battlefield and the Lincoln Memorial on the Mall in Washington, D.C.

48. I have come across at least five different references to the first Memorial Day celebration—some in France and some in the United States—but

they all come after the 1868 Gettysburg claim made in Unrau's incredibly careful book. See Unrau, *Administrative History*, 23.

49. Order issued by John A. Logan, Commander in Chief, Grand Army of the Republic, May 5, 1868, quoted in McLaughlin, *Gettysburg*, 483.

50. The casualty figures are taken from the 1994 *Information Please Almanac* (New York: Houghton Mifflin, 1994), 389.

51. Holt, *American Military Cemeteries*, 3.

52. John Harris, *Silent Cities: An Exhibition of Memorial and Cemetery Architecture of the Great War* (London: Royal Institute of British Architects, 1977), 3.

53. Curl, *A Celebration of Death*, 317.

54. Borg, *War Memorials*, 128.

55. Thomas Laqueur, "Memory and Naming in the Great War," in *Commemorations: The Politics of National Identity*, ed. John R. Gillis (Princeton: Princeton University Press, 1994), 156.

56. Naming was not entirely new as a memorial trope. Ancient Greeks used casualty lists, the Swiss listed the dead at Lucerne in 1792, and local communities in the United States listed names of Civil War dead; but in these instances the names were used as inscriptions on ornamental, symbolic memorial forms. In Greece the names were carved into stelae, in Switzerland they were carved into columns, and after the Civil War they were engraved in bronze plaques at the bases of statues and obelisks.

57. Laqueur, "Memory and Naming," 152.

58. Borg, *War Memorials*, 141.

59. Secretary of War, *Program of the Ceremonies attending the Burial of an Unknown and Unidentified American Soldier Who Lost His Life during the World War* (Washington, D.C., 1921).

60. James Mayo, *War Memorials as Political Landscape: The American Experience and Beyond* (New York: Praeger, 1988), 94. Initially the guard was a ceremonial daytime shift, but since 1937 the tomb has had twenty-four-hour "protection."

61. This characteristic of U.S. World War I memorials does not, of course, imply that the veterans of this war were always treated with the respect that they felt they deserved. The 1932 march on Washington of the Bonus Expeditionary Force, is a hallmark in the history of American veterans.

62. Theodore Roosevelt, "Open Letter to Dr. H. Holbrook Curtis," *American City*, May 18, 1916, 219.

63. Bureau of Memorial Buildings, *Community Buildings as War Memorials* (New York: War Camp Community Service, 1920), 2.

64. *American City*, July 20, 1918, cover.

65. There is no comprehensive study of World War I memorials; neither the American Legion's historian nor the Battle Monuments Commission was

able to provide me with any useful information about numbers or kinds of memorials in the United States. The best evidence for the kinds of memorials erected—apart from an extensive search of municipal records across the country—is the memorials that survive and the memorials written about in city planning journals such as *American City* or *The Rotarian*.

66. Mayo, *War Memorials as Political Landscape*, 80. It is a heartbreaking irony that the plaza that joins these buildings has become a crowded tent city for homeless people, and that many of the homeless men claim to be Vietnam veterans. The monument to the veterans of the earlier war has provided public benches for veterans of the later war to live under.

67. Bureau of Memorial Buildings, *Community Buildings as War Memorials*, 4.

68. Quoted in Karal Ann Marling and John Wetenhall, *Iwo Jima: Monuments, Memories, and the American Hero* (Cambridge: Harvard University Press, 1991).

69. George Kennan had just coined the term "containment" when Nixon gave this speech. President Eisenhower refused to speak because he was disgusted by the crass self-promotion of the Marine Corps that he saw in the Iwo Jima memorial. See Marling and Wetenhall, *Iwo Jima*, 19.

70. These anxieties were not, however, entirely gone. In 1946 sculptor James Earl Fraser wrote—in a debate in *The Rotarian*—that living memorials would some day die and that the memory of the war would go with them. James Earl Fraser, "Let Our New Monuments Inspire—And Endure," *The Rotarian*, February 1946, 24.

71. The remains of 175,000 casualties of World War II—61 percent of the recovered bodies—were buried at home in their local cemeteries.

72. While there is extensive documentation of all memorials erected after the Vietnam War and the guide books to Vietnam memorials are almost obsessive, there is no published guide to World War II memorials.

73. James Dahir, *Community Centers as Living War Memorials* (New York: Russell Sage, 1946), 16.

74. Charles B. Stevenson, "Survey of War Memorial Plans of 500 Cities and Towns," *Toledo City Journal*, February 23, 1946.

75. S/Sgt. R. V. W., USMC, "Letter of the Week," *Saturday Evening Post*, October 7, 1944, quoted in Dahir, *Community Centers*, 18.

76. Janet Darling, "What Is an Appropriate War Memorial?" *House Beautiful*, January 1945, 42–43

77. Joseph Hudnut, "The Monument Does Not Remember," *Atlantic Monthly*, September 1945, 55–59.

78. In England, to negotiate the tough battle between the traditionalists in charge of the Imperial War Graves Commission and the public push for useful memorials, the commission established the National Land Fund in

1946. This fund bought land and houses in the countryside. Historian George Mosse argues that "this memorial democratized, as it were, the commemoration of the fallen by making the English rural heritage accessible to all; no longer was the war memorial an abstract symbol confined to one specific location as the focus of commemorative ceremonies, though the cenotaph, erected after the First World War, continued to perform this function." See Mosse, *Fallen Soldiers*, 221.

79. Laura Beam, "The War Memorial," *Journal of American Association of University Women* 39 (September 1945).

80. Ira Hayes, a Native American soldier and the only nonwhite man in the image, survived for only a few years after the dedication of the memorial. He died drunk and desperate in 1955 on the reservation where he was raised; like everything connected with the Iwo Jima Memorial, his life was not what the Marine Corps memorializers needed it to be, so they simply reinvented it. Marling and Wettenhall's discussion of his life is good (*Iwo Jima*, 170).

81. These are a few of the things left at the Wall in the first days of May 1990. VVMC, Accession 452.

82. Gillis, ed., *Commemorations*, 13.

CHAPTER 3. SEASHELL MONUMENTS AND CITIES FOR THE SILENT

1. The broad sheet is quoted in Gary Wills's wonderful, helpful discussion of Lincoln and the culture of death, *Lincoln at Gettysburg: The Words That Remade America* (New York: Simon and Schuster, 1992), 67.

2. Wills is not sure that Lincoln attended the dedication, but Oak Ridge Cemetery historian Robert Gramm assured me that there is "abundant" evidence of his presence on May 24, 1860. Robert Gramm, Oak Ridge Cemetery historian, telephone conversation with author, February 3, 1994.

3. Wills, *Lincoln at Gettysburg*, 67.

4. James C. Conkling, address delivered at the Oak Ridge Cemetery dedication, May 24, 1860, from the files of the Oak Ridge Cemetery, Springfield, Illinois (see Blanche Linden-Ward, *Silent Cities on a Hill: Landscapes of Memory and Boston's Mount Auburn Cemetery* [Columbus: Ohio State University Press, 1989], 16). "Cemetery" in this context is something of a misnomer because it comes from the synonyms *ecclesia* and *cimeterium*, "of the church."

5. James T. Farrell, *Inventing the American Way of Death: The Development of the Modern Cemetery, 1830–1920* (Philadelphia: Temple University Press, 1980), 112.

6. In 1815 in Baltimore the cornerstone was set for a memorial column to commemorate the heroes of the War of 1812, and in 1829, also in Baltimore, a similar marble column was dedicated to the memory of George Washington.

7. Linden-Ward, *Silent Cities on a Hill*, 128, 172.

8. Joseph Story, address delivered on the dedication of Mount Auburn Cemetery, September 24, 1831, quoted in Stanley French, "The Cemetery as Cultural Institution: The Establishment of Mount Auburn and the 'Rural Cemetery' Movement," in *Death in America*, ed. David Stannard (Philadelphia: University of Pennsylvania Press, 1975), 78.

9. Linden-Ward, *Silent Cities on a Hill*, 109.

10. A granite monument to the battle at Bunker Hill was constructed in 1825, but it quickly fell into disrepair. Linden-Ward argues that the time and money expended in building this monument persuaded Bostonians to turn to more manageable, personal commemorations in the form of cemeteries. Other scattered early monuments were equally disappointing to citizens striving to mark the landscape with enduring emblems of national pride. For detailed discussions of early monuments see Linden-Ward, *Silent Cities on a Hill*, 105–30; and Edward Linenthal, *Sacred Ground: Americans and Their Battlefields* (Chicago: University of Illinois Press, 1991).

11. For example, Jacob Bigelow, the cemetery's most ardent promoter, had recently had to decide where to bury his older brother. Joseph Story, the speaker at the dedication ceremonies, erected his family monument—an obelisk carved with Egyptian images—on Narcissus Path (Linden-Ward, *Silent Cities on a Hill*, 219–20).

12. Ibid., 4.

13. Ibid. As George Herbert (quoted in ibid.) wrote in 1633,

> Death, thou wast once an uncouth, hideous thing
> Nothing but bones
> The sad effect of sadder groans:
> Thy mouth was open, but thou couldst not sing.

14. Ibid., 107.

15. There were, of course, some graves marked with modest obelisks and embellished stelae as early as 1770, but these were the exception and not the rule. For a discussion of the elaboration of headstone decorations, see Richard E. Meyer, ed., *Cemeteries and Gravemarkers: Voices of American Culture* (Ann Arbor: UMI Research Press, 1989); Alan Ludwig, *Graven Images: New England Stonecarving and Its Symbols, 1650–1815* (Middletown, Conn.: Wesleyan University Press, 1966); and Terry Jordan, *Texas Graveyards: A Cultural Legacy* (Austin: University of Texas Press, 1982).

16. The willow-and-urn motif also became a popular decorative element in furniture design and other domestic arts.

17. French, "The Cemetery as Cultural Institution," 73.

18. Linden-Ward, *Silent Cities on a Hill*, 111.

19. See Barry Schwartz, *George Washington: The Making of an American*

Symbol (New York: Free Press, 1987). The chapter entitled "Death of a Hero" is particularly interesting in this context.

20. Linden-Ward, *Silent Cities on a Hill*, 33; Charles Fraiser, quoted in French, "The Cemetery as Cultural Institution," 81; ibid., 80; Joseph Story, quoted in ibid., 80; ibid., 81.

21. This lack of specificity does not, however, imply that the memories constructed by the rural cemetery movement were democratically shared. Because there are virtually no references to race in the extensive literature about these cemeteries, the past they were making, the nation they were building, and the bodies they were burying were likely to have been white. African American and Native American bodies and memories were simply not a part of the imagined community being forged in these cemeteries. It is interesting to note that in the abundance of eighteenth- and nineteenth-century graveyard poetry, one of the most frequently reprinted poems is Philip Freneau's "The Indian Burying Ground," which ponders admiringly about the liveliness of the Indian dead as compared to the white dead. This admiration is compelling in relation to the funerary practices of Native Americans and other Americans.

22. Stanley French argues that the rural cemetery movement "supplied a great impetus for the development of sculpture in America." French, "The Cemetery as Cultural Institution," 81.

23. "Cemetery Travelogues: VIII. Havana," *Park and Cemetery* 38 (January 1929): 306, quoted in John Matturri, "Windows in the Garden: Italian-American Memorialization and the American Cemetery," in *Ethnicity and the American Cemetery* (Bowling Green: Bowling Green State University Popular Press, 1993), 14. Nearly all histories of American cemetery and funerary practices have explored the influence of the cemeteries created by the rural cemetery movement. The scholarship falls into three broad categories: richly detailed histories of the iconography of grave markers and headstones; histories of theological and cosmological explanations of death and the afterlife; and histories of the funerary and cemetery businesses. The Mount Auburn Cemetery is in many ways the centerpiece of these histories, because it so radically changed expectations about the place of the dead. Even as the rural cemetery was gradually replaced by more of the simply landscaped, uninterrupted lawns that have dominated twentieth-century cemetery design, these same principles continued to shape the work of burying the dead. Stanley French argues that the 1845 Spring Grove Cemetery in Cincinnati, Ohio, is the first example of the "lawn cemeteries" that would dominate the twentieth century. It was the first cemetery to abolish inner fencing and to try to regularize monuments and headstones. Occasionally, as at Mount Auburn, lots were sold individually to the less well-to-do, but the great majority of the cemetery was organized into family plots. French's excellent essay, "The Cemetery

as Cultural Institution," is a particularly good introduction to the history of this cemetery and to the general history of American cemeteries.

24. Matturri, "Windows in the Garden," 16.

25. The words printed on the sign are quoted in John C. Power, *Abraham Lincoln: His Great Funeral Cortege, From Washington to Springfield* (Springfield, Ill.: privately published, 1872), 167. Another manifestation of nineteenth-century interest in forging memories of the dead was the practice of taking photographs of the dead. Lincoln was much photographed after he died, as were a growing number of middle-class Americans. Set up in typical Victorian poses, many corpses were photographed with family members and in individual portraits. See Peter Hujar, *Portraits in Life and Death* (New York: Da Capo, 1976).

26. For more details, see Power, *Abraham Lincoln*, 160–72.

27. Gary Laderman, "Abraham Lincoln's Hallowed and Hollowed Body: The Anatomy of a Transitional Symbol in the History of Attitudes toward Death in America" (paper presented at the annual meeting of the American Studies Association, Boston, Mass., November 3–5, 1993).

28. Brown and Alexander was one of three "embalmers of the dead" listed in the 1865 Washington directory; all of these firms were busy improving their technologies and popularity through work on Civil War soldiers. See Robert Habenstein and William Lamers, *The History of American Funeral Directing* (Milwaukee: Bulfin Printers, 1955), 332.

29. There are two different lines of development for the need to preserve the dead. The first has its roots in ancient customs that connected the status of the dead person with the number of days in which he or she lay "in state" as a show of respect and in the very different need among the poor to preserve the body while enough money for a "decent Christian burial" was raised. See Habenstein and Lamers, *The History of American Funeral Directing*. There is a correspondence here between Lincoln's body and the body of the ordinary soldier.

30. No statistics were kept on the numbers of soldiers returned home, but the claims of the embalmers indicate that there was great demand for their services. See Habenstein and Lamers, *The History of American Funeral Directing*, 332.

31. LeRoy Bowman also makes the compelling argument that the redevelopment of embalming as a central element in the funerary business has lead to increasing emphasis on the bodies of the dead. A new interest came out of the same historical moment that inspired the similar shift in public memorial traditions. Bowman writes, "during the Civil War the greatest impetus to undertaking was provided in the need to preserve the remains of those killed in combat until they could be delivered to their families and buried."

See LeRoy Bowman, *The American Funeral: A Study in Guilt, Extravagance, and Sublimity* (Westport, Conn.: Greenwood Press, 1959), 117.

32. It is worth remembering here that the family was the central organizing element of the graveyard, and a high premium was placed on burying family members together. See Habenstein and Lamers, *The History of American Funeral Directing;* Meyer, *Cemeteries and Gravemarkers;* and Bowman, *The American Funeral.*

33. Habenstein and Lamers, *The History of American Funeral Directing,* 330. Habenstein and Lamers have constructed an amazingly detailed account of the history of embalming in the nineteenth century.

34. Local newspapers were full of details about the color and texture of his skin. See Laderman, "Abraham Lincoln's Hallowed and Hollowed Body."

35. Laderman makes a wonderful argument about this tour as a great advertisement for embalming, and he makes the point that this embalming met with mixed reviews, particularly as the days wore on. Reports in newspapers indicate that the contents of the open coffin were pretty gruesome and certainly undignified in the last days.

36. The towering monument to Lincoln at Oak Ridge was not completed until 1874; it has since been rebuilt three times.

37. This key observation was articulated by James Farrell. See Farrell, *Inventing the American Way of Death,* 3.

38. Ann Douglas, "Heaven Our Home: Consolation Literature in the Northern United States, 1830–1880," in *Death in America,* ed. David Stannard (Philadelphia: University of Pennsylvania Press, 1975), 49.

39. Bowman, *The American Funeral,* 117.

40. Ibid.

41. This interest in the business of burying the dead is terribly important, but in their focus on this question, scholars have missed other essential stories in the history of American funerary traditions. James Farrell's *Inventing the American Way of Death* is a careful witness to the transformation of death ways with the professionalization of the mortuarial business. LeRoy Bowman's *The American Funeral* is a insightful sociological study of the funeral and examines similar themes about "urban evasion of evidences of death" and "escapist attitudes." Bowman argues, however, that professionalization does not actually alienate mourners from their grieving or from death. He argues instead that the idea on which these complaints in the scholarship are predicated—that funerals and cemeteries can assuage real grief—is a "fiction promulgated by funeral directors" (10).

42. Habenstein and Lamers, *The History of American Funeral Directing,* 497.

43. Farrell, *Inventing the American Way of Death*, 130.

44. O. C. Simonds as quoted in Farrell, *Inventing the American Way of Death*, 125.

45. The list comes from a longer list of the kinds of things that are typically left on graves in the African-American tradition in John Michael Vlach, *The Afro-American Tradition in Decorative Arts* (Cleveland: Cleveland Museum of Art, 1978), 139.

46. Matturri, "Windows in the Garden," 14; Ray F. Wyrick, *Park and Cemetery*, quoted in Matturri, "Windows in the Garden," 14.

47. Robert Hertz, *Death and the Right Hand*, trans. Rodney and Claudia Needham (Glencoe, Ill.: Free Press, 1960), 77.

48. In the 1970s there was a brief flurry of research into less mainstream funerary traditions. Of particular interest were rural folk traditions in the South and Southwest that involved elaborate grave decoration. There is tremendous potential for more research into each of these practices, but a valuable beginning has been made.

49. Vlach, *The Afro-American Tradition in Decorative Arts*, 139.

50. Ibid.

51. Vlach and others have noted that the graves of small children were particularly likely to be decorated with toys and other personal belongings of the child. (This observation resonates with the enormous number of toys left at the Wall.) Vlach, *The Afro-American Tradition in Decorative Arts*, 53. Vlach argues that the traditions are essentially indistinguishable.

52. Georgia Writers, *Drums and Shadows*, quoted in Vlach, *The Afro-American Tradition in Decorative Arts*, 136.

53. Vlach, *The Afro-American Tradition in Decorative Arts*, 143.

54. Ibid., 144.

55. The best sources here include L. V. Grinsell, "The Breaking of Objects as Funerary Rite," *Folklore* 72 (September 1961): 475–91; Jordan, *Texas Graveyards*, and "Roses So Red and Lilies So Fair: Southern Folk Cemeteries in Texas," *Southwestern Historical Quarterly* 83 (1980): 227–58; Beverly Kremenak-Pecohci, "At Rest: Folk Art in Texas Cemeteries," in *Folkart in Texas* (Dallas: Southern Methodist University Press, 1985), 52–63; Robert Farris Thompson, *Flash of the Spirit: African and Afro-American Art and Philosophy* (New York: Random House, 1983); Vlach, *The Afro-American Tradition in Decorative Arts*; and John O. West, "Folk Grave Decorations along the Rio Grande," in *Folkart in Texas* (Dallas: Southern Methodist University Press, 1985), 46–51.

56. Karen Krepps, "Black Mortuary Practices in Southeast Michigan," (Ph.D. diss., Wayne State University, 1990), 77, 83.

57. There are a variety of African American funeral practices that involve

protecting grave sites and coffins from vandals and from the disrespect of funeral professionals.

58. John McCarthy, "Material Culture and Performance: African-American Community, Ethnicity, and Agency in the Burial Practices at the First African Baptist Church Cemeteries, Philadelphia, 1810–1841" (paper delivered at the Winterthur Material Culture Conference, Winterthur, Delaware, October 1993). This paper is a good start in the work to document, if not interpret, these practices.

59. Matturri, "Windows in the Garden," 17, 18

60. Ibid.

61. One frustrated funeral manager asked, in a trade journal, "How am I going to convince an illiterate foreigner, full of sentiment and emotion, that a 'studied composition in the tablet type with the decor in the current modern influence is' better for the grave of the child than the carved Lamb for which the soul of him yearns?" Matturri, "Windows in the Garden," 30.

62. Of course, Mexican American culture is not homogeneous; there are, however, enough similarities in the available research to make a general discussion useful. I have found only one close case study of these practices in a particular community, but that study is wonderful. Lynn Gosnell and Suzanne Gott study the symbolic life of a large Catholic cemetery in San Antonio, Texas. They see the contemporary grave decoration as "evidence of a dynamic and artful communication process based within family and community." Lynn Gosnell and Suzanne Gott, "San Fernando Cemetery: Decorations of Love and Loss in a Mexican-American Community," in *Cemeteries and Gravemarkers: Voices of American Culture*, ed. Richard E. Meyer (Ann Arbor: UMI Research Press, 1989), 217.

63. Ibid., 221.

64. Ibid.

65. For Chinese Americans, "ancestor worship" is central to funerary traditions; the relationship of the living to their dead ancestors is intense, and the bonds between them are tight. A crude description of the relationship suggests that the fates of the living are in the hands of the dead, and the dead have needs very much like the living; and the dead will help the living if shown the proper respect. Formal ceremonial rites involve the offering of tea and food and flowers and other personal items. The extent to which Buddhist or Taoists or Christian Chinese Americans have continued to practice these rituals in unclear. For more on ancestor worship, see Francis L. K. Hsu, *Under the Ancestor's Shadow* (New York: Columbia University Press, 1948); and Nanette Napoleon Purnell, "Oriental and Polynesian Cemetery Traditions in the Hawaiian Islands," *Ethnicity and the American Cemetery*, ed. Richard E. Meyer (Bowling Green, Ohio: Bowling Green State University Popular Press,

1993). These works are a beginning, but much more research, which would be fascinating to conduct, is needed.

66. Jordan, *Texas Graveyards*, 21.

67. It is worth noting that Jordan does not mention other forms of grave decoration in Mexican American cemeteries either in his discussion of Texas cemeteries or in his chapter about Mexican cemeteries.

68. Jordan, *Texas Graveyards*, 25.

69. Items left at the Wall on August 28, 1988. VVMC, Accession 382. Perishable items left at the Wall are recorded in the collection, but they are not saved.

70. John E. Bodnar, *Remaking America: Public Memory, Commemoration, and Patriotism in the Twentieth Century* (Princeton: Princeton University Press, 1992), 20. Bodnar's arguments about local memorial practices are richly textured, and his work to define the boundaries of public memory is quite valuable. It is surprising that he dismisses the Vietnam Veterans Memorial as a product of official commemoration, because the Wall is, in many ways, a place of contest between the vernacular memory and official memory, which are the organizing principles of his argument.

CHAPTER 4. THE THINGS

1. The items in the list were left at the Wall on November 12, 1989. VVMC, Accession 435.

2. Laura Palmer, *Shrapnel in the Heart: Letters and Remembrances from the Vietnam Veterans Memorial* (New York: Vintage Books, 1987), 34.

3. General S. L. A. Marshal, quoted in Lawrence Baskir and William A. Strauss, *Chance and Circumstance: The Draft, the War, and the Vietnam Generation* (New York: Knopf, 1978), 8. Baskir and Strauss go on to argue: "Poorly educated, low-income whites and poorly educated low-income blacks together bore a vastly disproportionate share of the burdens of Vietnam." Low-income draft-age men were twice as likely to fight in Vietnam as middle- and upper-class men. Baskir and Strauss, *Chance and Circumstance*, 9. And until 1967 nearly 20.6 percent of all those killed in action were African American—this percentage was twice their percentage in the population as a whole. See Christian Appy, *Working-Class War: American Combat Soldiers and Vietnam* (Chapel Hill: University of North Carolina Press, 1993), 22. From the note that accompanied the beer for Barnett, we do know that the friends were not of the same race, but the foregrounding of this difference in the note indicates that this mourner felt a compelling connection to the dead despite the different contexts from which he and his friend came.

4. Three people have committed suicide at the Wall since it was dedicated in 1982. All three were male Vietnam Veterans. See Peter Goldman and Tony Fuller, *Charlie Company: What Vietnam Did to Us* (New York: Morrow, 1983).

5. Walter Capps, *The Unfinished War: Vietnam and the American Conscience* (Boston: Beacon Press, 1982), 1.

6. George Herring, *America's Longest War: The United States and Vietnam, 1950–1975* (New York: Knopf, 1979), 275.

7. Personal testimony of Fred Downs, quoted in Capps, *The Unfinished War*, 96.

8. David Guynes, in a letter reprinted in Lydia Fish, *The Last Firebase*: *A Guide to the Vietnam Veterans Memorial* (Shippensburg, Penn.: White Mane Publishing, 1987), 55.

9. These things listed were left at the Wall on June 6, 1991. VVMC, Accession 505.

10. Mary Douglas, "No Free Gifts," foreword to *The Gift*, by Marcel Mauss, trans. W. D. Halls (New York: Norton, 1990), ix.

11. Marcel Mauss, *The Gift*, trans. W. D. Halls (New York: Norton, 1990), 3. Mauss argues, however, that in modern industrial societies, these relationships are disassociated, fragmented by elaborate structures of economic exchange. He writes that "we live in societies that draw a strict distinction between real rights and personal rights, things, and persons . . . such a separation is basic: it constitutes the essential condition for . . . our system of property, transfer and exchange" (47). But, as Mary Douglas argues in her foreword to *The Gift*, Mauss's work to read the gift in modern societies gets hung up on this separation; he does not manage to build a strong theoretical frame for the gift as a lively social tool in modern societies. The Wall might, in fact, be a useful place to explore the strengths and limitations of Mauss's theory for modern societies.

12. Herring, *America's Longest War*, 273; Capps, *The Unfinished War*, 94.

13. These things were left at the Wall around July 15, 1990. VVMC, Accession 462. They represent a random sample of the things in the collection.

14. Tim O'Brien, *The Things They Carried* (New York: Houghton Mifflin, 1990), is one of many novels about the problem of remembering the Vietnam War.

15. Newspaper clippings from local papers are left at the Wall all the time; I would guess from my study of the VVMC logs that, after POW/MIA paraphernalia and dog tags, the clippings are the third most prevalent kind of offering.

16. The names Calvin Robinson and Charles John Robinson are carved on panel 35w.

17. Little research has been published on the evolution of the dog tag in the United States. Here I am working from Thomas Laqueur's essay "Mem-

ory and Naming in the Great War," in *Commemorations: The Politics of National Identity*, ed. John R. Gillis (Princeton: Princeton University Press, 1994). According to Laqueur's research, the first dog tags were issued by the British Army's newly formed Graves Registration Committee in 1901. His best evidence is a record of the first British dog tag, which was traced by military collector C. C. Sweeting.

18. VVMC, Accession 286.

19. This figure comes from a rough reading of the logs; the logs do not always give the name on the dog tag, so they do not give an entirely accurate account of how many belonged to people named on the Wall.

20. It seems likely that because so many, fifty-eight thousand, Vietnam veterans took their own lives after the war—and because there is no memorial of this loss—that some of these dog tags might bear the names of some of these veterans.

21. VVMC, Accession 286.

22. Laura Palmer, "The Wall: The Inexplicable Undertow of the Vietnam Veterans Memorial Draws Visitors in Search of Solace," *GQ*, July 1987, 138.

23. Anheuser-Busch supplied Budweiser to Americans in Vietnam through the post exchanges throughout the war; it was the most readily available American beer in Vietnam. Dr. William J. Volmar, Company Historian for Anheuser-Busch, telephone conversation with author, February 24, 1994. If it were shared brand loyalty that gave meaning to the objects left at the Wall, the corporate sponsors of the war would have won a stunning, and alarming, victory. However, loyalty to particular brands and corporations is the exception rather than the rule.

24. VVMC, Accessions 474–83. This letter and Colt 45 can are part of the selection that Guynes and Felton show to visitors to the collection.

25. Some nursing mothers line their bras with these pads to absorb milk leaks.

26. Duery Felton, conversation with author, Lanham, Md., February 27, 1991.

27. Ibid. Felton talked about the cryptic, inside jokes that these things convey. He suggested that many other things could possibly be emblematic in the same way, but he had only his experience and conversations with other veterans about various things left at the Wall to go on.

28. John R. Gillis, ed., *Commemorations: Politics and National Identity* (Princeton: Princeton University Press, 1994), 17.

CHAPTER 5. "YOU ARE NOT FORGOTTEN"

1. Items left at the Wall on December 4, 1990. VVMC, Accession 483.

2. This movie has been written about extensively; see Leonard Quart, "The

Deer Hunter: The Superman in Vietnam," in *From Hanoi to Hollywood: The Vietnam War in American Film*, ed. Linda Dittmar and Gene Michaud (New Brunswick, N.J.: Rutgers University Press, 1990), 159–68.

3. Historian George Mosse argues that it is just this kind of patriotic hymn that articulated and built the foundation for militant nationalism in early-nineteenth-century Europe. See George Mosse, *Fallen Soldiers: Reshaping the Memory of the World Wars* (New York: Oxford University Press, 1990), 20–21.

4. Rick Berg, "Covering Vietnam in an Age of Technology," in *The Vietnam War and American Culture*, ed. John Carlos Rowe and Rick Berg (New York: Columbia University Press, 1991), 141.

5. Alexander Kendrick, *The Wound Within: America in the Vietnam Years, 1945–1974* (Boston: Little, Brown, 1974), 396.

6. Kurt Anderson, "A Homecoming at Last," *Time*, November 22, 1982, 45.

7. With few exceptions the grief at the Wall seems to be grief about what the war did to Americans and America. Although there is plenty of regret expressed at the Wall, the debate at the memorial focuses on the cost of the war at home rather than the cost of the war in Vietnam or for the Vietnamese, the Laotians, and the Cambodians. This lack of attention to the plight of the people for whom we were ostensibly fighting is strong evidence that Americans are grieving for the domestic changes wrought by the war rather than for the broad consequences of the war itself.

8. Officially the POW/MIA organizations are concerned about both the missing and the prisoners, but the POWs are the real focus of the movement. There is little interest in MIAs who are not thought to have been taken as prisoners.

It is interesting and worth noting that although many academic histories and cultural analyses of the legacy of the Vietnam War have been written, the POW/MIA issue and the burning question of the effects of Agent Orange have not been compelling, either metaphorically or institutionally, parts of the story in these studies. John Carlos Rowe and Nick Berg, *The Vietnam War and American Culture* (New York: Columbia University Press, 1991); Loren Baritz, *Backfire: A History of How American Culture Led Us into Vietnam and Made Us Fight the Way We Did* (New York: Ballantine, 1985); Susan Jeffords, *The Remasculinization of America: Gender and the Vietnam War* (Bloomington: University of Indiana Press, 1989); Myra MacPherson, *Long Time Passing: Vietnam and the Haunted Generation* (Garden City, N.Y.: Doubleday, 1984); and Richard Morris and Peter Ehrenhaus, eds., *Cultural Legacies of Vietnam: Uses of the Past in the Present* (Norwood, N.J.: Ablex Publishing, 1990), all build elaborate arguments about the legacy of the war without any serious attention to the POW/MIA situation or the Agent Orange issue.

9. H. Bruce Franklin, "The POW/MIA Myth," *The Atlantic Monthly*, De-

cember 1991, 45. Both H. Bruce Franklin, *MIA or Mythmaking in America* (Brooklyn, New York: Lawrence Hill, 1992); and Monika Jensen-Stevenson and William Stevenson, *Kiss the Boys Goodbye: How the United States Betrayed Its Own POWs in Vietnam* (New York: Plume Books, 1991), reconstruct lengthy—if quite different—histories of the constant official and civilian attention paid to this issue since 1969.

10. Of course, the slim likelihood of prisoners surviving for twenty years and the problem of the motivation of the Vietnamese and Laotians for continuing to keep prisoners are not seen as logical flaws by the POW/MIA supporters; they are amazed that the issue has not incited more outrage. See Jensen-Stevenson and Stevenson, *Kiss the Boys Goodbye;* and Nigel Cawthorne, *The Bamboo Cage: The Full Story of the American Servicemen Still Held Hostage in South-East Asia* (London: Leo Cooper, 1991). The research that takes an opposing opinion is so busy countering the barrage of POW information and misinformation that it does not address the question of why this issue continues to be so compelling. See Franklin, *MIA or Mythmaking in America*.

11. The claims that the POW/MIA movement makes about the cruelty of the Vietnamese are laced with all too familiar racial stereotypes. For a useful history of the wartime manipulations of these racist images, see John W. Dower, *War without Mercy: Race and Power in the Pacific War* (New York: Pantheon, 1986).

12. This is a generic list of the kinds of things that were left at the Wall on November 11, 1992.

13. It is of course important to note that Vietnam veterans are not the only American veterans to end their war mad or the first Americans to resist the military. The 1863 Civil War draft riots in New York City and the 1932 march on Washington made by veterans of World War I are important precedents for this kind of protest. See Iver Bernstein, *The New York City Draft Riots: Their Significance for American Society and Politics in the Age of the Civil War* (New York: Oxford University Press, 1990). I am not arguing that this kind of protest is new, but rather that the particular form of this protest is worth reading in its moment.

14. Bobbie Ann Mason's novel *In Country* (New York: Harper and Row, 1985) uses the metaphor of manhood poisoned by Agent Orange. The novel's central character is a young woman who feels left out of the heart of the culture because she did not go to Vietnam—her best friend is her Agent Orange–poisoned uncle.

15. Country Joe McDonald was an active voice in the antiwar movement; the patriotic ballads of Britt Small and Festival marked them as likely war supporters.

16. Speakers included Ron Barbaro, Harry G. Robinson, James M. Ride-

nour, Reverend John Steer, Father Philip Salios, Rocky Bleier, Anni Booth Elais, Pamela Handrahan, Maya Ying Lin, Major General Edward Baca, Diane Carlson Evans, Terry Anderson, and Vice President Al Gore.

17. The pinup girl as the paragon of American female beauty and purity that American GIs were fighting to protect is an important part of the mythos of the American soldier. Jane Fonda's visiting Hanoi and posing astride an enemy missile was perceived by many soldiers and veterans as an unforgivable affront to American manhood. Despite her public apology many years later, Jane Fonda is hated by many Vietnam veterans.

18. This brought the number of Congressional Medals of Honor left at the Wall to two.

19. The official machinations around this issue are far too complicated to reproduce here. H. Bruce Franklin's singular account of these vastly snarled numbers games and policy positions, *MIA or Mythmaking in America*, provides a remarkable account of all of the details.

The first POWs involved in the Vietnam War were Nazi prisoners of war who had been held in the United States during the war and turned over to the French after the war. In the post–World War II treaties Nazi POWs were not freed as the Geneva Convention dictated they should be; instead they were used as laborers in the work of rebuilding Europe. The French used the Nazi POWs to try to rebuild their colonial bases; they sent the captured German soldiers to fight for French interests in Vietnam.

20. Ibid., 26.

21. Ibid., 40.

22. Henry Cabot Lodge called for "the early release of prisoners of war on both sides" (ibid., 57).

23. Richard Nixon, "The President's News Conference on Foreign Policy, March 4, 1971," quoted in ibid., 389.

24. Ibid., 50, 51. Not surprisingly Sybil Stockdale's involvement with the League brought her into close contact with H. Ross Perot and cemented a friendship that would eventually lead to Perot's asking her husband, Admiral James Stockdale, to be his running mate in the 1992 presidential election.

25. Janet Lee Koenigsmen, "Mobilization of a Conscience Constituency: VIVA and the POW/MIA Movement" (Ph.D. diss., Kent State University, 1987), 6.

26. Franklin, *MIA or Mythmaking in America*, 56. This bracelet campaign worked so well that it has inspired similar campaigns in struggles across the political spectrum, including the fight to free political prisoners in South Africa and the fight to find a cure for AIDS. The introduction of the bracelets in the immediate wake of the killings at Kent State, on May 4, 1970, could hardly have been more appropriate; the conservative pro-war activists desperately needed to mark themselves as patriots working for a humanitarian cause.

27. George C. Herring, *America's Longest War: The United States and Vietnam, 1950–1975* (New York: Knopf, 1986), 257.

28. Franklin, *MIA or Mythmaking in America*, 17.

29. Getting an accurate figure for POW/MIAs in Vietnam is nearly impossible. Virtually every source provides different numbers. I rely, throughout this discussion, on H. Bruce Franklin's careful research.

30. Franklin, *MIA or Mythmaking in America*, 14.

31. Ibid.

32. Ibid., 85, 84.

33. Koenigsmen, "Mobilization of a Conscience Constituency"; Ethan Seidman, "The POW/MIA Lobby," *The Atlantic Monthly*, December 1991, 75.

34. The truly hard-core POW activists in the 1990s have disavowed the League and VIVA entirely as instruments of the United States government. See Jensen-Stevenson and Stevenson, *Kiss the Boys Goodbye*, 225.

35. On people's continued belief in POWs, see Franklin, *MIA or Mythmaking in America*, 3; on the five organizations preserving the memory of POWs, see "The POW/MIA Lobby," 75. The organization Operation Rescue, founded in 1981, shares more than a name with the antiabortion movement group. The relationship of the politics and the use of the idea of the body of the citizen in these movements is deeply suggestive.

36. Ronald Reagan as quoted by Bo Gritz, quoted in Charles J. Patterson and Colonel G. Lee Tippin, *The Heroes Who Fell from Grace: The True Story of Operation Lazarus, the Attempt to Free American POW's from Laos in 1982* (Canton, Ohio: Daring, 1985), 102.

37. The POW/MIA movies have been written about a great deal. For a start see Jeffords, *The Remasculinization of America;* Franklin, *MIA or Mythmaking in America;* and Gregory A. Waller, "Rambo: Getting to Win This Time," in *From Hanoi to Hollywood: The Vietnam War in American Film*, ed. Linda Dittmar and Gene Michaud (New Brunswick, N.J.: Rutgers University Press, 1990).

38. Duery Felton, conversation with author, Lanham, Md., July 1992. The Park Service was worried about the rubbings wearing away at the granite and the prospect of having to replace the panel eventually.

39. Lydia Fish, *The Last Firebase: A Guide to the Vietnam Veterans Memorial* (Shippensburg, Penn.: White Mane Publishing, 1987), 43.

40. Ibid.

41. Lawrence L. Knutson, "Presence of Peddlers by the Vietnam Wall Infuriates Some Vets," *Detroit Free Press*, July 22, 1993, 6A.

42. For every possible POW or MIA or KIA/BNR there are at least a thousand homeless veterans on American streets (see Franklin, "The POW/MIA Myth," 46), but for the veterans rallying at the Wall, the real suffering of homeless veterans has been displaced by the imagined suffering in Vietnam.

43. This is a sampling of the kinds of POW/MIA artifacts that get left at the Wall. The sample is pulled from the MARS log records.

44. As noted in chapter 4, the accounting of artifacts left before 1985 is quite poor. It is possible, quite likely in fact, that bracelets were left at the Wall between 1982 and 1984, but there is no record of them. My survey of the VVMC logs make it clear that the frequency with which bracelets were left increased steadily between 1985 and 1992.

In 1985, roughly 108 bracelets were left at the Wall, 114 were left in 1986, 148 were left in 1987, 250 were left in 1988, 259 were left in 1989, 257 were left in 1990, 278 were left in 1991, and 269 were left in the first ten months of 1992. I suspect that these numbers are not entirely reliable because the sheer volume of bracelets left makes them less interesting for the volunteers to record in the log books. But these numbers provide a relatively accurate general sense of the volume of bracelets left at the Wall.

45. Of course, remembering, being unable to forget, haunts many veterans. One veteran who holds vigil at the Wall while working two jobs recently told a visitor to the memorial that he spends his nights in the tent selling POW things and talking to visitors because he is afraid that too much idle time at home would let the memory of a seventeen year old girl he killed come back to haunt him.

46. These things were left at the Wall in May 1990. VVMC, Accession 452.

47. Since 1968, "no more Vietnams" has been a rallying cry for nearly every political affiliation imaginable: it was used repeatedly by antiwar activists on the left to warn against the domestic cost of U.S. involvement in Central America and by hawks during the Gulf War to warn against the dangers of a timid, limited entry into war.

EPILOGUE

1. If it is in fact true that the building was bombed by working-class white men enraged by their shifting social position, then there are further resonances between the things left at the Wall and the things left at the bombing site.

2. These gifts are being saved by the Oklahoma City Memorial Commission with the hope that they will be incorporated, somehow, into the memorial design. In an interesting twist on the practice of carrying gifts, they started as a response to what was not in official memorials and other forms of public memory, but they will soon become the official memorial itself.

3. This is a sampling of things left at the Wall in the fall of 1988. VVMC, Accessions 371–91.

SELECTED BIBLIOGRAPHY

MATERIAL CULTURE: THEORY AND METHODS

Anderson, Jay. "Immaterial Material Culture." *Folklore* 21 (1977): 1–13.

Ames, Kenneth. *Beyond Necessity: Art in the Folk Tradition*. Lawrence: University Press of Kansas, 1977.

———. "Meaning in Artifacts." *Journal of Interdisciplinary History* 9, no. 1 (1978): 19–46.

———. "Material Culture as Nonverbal Communication." *Journal of American Culture* 3 (winter 1980): 619–41.

———. *Death in the Dining Room and Other Tales of Victorian Culture*. Philadelphia: Temple University Press, 1993.

Bakhtin, M. M. *The Dialogic Imagination*. Ed. Michael Holquist. Trans. Caryl Emerson and Michael Holquist. Austin: University of Texas Press, 1981.

Bronner, Simon J. "From Neglect to Concept: An Introduction to the Study of Material Aspects of American Folk Culture." *Folklore Forum* 12 (1979): 117–32.

———. *American Material Culture and Folklife: A Prologue and a Dialogue*. Ann Arbor: UMI Research Press, 1985.

———, ed. *Grasping Things: Folk Material Culture and Mass Society in America*. Lexington: University Press of Kentucky, 1986.

———. *Consuming Visions: Accumulation and Display of Goods in America, 1880–1920*. New York: Norton, 1989.

Carson, Barbara, and Gary Carson. "Things Unspoken: Learning Social History through Artifacts." In *Ordinary People and Everyday Life*, ed. James B. Gardner and George Rollie Adams. Nashville, Tenn.: AASLH, 1983.

Cotter, John, "Above Ground Archaeology." *American Quarterly* 26 (1974): 266–80.

Csikszentmihalyi, Mihaly, and Eugene Halton-Rochberg. *The Meaning of*

Things: Domestic Symbols and the Self. Cambridge: Cambridge University Press, 1981.

Culler, Jonathan. "Junk and Rubbish: A Semiotic Approach." *Diacritics* 15 (fall 1982): 2–12.

Czach, Marie. "At Home: Reconstructing Everyday Life through Photographs and Artifacts." *Afterimage* 5 (September 1977).

Deetz, James. *Invitation to Archaeology.* Garden City, N.Y.: Doubleday, 1967.

Douglas, Mary, and Baron Isherwood. *The World of Goods: Towards an Anthropology of Consumption.* New York: Basic, 1979.

Ellsworth, Lucius, and Maureen O'Brien, eds. *Material Culture: Historical Agency and the Historian.* Philadelphia: Reprint Book Service, 1969.

Fagan, Brian M. *The Great Journey.* London: Thames and Hudson, 1987.

Fleming, McClung E. "Artifact Study: A Proposed Model." *Winterthur Portfolio* 9 (June 1974): 153–73.

Geertz, Clifford, ed. *Myth, Symbol, and Culture.* New York: Norton, 1974.

Glassie, Henry. "Meaningful Things and Appropriate Myths: The Artifact's Place in American Studies." *Prospects* 3 (1977): 1–49.

———. "Folkloristic Study of the American Artifact: Objects and Objectives." In *Handbook of American Folklore,* ed. Richard M. Dorson. Bloomington: University of Indiana Press, 1983.

Gordon, Beverly. "The Whimsey and Its Contexts: A Multi-Cultural Model of Material Culture Study." *Journal of American Culture* 9 (spring 1986): 61–76.

Gould, Richard A., and Michael B. Schiffer, eds. *Modern Material Culture: The Archaeology of Us.* New York: Academic Press, 1981.

Hamp, Steven. "Meaning in Material Culture." *Living History Farms Bulletin* 9 (May 1980): 9–13.

Herman, Brenard L. "The 'Bricoleur' Revisited." Paper delivered at the Winterthur Material Culture Conference, Winterthur, Delaware, October 1993.

Hudson, Luanne B. "Modern Material Culture Studies: Anthropology as Archaeology." *American Behavioral Scientist* 23 (September 1984): 31–39.

Karp, Ivan, and Steven D. Lavine, eds. *Exhibiting Cultures: The Poetics and Politics of Museum Display.* Washington, D.C.: Smithsonian Institution Press, 1991.

Kouwenhoven, John. *Made in America.* Garden City, N.Y.: Doubleday, 1948.

———. "American Studies: Words or Things?" In *American Studies in Transition,* ed. Marshall Fishwick. Philadelphia: University of Pennsylvania Press, 1964.

Lantham, Richard S. "The Artifact as Cultural Cipher." In *Who Designs America? The American Civilization Conference at Princeton,* ed. Laurence B. Holland. New York: Anchor, 1966.

Lears, Jackson T. J. *No Place of Grace: Antimodernism and the Transformation of American Culture, 1880–1920*. New York: Pantheon, 1981.
————, ed. *The Culture of Consumption: Critical Essays in American History, 1880–1980*. New York: Pantheon, 1983.
Lévi-Strauss, Claude. *Structural Anthropology 2*. Trans. M. Layton. London: Penguin, 1977.
Lylle, Charles T. "The Artifact and American History: An Examination of the Use of the Artifact for Historical Evidence." Master's thesis, University of Delaware, 1971.
Mayo, Edith, ed. *American Material Culture: The Shape of Things around Us*. Bowling Green, Ohio: Bowling Green State University Popular Press, 1984.
McCracken, Grant. *Culture and Consumption: New Approaches to the Symbolic Character of Consumer Goods and Activities*. Bloomington: University of Indiana Press, 1988.
Miller, Daniel. *Material Culture and Mass Consumption*. Oxford: Basil Blackwell, 1987.
Orvell, Miles. *The Real Thing: Imitation and Authenticity in American Culture, 1880–1940*. Chapel Hill: University of North Carolina Press, 1989.
Pearce, Susan M. *Museum Studies in Material Culture*. Washington, D.C.: Smithsonian Institution Press, 1989.
Place, Linda Punk. "The Object as Subject." *American Quarterly* 26 (1974): 281–94.
Prown, Jules. "Mind in Matter: An Introduction to Material Culture Theory and Method." *Winterthur Portfolio* 17 (1982): 1–19.
Quimby, Ian M. G., ed. *Material Culture and the Study of American Life*. New York: Norton, 1978.
Rathje, William L. "A Manifesto for Modern Material Culture Studies." In *Modern Material Culture: The Archaeology of Us*, ed. Richard A. Gould and Michael B. Schiffer. New York: Academic Press, 1981.
Schlereth, Thomas J. *Artifacts and the American Past: Techniques for the Historian*. Nashville, Tenn.: AASLH, 1980.
————, ed. *Material Culture Studies in America*. Nashville, Tenn.: AASLH, 1982.
————. *Material Culture: A Research Guide*. Lawrence: University Press of Kansas, 1985.
————. *Cultural History and Material Culture: Everyday Life, Landscapes, Museums*. Ann Arbor: UMI Research Press, 1990.
Schuler, Robert L. *Historical Archaeology: A Guide to Substantive and Theoretical Contributions*. Farmingdale, N.Y.: Baywood, 1978.
Tilley, Christopher, ed. *Reading Material Culture: Structuralism, Hermeneutics, and Post-Structuralism*. Oxford: Basil Blackwell, 1989.

Upton, Dell. "Material Culture Studies: A Symposium." *Material Culture* 17 (summer/winter 1985): 2 ff.

Williams, Raymond. *Culture and Society, 1780–1950*. New York: Columbia University Press, 1983.

VIETNAM WAR HISTORY

Appy, Christian. *Working Class War: American Combat Soldiers and Vietnam*. Chapel Hill: University of North Carolina Press, 1993.

Baskir, Lawrence, and William A. Strauss. *Chance and Circumstance: The Draft, the War, and the Vietnam Generation*. New York: Knopf, 1978.

Bergerud, Eric. *Red Thunder, Tropic Lighting: The World of a Combat Division in Vietnam*. New York: Penguin Books, 1994.

Braestrup, Peter, ed. *Vietnam as History: Ten Years after the Paris Peace Accords*. Washington, D.C.: University Press of America, 1984.

Butterfield, Fox. "The New Vietnam Scholarship." *New York Times Magazine*, February 13, 1983, 26–32.

Cooper, Chester A. *The Lost Crusade: American in Vietnam*. New York: Dodd, Mead, 1970.

Emerson, Gloria. *Winners and Losers: Battles, Retreats, Gains, Losses, and Ruins from a Long War*. New York: Random House, 1976.

FitzGerald, Frances. *Fire in the Lake: The Vietnamese and the Americans in Vietnam*. Boston: Little, Brown, 1972.

Gelb, Leslie H., and Richard K. Betts. *The Irony of Vietnam: The System Worked*. Washington, D.C.: Brookings Institution, 1979.

Gitlin, Todd. *The Whole World Is Watching*. Berkeley: University of California Press, 1980.

Halberstam, David. *The Best and the Brightest*. New York: Random House, 1972.

Harris, Louis. *The Anguish of Change*. New York: Norton, 1973.

Herring, George C. *America's Longest War: The United States and Vietnam, 1950–1975*. New York: Knopf, 1979.

———. "Sources for Understanding the Vietnam Conflict." *Society of American Foreign Relations Newsletter*, March 16, 1985.

Karnow, Stanley. *Vietnam: A History*. New York: Penguin Books, 1983.

Lubell, Samuel. *The Hidden Crisis in American Politics*. New York: Norton, 1973.

Lunch, William L., and Peter W. Sperlich. "Public Opinion and the War in Vietnam." *Western Political Quarterly* 32 (March 1979), 21–44.

Maclear, Michael. *The Ten Thousand Day War: Vietnam, 1945–1975*. New York: St. Martin's, 1981.

MacPherson, Myra. *Long Time Passing: Vietnam and the Haunted Generation*. Garden City, N.Y.: Doubleday, 1984.

Podhoretz, Norman. *Why We Were in Vietnam*. New York: Simon and Schuster, 1982.

Powers, Thomas. *'Nam, the War at Home: Vietnam and the American People, 1964–1968*. Boston: Hall, 1973.

Salisbury, Harrison, ed. *Vietnam Reconsidered: Lessons from a War*. New York: Harper and Row, 1984.

Sanders, Jacquin. *The Draft and the Vietnam War*. New York: Walker, 1966.

Schlesinger, Arthur. *The Bitter Heritage: Vietnam and American Democracy, 1941–1966*. Boston: Houghton Mifflin, 1966.

Stevens, Robert. *Vain Hopes, Grim Realities: The Economic Consequences of the Vietnam War*. New York: New Viewpoints, 1976.

THE VIETNAM VETERANS MEMORIAL*

Adams, William. "Remembering Vietnam." *Democracy* 3 (1983): 73–77.

Allen, Leslie. "Offerings at the Wall." *American Heritage* 46 (February/March 1995): 92–100 ff.

Allen, Thomas. *Offerings at the Wall: Artifacts from the Vietnam Veterans Memorial Collection*. Atlanta, Ga.: Turner Publishing, 1995.

Anderson, Kurt. "A Homecoming at Last: Vietnam Veterans Converge on Washington in Quest of Catharsis and Respect." *Time*, November 22, 1982, 44–46.

———. "Hush, Timmy—This Is Like a Church." *Time*, April 15, 1985, 61.

Ashabranner, Brent. *Always to Remember: The Story of the Vietnam Veterans Memorial*. New York: Scholastic, 1988.

Barker, Karlyn. "At the Wall, Sympathy and Sorrow." *Washington Post*, November 11, 1989.

Beardsley, John. "Personal Sensibilities in Public Places." *Artforum* (summer 1981): 43–45.

Bee, John D. "Eros and Thanos: An Analysis of the Vietnam Memorial." In *Vietnam Images: War and Representation*, ed. James Walsh and James Aulich. New York: St. Martin's, 1989.

"Black Gash of Shame" (editorial). *New York Times*, April 14, 1985.

Blum, Shirley Neilson. "The National Vietnam War Memorial." *Arts Magazine* 59 (December 1984): 124–28.

Bragg, Rick. "On the Walls, Memories of Slain Are Kept." *New York Times*, January 28, 1994.

Braithwaite, Charles. "Cultural Communication among Vietnam Veterans: Ritual, Myth, and Social Drama." In *Cultural Legacies of Vietnam: Uses of the*

*There are literally hundreds of Vietnam War histories out there—this is a selection with a particular interest in the war in relation to the home front.

Past in the Present, ed. Richard Morris and Peter Ehrenhaus. Norwood, N.J.: Ablex Publishing, 1990.

Brisbaine, Arthur. "A Cycle of War and Remembrance." *Washington Post*, November 12, 1984.

Brown, Melissa. "Memorials, Not Monuments." *Progressive Architecture* 66 (September 1985): 43 ff.

Broyles, William. "A Ritual for Saying Goodbye." *U.S. News & World Report*, November 10, 1986, 19.

Buckley, Christopher. "The Wall." *Esquire*, September 1985, 65–73.

Bumiller, Elizabeth. "The Memorial, Mirror of Vietnam." *Washington Post*, November 9, 1984.

Carhart, Tom. "Insulting Vietnam Vets." *New York Times*, October 24, 1981.

Carlson, Peter. "Back to the Wall." *Washington Post Magazine*, November 6, 1988, 34–37.

Chua-Eoan, Howard. "Along the Wall, Gifts from the Heart." *People*, June 1, 1992, 109 ff.

Clardy, Jim. "Warehouse Is Giant Scrapbook for Mementos Left at the Vietnam Wall." *Washington Times*, May 28, 1990.

Clay, Grady. "The Vietnam Veterans Memorial Competition." *Harvard Magazine*, no. 87 (1985): 56a–h.

Codrington, Andrea. "Moveable Memorials?" *ID* 40 (May/June 1993), 28.

Coleman, Jonathan. "First She Looks Inward." *Time*, November 6, 1989, 90–94.

Corman, James. "Reflections of a War: Vietnam Veterans Memorial Collection." *National Parks* 60 (March/April 1986): 20–25.

Danto, Arthur C. "The Vietnam Veterans Memorial." *The Nation*, August 31, 1985, 152–55.

Ellis, Caron Schwartz. "So Old Soldiers Don't Fade Away: The Vietnam Veterans Memorial." *Journal of American Culture* 15 (summer 1992): 25–30.

Ezell, Edward Clinton. *Reflections on the Wall: The Vietnam Veterans Memorial.* Harrisburg, Penn.: Stackpole, 1987.

Fish, Lydia. *The Last Firebase: A Guide to the Vietnam Veterans Memorial.* Shippensburg, Penn.: White Mane Publishing, 1987.

Forgery, Benjamin. "Battle Won for War Memorials: CFA Approves Women's Vietnam, Black Patriots Designs." *Washington Post*, September 20, 1991.

Foss, Sonja. "Ambiguity as Persuasion: The Vietnam Veterans Memorial." *Communication Quarterly* 34 (summer 1986): 326–40.

Foster, Gaines M. "Coming to Terms with Defeat: Post-Vietnam America and the Post–Civil War South." *Virginia Quarterly Review* 66 (1990): 17–35.

Fox, Terrance. "The Vietnam Veterans Memorial: Ideological Implications." In *Vietnam Images: War and Representation*, ed. Jeffery Walsh and James Aulich. London: St. Martin's, 1989.

Glowen, Ron. "Going to the Wall." *Artweek*, March 28, 1991, 3.

Goulait, Bert. "Personal Effects." *Soldiers*, May 1986, 28–30.

Graves, Louise. *Let Us Remember: The Vietnam Veterans Memorial*. Washington, D.C.: Department of the Interior, 1984.

Grewing, Colleen. "A Living Memorial: A Growing Collection of Some 15,000 Personal Mementos Left at the Wall Has Become a Unique Social History of Everyday Man." *Washington Monthly*, November 1990, 22.

Griswold, Charles. "The Vietnam Veterans Memorial and the Washington Mall: Philosophical Thoughts on Political Iconography." *Critical Inquiry* 12 (summer 1986): 688–719.

———. *Warrior and Statesmen: Symbolism in the Vietnam Veterans Memorial and Nearby Monuments*. Bethesda, Md.: published by the author, 1990.

Grunwald, Lisa. "Facing the Wall." *Life*, November 15, 1992, 24–29.

Guido, Michelle. "A Wall Divided by Commercialism." *San Jose Mercury News*, March 14, 1991.

Haines, Harry W. "What Kind of War? An Analysis of the Vietnam Veterans Memorial." *Critical Studies in Mass Communications* 3 (1986): 1–20.

———. "Mediated Vietnam: The Politics of Postwar Representations." Ph.D. diss., University of Utah, 1987.

Harbutt, Charles. "The Things They Left Behind." *New York Times Magazine*, November 12, 1995, 83–85.

Hart, Fredrick. "Letter to the Editor." *Art in America*, November 1983, 5.

Hess, Elizabeth. "A Tale of Two Memorials." *Art in America*, April 1983, 120–27.

Hoekema, David. "A Wall for Remembering." *Commonwealth*, July 15, 1983, 397–99.

Holm, Tom. "Intergenerational Rapprochement among American Indians: A Study of Thirty-Five Indian Veterans of the Vietnam War." *Journal of Political and Military Sociology* 12 (1984): 161–70.

Howett, Catherine M. "The Vietnam Veterans Memorial: Public Art and Politics." *Landscape* 28 (1985): 1–9.

Hubbard, William. "A Meaning for Monuments." *The Public Interest* 74 (winter 1984): 17–30.

Jeppeson, Marsha, Enrico Pucci, and Carole Blair. "Public Memorializing in Postmodernity: The Vietnam Veterans Memorial as Prototype." *Quarterly Journal of Speech* 77 (August 1991): 263–88.

Katakis, Michael. *The Vietnam Veterans Memorial*. New York: Crown, 1988.

Knutson, Lawrence L. "Presence of Peddlers by the Vietnam Wall Infuriates Some Vets." *Detroit Free Press*, July 22, 1993.

Krohn, Franklin B. "Vietnam Veterans Memorial: Universal Symbolism." *Etc* 50 (summer 1993): 165–67.

Lamb, David. "Hearts Meet History at 'the Wall' of Vietnam." *Los Angeles Times*, August 13, 1990.

"Left at the Wall." *Economist*, October 31, 1992, 38.

Lescaze, Les. "Vietnam Legacy: Inspired by Memorial, Veterans of the War Come into Their Own." *Wall Street Journal*, April 4, 1985, 1.

Lin, Maya Ying. "Design Competition: Winning Designer's Statement." Washington, D.C.: Vietnam Veterans Memorial Fund, 1982.

———. "An Interview with Maya Lin." In *Unwinding the Vietnam War: From War into Peace*, ed. Reese Williams. Seattle: Real Comet, 1987.

Lindberg, Todd. "Of Arms, Men, and Monuments." *Commentary* 78 (October 1984): 51–56.

Lopez, Sal. *The Wall: Images and Offerings from the Vietnam Veterans Memorial*. New York: Collins, 1987.

Lundeed, Kathleen, "Immovable Type: Textual Sculpture in the Vietnam Veterans Wall and the Illuminations of Blake." Unpublished.

Malone, Maggie. "Up against the Wall, Architect M. Y. Lin." *Newsweek*, January 20, 1986, 6.

Marling, Karal Ann, and Robert Silberman. "The Statue near the Wall: The Vietnam Veterans Memorial and the Art of Remembering." *Smithsonian Studies in American Art* 1 (1987): 5–29.

Marling, Karal Ann, and John Wetenhall. "The Sexual Politics of Memory: The Vietnam Women's Memorial Project and 'The Wall.'" *Prospects* 14 (1989): 341–72.

McDonald, Jack, "Archaeology of Grief." *Archaeology* 46 (November/ December 1993): 96.

McIntyre, Mike. "Gifts of Grief." *San Diego Union*, May 14, 1989.

"Mementos at the Vietnam Memorial." *New York Times*, September 9, 1986.

Mills, Nicolaus. "Architectural Politics: The Vietnam Memorial." *Dissent* 31 (winter 1984): 24–26.

Morganthau, Tom. "Honoring Vietnam Veterans—At Last." *Newsweek*, November 22, 1982, 80–86.

Murolo, Priscilla. "Remembering Vietnam." *Radical History Review* 33 (1985): 182–85.

Neibuhr, Gustav. "More Than a Monument: The Spiritual Dimension of the Hallowed Walls." *New York Times*, November 11, 1994.

Norman, Michael. "Voices at the Wall." *The New York Time Magazine*, May 27, 1990, 16–19.

Palmer, Laura. *Shrapnel in the Heart: Letters and Remembrances from the Vietnam Veterans Memorial*. New York: Vintage Books, 1987.

———. "The Wall: The Inexplicable Undertow of the Vietnam Veterans Memorial Draws Visitors in Search of Solace." *GQ*, July 1987, 138–66.

Phillips, Patricia. "Vietnam Veterans Memorial, Vietnam Veterans Plaza." *Artforum* 24 (December 1985): 90–91.

Powell, Stewart. "A Sacred Place on the Potomac: Collection of Mementos Left at the Vietnam Veterans Memorial." *U.S. News & World Report*, November 10, 1986, 16–18.

Rathbun, Elizabeth. "A Living Museum." *Federal Times*, November 18, 1985, 22–23.

Reston, James. "Monument Glut." *New York Times Magazine*, September 10, 1995, 48–49.

Scott, Grant F. "Mediations in Black: The Vietnam Veterans Memorial." *Journal of American Culture* 13 (fall 1990): 37–40.

Scruggs, Jan C, and Joel Swerdlow. *To Heal a Nation: The Vietnam Veterans Memorial*. New York: Harper and Row, 1985.

Spencer, Duncan. *Facing the Wall: Americans at the Vietnam Memorial*. New York: Macmillan, 1986.

Sorkin, Michael. "What Happens When a Woman Designs a War Monument?" *Vogue*, May 1983, 120–22.

Strait, Jerry L. *Vietnam War Memorials: An Illustrated Reference to Veterans' Tributes throughout the United States*. Jefferson, N.C.: McFarland, 1988.

Sturken, Marita. "The Wall, the Screen, and the Image: The Vietnam Veterans Memorial." *Representations* 35 (1991): 118–42.

———. "Cultural Memory and Identity Politics: The Vietnam War, AIDS, and Technologies of Memory." Ph.D. diss., University of California, Santa Cruz, 1992.

"Vietnam Memorial: America Remembers." *National Geographic*, May 1985, 557.

"Vietnam Memorial Gathers Own Collection of Artifacts." *New York Times*, November 10, 1991.

Von Eckhardt, Wolf. "The Vietnam Veterans Memorial in Washington." Unpublished, 1986.

Wagner-Pacifici, Robin, and Barry Schwartz. "The Vietnam Veterans Memorial: Commemorating a Difficult Past." *American Journal of Sociology* 97 (September 1991): 376–420.

Walker, Susan. "The Vietnam Veterans Memorial and MARS Dedicated to Keeping the Memories Alive." *Stars and Stripes*, January 15, 1990, 9.

Williams, Lorna. "Tears and Tributes." *Military Lifestyle* 19, no. 10 (November/December 1987).

Wolfe, Tom. "Art Disputes War: The Battle of the Vietnam Memorial." *Washington Post*, October 13, 1982.

FUNERARY TRADITIONS

Aries, Philippe. *Western Attitudes toward Death: From the Middle Ages to the Present*. Baltimore: Johns Hopkins University Press, 1974.

———. *The Hour of Our Death*. Trans. Helen Weaver. New York: Knopf, 1981. Originally published as *L'Homme devant la mort* (Paris: Éditions du Seuil, 1977).

Bender, Thomas. "The Rural Cemetery Movement: Urban Travail and the Appeal of Nature." *New England Quarterly* 47 (June 1974): 196–211.

Bergman, Edward F. *Woodlawn Remembers: Cemetery of American History*. Utica, N.Y.: North Country, 1989.

Bowman, LeRoy. *The American Funeral: A Study in Guilt, Extravagance, and Sublimity*. Westport, Conn.: Greenwood Press, 1959.

Conkling, James C. "Oak Ridge Cemetery Dedication Speech." Files of Oakridge Cemetery, Springfield, Illinois.

Darnall, Margaretta J. "The American Cemetery as Picturesque Landscape: Bellefontaine Cemetery, St. Louis." *Winterthur Portfolio* 18 (winter 1983): 249–69.

Dickinson, Robert. *Final Placement: A Guide to the Deaths, Funerals, and Burials of Notable Americans*. Algonac, Mich.: Reference Publications, 1982.

Douglas, Ann. "Heaven Our Home: Consolation Literature in the Northern United States, 1830–1880." In *Death in America*, ed. David Stannard. Philadelphia: University of Pennsylvania Press, 1975.

Dye, Nancy Schram, and Daniel Blake Smith. "Mother Love and Infant Death, 1750–1920." *Journal of American History* 73 (September 1986): 329–53.

Farrell, James T. *Inventing the American Way of Death: The Development of the Modern Cemetery, 1830–1920*. Philadelphia: Temple University Press, 1980.

French, Stanley. "The Cemetery as Cultural Institution: The Establishment of Mount Auburn and the 'Rural Cemetery' Movement." In *Death in America*, ed. David Stannard. Philadelphia: University of Pennsylvania Press, 1975.

Gosnell, Lynn, and Suzanne Gott. "San Fernando Cemetery: Decorations of Love and Loss in a Mexican-American Community." In *Cemeteries and Gravemarkers: Voices of American Culture*, ed. Richard E. Meyer. Ann Arbor: UMI Research Press Press, 1989.

Grinsell, L. V. "The Breaking of Objects as Funerary Rite." *Folklore* 72 (September 1961): 475–91.

Habenstein, Robert, and William Lamers. *The History of American Funeral Directing*. Milwaukee: Bulfin Printers, 1955.

Hertz, Robert. *Death and the Right Hand*. Trans. Rodney and Claudia Needham. Glencoe, Ill.: Free Press, 1960.

Holloway, Joseph, ed., *Africanisms in American Culture*. Bloomington: Indiana University Press, 1990.

Hsu, Francis L. K. *Under the Ancestor's Shadow*. New York: Columbia University Press, 1948.

Hujar, Peter. *Portraits in Life and Death*. New York: Da Capo, 1976.

Huntingdon, Richard, and Peter Metcalf. *Celebrations of Death: The Anthropology of Mortuary Ritual*. Cambridge: Harvard University Press, 1979.

Jackson, Kenneth T., and Camilo Jose Vergara. *Silent Cities: The Evolution of the American Cemetery*. Princeton: Princeton Architectural Press, 1989.

Jordan, Terry. "Roses So Red and Lilies So Fair: Southern Folk Cemeteries in Texas." *Southwestern Historical Quarterly* 83 (1980): 227–58.

———. *Texas Graveyards: A Cultural Legacy*. Austin: University of Texas Press, 1982.

Kleinberg, S. L. "Death and the Working Class." *Journal of Popular Culture* 11 (summer 1977): 193–209.

Kremenak-Pecohci, Beverly. "At Rest: Folk Art in Texas Cemeteries." In *Folkart in Texas*. Dallas: Southern Methodist University Press, 1985.

Krepps, Karen. "Black Mortuary Practices in Southeast Michigan." Ph.D. diss., Wayne State University, 1990.

Laderman, Gary. "Abraham Lincoln's Hallowed and Hollowed Body: The Anatomy of a Transitional Symbol in the History of Attitudes toward Death in America." Paper presented at the 1993 American Studies Association Conference, Boston, Mass., November 3–5, 1993.

Lesy, Michael. *Wisconsin Death Trip*. New York: Pantheon, 1973.

Linden-Ward, Blanche. *Silent Cities on a Hill: Landscapes of Memory and Boston's Mount Auburn Cemetery*. Columbus: Ohio State University Press, 1989.

Ludwig, Alan. *Graven Image: New England Stone Carving and Its Symbols, 1650–1815*. Middleton, Conn.: Wesleyan University Press, 1966.

Matturri, John. "Windows in the Garden: Italian-American Memorialization and the American Cemetery." In *Ethnicity and the American Cemetery*, ed. Richard E. Meyer. Bowling Green, Ohio: Bowling Green State University Popular Press, 1993.

McCarthy, John. "Material Culture and Performance: African-American Community, Ethnicity, and Agency in the Burial Practices at the First African Baptist Church Cemeteries, Philadelphia, 1810–1841." Paper delivered at the Winterthur Material Culture Conference, Winterthur, Delaware, October 1993.

McGrath, Robert L. "Death Italo-American Style: Reflections on Modern Martyrdom." *Markers* 4 (1987): 107–13.

Meyer, Richard E., ed. *Cemeteries and Gravemarkers: Voices of American Culture*. Ann Arbor: UMI Research Press, 1989.

————, ed. *Ethnicity and the American Cemetery*. Bowling Green, Ohio: Bowling Green State University Popular Press, 1993.

Mitford, Jessica. *The American Way of Death*. New York: Simon and Schuster, 1963.

Mossman, B. C. *The Last Salute: Civil and Military Funerals, 1921–1969*. Washington, D.C.: Department of the Army, 1972.

Power, John C. *Abraham Lincoln: His Great Funeral Cortege, from Washington to Springfield*. Springfield, Ill.: privately published, 1872.

Sloane, David C. *The Last Great Necessity: Cemeteries in American History*. Baltimore: Johns Hopkins University Press, 1991.

Stannard, David, ed. *Death in America*. Philadelphia: University of Pennsylvania Press, 1975.

————. *The Puritan Way of Death: A Study in Religion, Culture, and Social Change*. New York: Oxford University Press, 1977.

Thompson, Robert Farris. *Flash of the Spirit: African and Afro-American Art and Philosophy*. New York: Random House, 1983.

Vlach, John Michael. *The Afro-American Tradition in Decorative Arts*. Cleveland: Cleveland Museum of Art, 1978.

Warner, William L. *The Living and the Dead: A Study in the Symbolic Life of Americans*. New Haven: Yale University Press, 1959.

West, John O. "Folk Grave Decorations along the Rio Grande." In *Folkart in Texas*. Dallas: Southern Methodist University Press, 1985.

WAR MEMORIALS AND MEMORIALIZING

American Battle Monuments Commission. *American Armies and Battlefields in Europe*. Washington, D.C.: United States Government Printing Office, 1938.

Barber, Bernard. "Place, Symbol, and Utilitarian Functions in War Memorials." *Social Forces* 28 (1949): 64–68.

Beam, Laura. "The War Memorial." *Journal of the American Association of University Women* 39 (September 1945).

Berryman, Sue E. *Who Serves? The Persistent Myth of the Underclass Army*. Boulder, Colo.: Westview, 1988.

Bodnar, John E. *Remaking America: Public Memory, Commemoration, and Patriotism in the Twentieth Century*. Princeton: Princeton University Press, 1992.

————. "Public Memory in an American City: Commemoration in Cleveland." In *Commemorations: The Politics of National Identity*, ed. John R. Gillis. Princeton: Princeton University Press, 1994.

Boorman, Derek. *At the Going Down of the Sun: British First World War Memorials*. York, England: Ebor Press, 1988.

Borg, Alan. *War Memorials: From Antiquity to the Present.* London: Leo Cooper, 1991.

Bureau of Memorial Buildings. *Community Buildings as War Memorials.* New York: War Camp Community Service, 1920.

Commission of Fine Arts. *Report to the Senate and the House of Representatives concerning the Thomas Jefferson Memorial.* Washington, D.C.: Commission of Fine Arts, 1939.

Creighton, Thomas H. *The Architecture of Monuments: The Franklin Delano Roosevelt Memorial Competition.* New York: Reinhold, 1962.

Curl, James Stevens. *A Celebration of Death: An Introduction to Some of the Buildings, Monuments, and Settings of Funerary Architecture in the Western European Tradition.* London: Constable, 1980.

"Current Trends in War Memorials." *American City,* July 1945, 5.

Dahir, James. *Community Centers as Living War Memorials.* New York: Russell Sage, 1946.

Darling, Janet. "What Is an Appropriate War Memorial?" *House Beautiful,* January 1945, 42–43.

Doezema, Marianne, and June Hargrove. *The Public Monument and Its Audience.* Cleveland: Cleveland Museum of Art, 1977.

Douglas, O. W. "Playgrounds and Recreation Centers as Memorials." *American City,* September 1916, 88.

"Dramatic Memorial Fountain for Cleveland." *American City,* August 1945, 111.

Emerson, Bettie A. C. *Historic Southern Monuments.* New York: Neale Publishing, 1911.

Fraser, James Earl. "Let Our New Monuments Inspire—And Endure." *The Rotarian,* February 1946, 24–25, 51–52.

Fussell, Paul. *The Great War and Modern Memory.* New York: Oxford University Press, 1975.

Gardener, Alexander. *Gardener's Photographic Sketch Book of the War.* 1868.

Garland, Robert. *The Greek Way of Death.* London: Duckworth, 1985.

"Give the Veterans a Voice as to War Memorials in Their Communities." *American City,* August 1945.

Gurney, Gene. *Arlington National Cemetery: A Picture Story of America's Most Famous Burial Grounds from the Civil War to President John F. Kennedy's Burial.* New York: Crown, 1965.

Hanna, Michael R. "What Service Men and Women Favor in War Memorials." *American City,* August 1945, 107.

Harris, John. *Silent Cities: An Exhibition of the Memorial and Cemetery Architecture of the Great War.* London: Royal Institute of British Architects, 1977.

Harrison, Kathleen Georg. "This Grand National Enterprise." Special Collections, Gettysburg National Military Park, Gettysburg, Pennsylvania.

Herrold, George H. "State Center and War Memorial for St. Paul." *American City*, June 1945, 118.

Hill, Charles. "Man Thinking—Nation and Universe: The Einstein Memorial at the National Academy of Sciences." *American Studies International* 28 (April 1990), 2–12.

Holt, Dean W. *American Military Cemeteries: A Comprehensive Illustrated Guide to the Hallowed Grounds of the United States, Including Overseas.* Jefferson, N.C.: McFarland, 1992.

Horan, James. *Timothy H. O'Sullivan: America's Forgotten Photographer.* New York: Doubleday, 1966.

Hubbard, William. "A Meaning for Monuments." *The Public Interest* 74 (winter 1984), 17–30.

Hudnut, Joseph. "The Monument Does Not Remember." *The Atlantic Monthly*, September 1945, 55–59.

Janson, H. W. *The Rise and Fall of the Public Monument.* New Orleans: The Graduate School, Tulane University, 1976.

Kent State May 4 Memorial Design Competition. Kent, Ohio: Kent State University Press, 1988.

Laqueur, Thomas. "Memory and Naming in the Great War." In *Commemorations: The Politics of National Identity*, ed. John R. Gillis. Princeton: Princeton University Press, 1994.

Lewis, William Mather. "Useful Ones Best Honor the Hero." *The Rotarian*, February 1946, 26–27, 50–51.

"Liberty Buildings as Soldiers Memorials." *American City*, September 1918, 1.

"Living Memorials Advocated by Mayors' Conference." *American City*, August 1946, 83.

Marling, Karal Ann, and John Wetenhall. *Iwo Jima: Monuments, Memories, and the American Hero.* Cambridge: Harvard University Press, 1991.

Mayo, James. "War Memorials as Political Memory." *Geographical Review* 78 (January 1988), 62–75.

———. *War Memorials as Political Landscape: The American Experience and Beyond.* New York: Praeger, 1988.

McIntyre, Colin. *Monuments of War: How to Read a War Memorial.* London: Robert Hale, 1990.

McLaughlin, Jack. *Gettysburg: The Long Encampment.* New York: Appleton-Century, 1963.

Morgan, J. McDowell. *Military Medals and Insignia of the United States.* Glendale, Calif.: Griffin-Patterson, 1941.

Morris, Richard. "Memorializing among Americans: The Case of Lincoln's Assassination." Ph.D. diss., University of Wisconsin, Madison, 1986.

Patterson, John S. "A Patriotic Landscape: Gettysburg, 1863–1913." *Prospects* 7 (1982), 315–33.

Petrucelli, Fred. "Million Dollar Recreation Plant Planned as War Memorial for North Little Rock, Ark." *American City*, July 1946, 82, 137.

Pike, Martha, and Janice Armstrong. *A Time to Morn: Expressions of Grief in Nineteenth-Century America*. Brooklyn, N.Y.: Museums at Stonybrook, 1980.

"Proposed Liberty Memorial Square and Civic Center for Berkeley, California." *American City*, May 1919, 428–29.

Ragon, Michel. *The Space of Death: A Study of Funerary Architecture, Decoration, and Urbanism*. Trans. Alan Sheridan. Charlottesville: University Press of Virginia, 1983.

Rieth, Adolf. *Monuments to the Victims of Tyranny*. New York: Praeger, 1969.

Roosevelt, Theodore. "Memorials That Serve Mankind." *American City*, May 1916, 219.

Runsisvalle, Joseph. *Statues, Monuments, and Memorials Located in the Parks of the National Capital*. Washington, D.C.: Department of the Interior, 1977.

Sandage, Scott. "A Marble House Divided: The Lincoln Memorial, the Civil Rights Movement, and the Politics of Memory, 1939–1963." *Journal of American History* 8 (June 1993): 135–67.

Schwartz, Barry. "The Social Context of Commemoration: A Study in Collective Memory." *Social Forces* 61 (December 1982): 374–402.

Secretary of War, *Program of the Ceremonies attending the Burial of an Unknown and Unidentified American Soldier Who Lost His Life during the World War*. Washington, D.C., 1921.

Segal, David. *Recruiting for Uncle Sam: Citizenship and Military Manpower Policy*. Lawrence: University Press of Kansas, 1989.

Sontag, Susan. *Against Interpretation, and Other Essays*. New York: Farrar, Strauss, and Giroux, 1969.

Stevenson, Charles B. "Survey of War Memorial Plans of 500 Cities and Towns." *Toledo City Journal*, February 23, 1946.

Storrick, W. C. *Gettysburg: The Places, the Battle, the Outcome*. Harrisburg, Penn.: J. Horace McFarland, 1932.

"Trends in Living Memorials." *American City*, February 1946, 88.

Tuan, Yi-Fu. "The Significance of the Artifact." *Geographical Review* 70, no. 4 (1980): 462–72.

Unrau, Harlan. *Administrative History: Gettysburg National Military Park and Gettysburg National Cemetery, Pennsylvania*. Denver: National Park Service, 1991.

Webb, Anne Holliday. "What Type Memorial? Some Questions the Average Community May Consider When Discussing and Planning a Memorial to Its Boys and Girls Serving in World War II." *The American City*, February 1945, 63–65.

————, ed. *Commemoration through Community Services: Trends in Living Memorials*. New York: American City Magazine Co., 1946.

Whittick, Arnold. *War Memorials*. London: Country Life, 1946.

PUBLIC MEMORY AND NATIONALISM

Albanese, Catherine. "Requiem for Memorial Day: Dissent in the Redeemer Nation." *American Quarterly* 26 (1974): 386–98.

Alexander, Charles C. *Here the Country Lies: Nationalism and the Arts in Twentieth-Century America*. Bloomington: Indiana University Press, 1980.

Anderson, Benedict. *Imagined Communities: Reflections on the Origin and Spread of Nationalism*. London: Verso, 1983.

Bailyn, Bernard. *The Ideological Origins of the American Revolution*. Cambridge: Harvard University Press, 1967.

Bellah, Robert, "Civil Religion in America." *Daedalus* 96 (1967): 1–26.

Benjamin, Walter. *Illuminations*. Trans. Harry Zohn. New York: Schocken, 1969.

Bercovitch, Sacvan. *The American Jeremiad*. Madison: University of Wisconsin Press, 1978.

Bernstein, Iver. *The New York City Draft Riots: Their Significance for American Society and Politics in the Age of the Civil War*. New York: Oxford University Press, 1990.

Bodnar, John E. *Remaking America: Public Memory, Commemoration and Patriotism in the Twentieth Century*. Princeton: Princeton University Press, 1992.

Boorstin, Daniel. *The Americans: The National Experience*. New York: Random House, 1965.

Butler, Thomas, ed. *Memory: History, Culture, and the Mind*. Oxford: Basil Blackwell, 1989.

Curti, Merle. *Roots of American Loyalty*. New York: Columbia University Press, 1946.

Davies, Wallace Evan. *Patriotism on Parade: The Story of Veterans' and Hereditary Organizations in America, 1783–1900*. Cambridge: Harvard University Press, 1955.

Davis, Natalie Zemon, and Randolph Starns, eds. "Special Issue: Memory and Counter-Memory." *Representations* 26 (spring 1989).

Davis, Susan. *Parades and Power: Street Theater in Nineteenth-Century Philadelphia*. Philadelphia: Temple University Press, 1986.

Douglas, Ann. *Feminization of American Culture*. New York: Knopf, 1977.

Eco, Umberto. "Architecture and Memory." *Via* 8 (1986): 88–94.

Foucault, Michel. *The Foucault Reader*. Ed. Paul Rabinow. New York: Pantheon, 1984.

Frisch, Michael H. "American History and the Structures of Collective Memory: A Modest Exercise in Empirical Iconography." *The Journal of American History* 75 (March 1989): 1130–50.

Geary, James. *We Need Men: The Union Draft in the Civil War.* Dekalb: Northern Illinois University Press, 1991.

Gellner, Ernest. *Nations and Nationalism.* Oxford: Basil Blackwell, 1983.

Giddens, Anthony. *The Constitution of Society: Outline of the Theory of Structuration.* Cambridge: Polity Press, 1984.

Gillis, John R., ed. *Commemorations: The Politics of National Identity.* Princeton: Princeton University Press, 1994.

Glassberg, David. *American Historical Pageantry: The Uses of Tradition in the Early Twentieth Century.* Chapel Hill: University of North Carolina Press, 1990.

Halbwachs, Maurice. *On Collective Memory.* Trans. F. J. Ditter. New York: Harper and Row, 1980.

Hobsbawm, Eric, and Terrance Ranger, eds. *The Invention of Tradition.* Cambridge: Cambridge University Press, 1983.

———. *Nations and Nationalism since 1780: Programme, Myth, Reality.* Cambridge: Cambridge University Press, 1990.

Honey, Maureen. *Creating Rosie the Riveter: Class, Gender, and Propaganda During World War II.* Amherst: University of Massachusetts Press, 1984.

Hutton, Patrick. "Collective Memory and Collective Mentalities: The Halswachs-Aries Connection." *Historical Reflections/Réflexions Historiques* 15 (1988): 311–22.

Hyde, Lewis. *The Gift: Imagination and the Erotic Life of Property.* New York: Random House, 1979.

Kammen, Michael. *A Season of Youth: The American Revolution and the Historical Imagination.* New York: Knopf, 1978.

———. *Mystic Chords of Memory: The Transformation of Tradition in American Culture.* New York: Knopf, 1991.

Kennedy, David. *Over Here: The First World War and American Society.* New York: Oxford University Press, 1980.

Leuchtenberg, William. *The Perils of Prosperity, 1914–1932.* Chicago: University of Chicago Press, 1958.

Linenthal, Edward. *Sacred Ground: Americans and Their Battlefields.* Chicago: University of Illinois Press, 1991.

Lipsitz, George. *Time Passages: Collective Memory and American Popular Culture.* Minneapolis: University of Minnesota Press, 1990.

Mauss, Marcel. *The Gift.* Trans W. D. Halls. New York: Norton, 1990.

Mosse, George. *The Nationalization of the Masses: Political Symbolism and Mass Movements in Germany from the Napoleonic Wars through the Third Reich.* New York: H. Fertig, 1975.

————. *Fallen Soldiers: Reshaping the Memory of the World Wars*. New York: Oxford University Press, 1990.

Nora, Pierre. "Between Memory and History: *Les Lieux de Memoire*." *Representations* (spring 1989): 7–25.

Rothkrug, Lionel. "Religious Practices and Collective Perceptions: Hidden Homologies in the Renaissance and Reformation." *Historical Reflections/Réflexions Historiques* 7 (1980): 3–251.

Scarry, Elaine. *The Body in Pain: The Making and Unmaking of the World*. New York: Oxford University Press, 1985.

Schudson, Michael. *Watergate in American Memory: How We Remember, Forget, and Reconstruct the Past*. New York: Basic, 1992.

Schwartz, Barry. *George Washington: The Making of an American Symbol*. New York: Free Press, 1987.

Silber, Nina. *The Romance of Reunion: Northerners and the South, 1865–1900*. Chapel Hill: University of North Carolina Press, 1993.

Thelen, David. "Memory and American History." *Journal of American History* 75 (March 1989): 117–29.

Trachtenberg, Alan. *Reading American Photographs: Images as History, Mathew Brady to Walker Evans*. New York: Hill and Wang, 1989.

Turner, Victor. *Dramas, Fields, and Metaphors: Symbolic Action in Human Society*. Ithaca: Cornell University Press, 1974.

Turner, Victor, and Edith Turner. *Image and Pilgrimage in Christian Culture: Anthropological Perspectives*. New York: Columbia University Press, 1978.

Veblen, Thorstein. *An Inquiry into the Nature of Peace*. New York: Huebsch, 1917.

White, Hayden. *Metahistory: The Historical Imagination in Nineteenth Century Europe*. Baltimore: Johns Hopkins University Press, 1973.

Wills, Gary. *Lincoln at Gettysburg: The Words That Remade America*. New York: Simon and Schuster, 1992.

Wilson, Charles. *Baptized in Blood: The Religion of the Lost Cause, 1865–1920*. Athens: University of Georgia Press, 1980.

Zelinsky, Wilbur. *Nation into State: The Shifting Symbolic Foundations of American Nationalism*. Chapel Hill: University of North Carolina Press, 1988.

VIETNAM WAR LEGACY

Ackland, Len, ed. *Credibility Gap: A Digest of the Pentagon Papers*. Philadelphia: National Peace Literature Service, 1972.

Alter, Jonathan. "Vietnam the Unknown Soldier." *Newsweek*, June 4, 1984, 25.

Baker, Mark. *Nam: The Vietnam War in the Words of the Men and Women Who Fought There*. New York: Berkley, 1981.

Baritz, Loren. *Backfire: A History of How American Culture Led Us into Vietnam and Made Us Fight the Way We Did*. New York: Morrow, 1985.

Barry, John, and Ehrhart W. D., eds. *Demilitarized Zones: Veterans after Vietnam*. Perkasie, Penn.: East River Anthology, 1976.

Beidler, Philip D. *American Literature and the Experience of Vietnam*. Athens: University of Georgia Press, 1982.

Benson, Susan Porter, Stephen Brier, and Roy Rosenzweig, eds. *Presenting the Past: Essays on History and the Public*. Philadelphia: Temple University Press, 1986.

Berg, Rick. "Losing Vietnam: Covering the War in the Age of Technology." *Cultural Critique* 3 (spring 1986): 92–125.

Berryman, Sue E. *Who Serves? The Persistent Myth of the Underclass Army*. Boulder, Colo.: Westview, 1988.

Binkin, Martin, and Mark J. Eitelberg, eds. *Blacks and the Military*. Washington: Brookings Institution, 1982.

"Blacks Presence Ignored in Nation's Tribute to Vietnam Unknown Soldier." *Jet*, June 18, 1984, 54.

Brende, Joel Osler, and Erwin Randolph Parson. *Vietnam Veterans: The Road to Recovery*. New York: Plenum Press, 1985.

Broder, David. *The Party's Over: The Failure of Politics in America*. New York: Harper and Row, 1972.

Brooks, Colette. "Notes on American Mythology." *Partisan Review* 55 (1988): 309–321.

Capps, Walter. *The Unfinished War: Vietnam and the American Conscience*. Boston: Beacon Press, 1982.

Caputo, Phil. *A Rumor of War*. New York: Ballantine, 1977.

Cawthorne, Nigel. *The Bamboo Cage: The Full Story of the American Servicemen Still Held Hostage in South-East Asia*. London: Leo Cooper, 1991.

Christopher, Renny. "'I Never Really Became a Woman Veteran Until . . . I Saw the Wall': A Review of Oral Histories and Personal Narratives by Women Veterans of the Vietnam War." *Vietnam Generation* 1 (1989): 33–45.

Clarfene-Casten, Liane. "Anatomy of a Cover-Up: Charges That Investigation of Effects of Agent Orange on Vietnam Veterans Was Sabotaged by the Centers for Disease Control." *The Nation*, November 30, 1992, 658–62.

Clark, Michael. "Remembering Vietnam." *Cultural Critique* 3 (spring 1986): 4–11.

Dean, Eric T., Jr. "The Myth of the Troubled and Scorned Vietnam Veteran." *Journal of American Studies* 26 (1992): 59–74.

Dickstein, Morris. *Gates of Eden: American Culture in the Sixties*. New York: Basic, 1977.

Dittmar, Linda, and Gene Michaud, eds. *From Hanoi to Hollywood: The Viet-

nam War in American Film. New Brunswick, N.J.: Rutgers University Press, 1990.

Dorn, Edward, ed. *Who Defends America? Race, Sex, and Class in the Armed Forces*. Washington: Joint Center for Political Studies Press, 1989.

Dower, John. *War without Mercy: Race and Power in the Pacific War*. New York: Pantheon, 1986.

Doyle, Robert C. "Unresolved Mysteries: The Myth of the Missing Warrior and the Government Deceit Theme in Popular Captivity Culture of the Vietnam War." *Journal of American Culture* 15 (summer 1992): 1–18.

Dunn, Joe P. "The Vietnam War POW/MIAs: An Annotated Bibliography." *Bulletin of Bibliography* 45 (1988): 152–57.

Edelman, Bernard, ed. *Dear America: Letters Home from Vietnam*. New York: Norton, 1985.

Egendorf, Arthur. *Healing from the War: Trauma and Transformation after Vietnam*. Boston: Houghton Mifflin, 1985.

Ehrenhaus, Peter. "On Not Commemorating Vietnam: Problems in the Celebration of Failure." Paper presented at the annual meeting of the Speech Communication Association, Chicago, 1986.

Figley, Charles, and Seymour Leventman, eds. *Strangers at Home: Vietnam Veterans since the War*. New York: Praeger, 1980.

FitzGerald, Frances. *Cities on a Hill: A Journey through Contemporary American Cultures*. New York: Simon and Schuster, 1986.

Foster, Gaines. "Coming to Term with Defeat: Post-Vietnam America and the Post-Civil War South." *Virginia Quarterly Review* 66 (1990): 17–35.

Franklin, Bruce H. "The POW/MIA Myth." *The Atlantic Monthly*, December 1991, 45–81.

———. *M.I.A., or, Mythmaking in America*. Brooklyn, N.Y.: Lawrence Hill, 1992.

Freedman, Dan, and Jacqueline Rhoads. *Nurses in Vietnam: The Forgotten Veterans*. Austin, Tex.: Texas Monthly Press, 1987.

Garfield, Bob. "No Peace of Mind." *Advertising Age*, June 1986, 78.

Gilbert, James. *Another Chance: Postwar America, 1945–1968*. Philadelphia: Temple University Press, 1981.

———. *Cycle of Outrage: America's Reaction to the Juvenile Delinquent in the 1950s*. New York: Oxford University Press, 1986.

Gitlin, Todd. *The Sixties: Years of Hope, Days of Rage*. New York: Bantam, 1987.

Goldman, Peter, and Tony Fuller. *Charlie Company: What Vietnam Did to Us*. New York: Morrow, 1983.

Gruner, E. G. *Prisoners of Culture: Representing the Vietnam POW*. New Brunswick, N.J.: Rutgers University Press, 1993.

Haines, Harry. "The Pride Is Back: *Rambo, Magnum P.I.*, and the Return Trip to Vietnam." In *The Cultural Legacy of Vietnam: Uses of the Past in the Present*, ed. Richard Morris and Peter Erhenhaus. Norwood, N.J.: Ablex Publishing, 1990.

Harris, Louis. *The Anguish of Change*. New York: Norton, 1973.

Harris, Neil. *Cultural Excursions: Marketing Appetites and Cultural Tastes in Modern America*. Chicago: University of Chicago Press, 1990.

Hellman, John. *American Myth and the Legacy of Vietnam*. New York: Columbia University Press, 1986.

Helmer, John. *Bringing the War Home: The American Soldier in Vietnam and After*. New York: Free Press, 1974

Herr, Michael. *Dispatches*. New York: Knopf, 1977.

Herring, George C. "Vietnam, American Foreign Policy, and the Uses of History." *Virginia Quarterly Review* 66 (1990): 1–16.

Holm, Tom. "Culture, Ceremonials, and Stress: American Indian Veterans and the Vietnam War." *Armed Forces and Society* 12 (1986): 237–51.

Horne, A. D., ed. *The Wounded Generation: America after Vietnam*. Englewood Cliffs, N.J.: Prentice-Hall, 1981.

Jeffords, Susan. "Debriding Vietnam: The Resurrection of the White American Male." *Feminist Studies* 14 (1988): 525–43.

———. *The Remasculinization of America: Gender and the Vietnam War*. Bloomington: University of Indiana Press, 1989.

Jensen-Stevenson, Monika, and William Stevenson. *Kiss the Boys Goodbye: How the United States Betrayed Its Own POWs in Vietnam*. New York: Plume Books, 1991.

Johnson, Haynes. *Sleepwalking through History: America in the Reagan Years*. New York: Anchor, 1991.

Kearns, Doris. *Lyndon Johnson and the American Dream*. New York: Harper and Row, 1976.

Kendrick, Alexander. *The Wound Within: America in the Vietnam Years, 1945–1974*. Boston: Little, Brown, 1974.

Klein, Robert. *Wounded Men, Broken Promises*. New York: Macmillan, 1981.

Koenigsmen, Janet Lee. "Mobilization of a Conscience Constituency: VIVA and the POW/MIA Movement." Ph.D. diss., Kent State University, 1987.

Kovic, Ron. *Born on the Forth of July*. New York: McGraw-Hill, 1976.

Lifton, Robert. *Home from the War: Vietnam Veterans: Neither Victims nor Executioners*. New York: Simon and Schuster, 1973.

Lomperis, Timothy. *"Reading the Wind:" The Literature of the Vietnam War*. Durham, N.C.: Duke University Press, 1987.

Luker, Kristin. *Abortion and the Politics of Motherhood*. Berkeley: University of California Press, 1984.

MacPherson, Myra. *Long Time Passing: Vietnam and the Haunted Genera-tion*. Garden City, N.Y.: Doubleday, 1984.

Marcus, Greil. *Mystery Train: Images of America in Rock 'n' Roll Music*. New York: Dutton, 1975.

————. *Lipstick Traces: A Secret History of the Twentieth Century*. Cam-bridge: Harvard University Press, 1989.

Mason, Bobbie Ann. *In Country*. New York: Harper and Row, 1985.

May, Elaine Tyler. *Homeward Bound: American Families in the Cold War Era*. New York: Basic, 1986.

Morris, Richard, and Peter Ehrenhaus, eds. *Cultural Legacies of Vietnam: Uses of the Past in the Present*. Norwood, N.J.: Ablex Publishing, 1990.

Morrow, Lance. "War and Remembrance: Casualty from Vietnamese War In-terred." *Time*, June 11, 1984, 29.

Murphy, Edward F. *Vietnam Medal of Honor Heroes*. New York: Ballantine, 1987.

Nixon, Richard. *No More Vietnams*. New York: Arbor House, 1985.

Novick, Peter. *That Noble Dream: The "Objectivity Question" and the Amer-ican Historical Profession*. Cambridge: Cambridge University Press, 1988.

O'Brien, Tim. *The Things They Carried*. Boston: Houghton Mifflin, 1990.

Office of the Deputy Assistant Secretary of Defense for Military Manpower and Personnel Policy. *Hispanics in America's Defense*. Washington, D.C.: Department of Defense, 1990.

Patterson, Charles, and Colonel G. Lee Tippin. *The Heroes Who Fell from Grace: The True Story of Operation Lazarus, the Attempt to Free Ameri-can POWs from Laos in 1982*. Canton, Ohio: Daring, 1985.

Pells, Richard. *The Liberal Mind in the Conservative Age: American Intel-lectuals in the 1940s and 1950s*. New York: Harper and Row, 1985.

Pfaff, William. *Barbarian Sentiments: How the American Century Ends*. New York: Hill and Wang, 1989.

Phillips, Kevin. *Post-Conservative America: People, Politics, and Ideology in a Time of Crisis*. New York: Random House, 1982.

Quart, Leonard. "The Deer Hunter: The Superman in Vietnam." In *From Hanoi to Hollywood: The Vietnam War in American Film*, ed. Linda Dittmar and Gene Michaud. New Brunswick, N.J.: Rutgers University Press, 1990.

Rowe, John Carlos, and Rick Berg. *The Vietnam War and American Culture*. New York: Columbia University Press, 1991.

Scarry, Elaine. "Injury and the Structure of War." *Representations* 10 (1985): 1–52.

Schell, Jonathan. *Observing the Nixon Years: "Notes and Comments" from the New Yorker on the Vietnam War and the Watergate Crisis, 1969–1975*. New York: Pantheon, 1989.

Schlossstein, Steven. *The End of the American Century.* New York: Congdon and Weed, 1989.

Seidman, Ethan. "The POW/MIA Lobby." *The Atlantic Monthly*, December 1991, 75.

Severo, Richard, and Lewis Milford. *The Wages of War: When America's Soldiers Came Home—From Valley Forge to Vietnam.* New York: Simon and Schuster, 1989.

Sevy, Grace. "Lessons of the War: The Effects of Disillusionment on the Consciousness and Political Thinking of Conservative Women Veterans." *Minerva: Quarterly Report on Women and the Military* 2 (1986): 96–132.

Sheehan, Neil. *A Bright Shining Lie: John Paul Vann and America in Vietnam.* New York: Random House, 1988.

————. "Prisoners of the Past: Normalizing of Relations with Vietnam and the POW/MIA Myth." *The New Yorker*, May 24, 1993, 44–51.

Susman, Warren. *Culture as History: The Transformation of American Society in the Twentieth Century.* New York: Pantheon, 1984.

Terry, Wallace, ed. *Bloods: An Oral History of the Vietnam War by Black Veterans.* New York: Random House, 1984.

Treviso, Ruben. "Hispanics and the Vietnam War." In *Vietnam Reconsidered: Lessons from a War*, ed. Harrison Salisbury. New York: Harper and Row, 1984.

Van Devanter, Linda, and C. Morgan. *Home before Morning: The Story of an Army Nurse in Vietnam.* New York: Warner, 1983.

Walker, Keith. *Piece of My Heart: The Stories of Twenty-Six American Women Who Served in Vietnam.* Novato, Calif.: Presidio, 1985.

Walsh, Jeffrey, and James Aulich, eds. *Vietnam Images: War and Representation.* New York: St. Martin's, 1989.

Wheeler, John. *Touched with Fire: The Future of the Vietnam Generation.* New York: Franklin Watts, 1984.

Willenz, June A. "Women Veterans from the Vietnam War through the Eighties." *Minerva: Quarterly Report on Women and the Military* 6 (1988): 44–60.

Williams, Reese, ed. *Unwinding the Vietnam War: From War into Peace.* Seattle: Real Comet, 1987.

Wills, Gary. *Reagan's America: Innocents at Home.* Garden City, N.Y.: Doubleday, 1987.

INDEX

182   *Index*

cemeteries: Evergreen Cemetery Association,
47; Greenwood, 67; Hollywood, 137n.25;
Laurel Hill, 67; Magnolia, 70; Mount
Auburn, 51, 67–68, 71, 143n.23; National
Cemetery System, 43–44, 136n.22; Oak
Ridge, 66, 144n.36; San Fernando, 82–83,
84; Spring Grove, 143n.23. *See also* funerary practices; rural cemetery movement;
Soldiers' National Cemetery
cenotaphs, memorial, 54, 141n.78
Chinese Americans, funerary practices of, 65,
77, 147n.65
City Beautiful movement, 58
Civic Center (San Francisco), 58
Civil War, American, 4; battle of Gettysburg,
44; conscription during, 50–51, 152n.13;
Gettysburg Address, 37, 38, 52–53,
138n.47; photographs of dead soldiers,
136–37n.25; soldiers buried individually,
37, 38, 43–44; soldiers' identification
tags, 36; soldiers reburied at Gettysburg,
34–35, 36–37, 38, 44–45, 137n.25 (*see
also* Civil War memorials)
Civil War memorials: Confederate monuments, 128n.14; at Gettysburg, 34–35,
36–37, 38, 44–45; private funding for,
128n.10
Clay, Grady, 129n.17
Coffin Manufacturers Association, 75
columns, memorial, 41–42, 43, 55
community bonds, 36, 134n.4
Confederate Army, 44
Confederate monuments, 128n.14
Conklin, Charles, 75
Conkling, Mayor James C., 66
conscription, 50–51, 152n.13
containment (of communism), 140n.69
Cret, Paul P., 61
Curl, James, 41
Curtin, Governor Andrew G., 45, 46–47,
137nn.27–28

Daughters of the Confederacy, 19, 70,
131n.47, 137n.25
death: ancestor worship, 147n.65; Catholic
conception of, 81–82, 83; living as
helping dead, 78, 79–80, 81–82, 83;
masculinization of, 137n.25; Protestant
conceptions of, 69, 142n.13
Deer Hunter, The, 10, 103–4
Department of Defense, 115–16
Department of the Interior, 12
dog tags, 36, 97–98, 149–50n.17, 149n.15,
150nn.19–20
Dorman, Robert, 115
Douglas, Ann, 75

Douglas, Mary, 149n.11
Downs, Fred, 89
draft, military, 50–51, 152n.13

Eastwood, Clint, 118
Ecklbo, Garret, 129n.17
Egyptians, memorials of, 40, 41, 43
Eisenhower, Dwight D., 60
Elais, Anni Booth, 111, 153n.16
"Elegy Written in a Country Churchyard"
(Gray), 70
embalming, 64, 65, 72–73, 144nn.28–31,
145n.35
England, memorials in, 54, 140–41n.78
Evans, Diane Carlson, 19, 20, 153n.16
Evergreen Cemetery Association (Gettys-
burg), 47

familial bonds, 36, 134n.4
Farrell, James, 145n.41
Federal Conscription Act (1863), 50
Felton, Duery, 24, 131n.43, 132nn.53–54,
150n.27
Fine Arts Commission, 12, 19, 128–29n.15,
131n.45
First Blood, 119
Fleming, E. M., 133n.64
Fonda, Jane, 16, 112, 153n.17
Ford, Gerald, 11, 108
Fraiser, Charles, 70–71
France, Nazi POWs used by, 153n.19
Fraser, James Earl, 140n.70
Frederick II, Holy Roman Emperor, 42
French, Stanley, 143nn.22–23
French Revolution, 43, 136nn.19–20
Freneau, Philip: "Indian Burying Ground,
The," 143n.21
frontier cemeteries, 43, 136n.22
funeral directors, 65, 75–76, 145n.41
funerary practices, 4–5, 64–84; of African
Americans, 4, 65, 77, 78–81, 88, 146–
47n.57; bodies returned home, 54, 72–73,
144n.30; as businesslike, 74–75, 145n.41;
caskets, objects left in, 80–81; of Chinese
Americans, 65, 77, 147n.65; embalming/
preserving the dead, 64, 65, 72–73,
144nn.28–31, 145n.35; family plots,
143n.23, 145n.32; flowers and flags, 8,
71, 76, 92; funeral directors, 65, 75–76,
145n.41; of German Americans, 83; grave
decoration, 4 (*see also* graves, decoration
of); and grief, 75, 76, 145n.41; headstones (*see* headstone decorations/
inscriptions); histories of/research on,
143n.23, 146n.48; of Italian Americans,
65, 77, 78, 81–82, 88, 147n.61; Latin

willow-and-urn motif, 69, 142n.16
Wills, David, 45–47, 48–49, 51–52, 137nn.26–28, 138n.34, 141n.2
women, volunteer work of, 19, 70, 131n.47, 137n.25
World War I: meaning of, 127–28n.6; memorials to, 4, 37, 39, 54–58, 59, 139–40n.65, 139n.61; scale of violence in, 39, 54–55; veterans of, 139n.61, 152n.13
World War II: burials in local cemeteries, 140n.71; meaning of, 127–28n.6; memorials to, 4, 37, 58–62, 140n.72; number of MIAs, 115
World War Memorial Plaza (Indianapolis), 58
Wyrick, Ray F., 77–78

Ypres memorial (Lutyens), 55, 56

Zaire, conceptions of death in, 80
Zuni grave-site offerings, 78

Indexer:	Carol Roberts
Compositor:	Integrated Composition Systems
Text:	11/13.5 Caledonia
Display:	Franklin Gothic
Printer and binder:	Royal Book Manufacturing